The Revival of Death

Neither traditional religion nor modern medical procedures make sense of the personal experience of many who are dying or bereaved. In response, there has been a massive revival of interest in developing new ways of talking about death. This revival, while reinstating some traditional practices and retaining medical expertise, seeks ultimate authority elsewhere: in the individual self. The new death is personal, facilitated by palliative care, the life-centred funeral, and bereavement counselling.

How, though, are people to know how to die and to grieve? Is the modern self able to make free choices here? What role do professional carers and their theories play in shaping the experiences of people who are dying or bereaved? How do such people learn from each other? To what extent are they influenced by stereotypical ideas of the good death? Is it possible for the self to be in control when the body has lost control? Can the unique personality of the deceased be incorporated into traditional funeral ritual?

This is the first book comprehensively to examine the revival of death as a subject and relate it to theories of modernity and postmodernity. The book will interest not only social scientists but anyone learning to care for the dying, the dead or the bereaved.

Tony Walter was a freelance writer for many years before becoming a lecturer in sociology at the University of Reading. His publications include *Basic Income* (1988) and *Funerals: and how to improve them* (1990).

The Revival of Death

Tony Walter

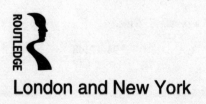

London and New York

First published 1994
by Routledge
11 New Fetter Lane, London EC4P 4EE

Simultaneously published in the USA and Canada
by Routledge
29 West 35th Street, New York, NY 10001

Typeset in Times by Michael Mepham, Frome, Somerset
Printed and bound in Great Britain
by Mackays of Chatham PLC, Chatham, Kent

British Library Cataloguing in Publication Data
A catalogue record for this book is available
from the British Library.

Library of Congress Cataloging in Publication Data
Walter, J.A. (Julian Anthony), 1948–
  The revival of death/Tony Walter
    p. cm.
  Includes bibliographical references and index.
  ISBN 0–415–08665–5: $55.00 (U.S.). – ISBN 0–415–11854–9
  (pbk.): $16.95 (U.S.)
  1. Thanatology. 2. Death – Social aspects. I. Title.
HQ1073.W35   1994
306.9–dc20   94–12148
                                                         CIP

ISBN 0–415–08665–5 (hbk)
ISBN 0–415–11854–9 (pbk)

Contents

Acknowledgements

In formal interview and informal conversation, so many people have both provided data and helped me analyse it that it is invidious to start naming some individuals and not others. But I would like to thank the several people in San Francisco, at St Christopher's Hospice (London) and at my own local hospice who have taken time to show me around, answer my questions and point me to literature I would never otherwise have found.

There has arisen over the past few years in Britain a small but growing number of sociologists interested in 'DDD' – death, dying and disposal. I have learnt much from discussions with Edward Bailey, Douglas Davies, David Field, Glennys Howarth, Nicky James, Peter Jupp, Rory Williams and especially Michael Young. I am also grateful to Chris Rojek for his invitation to write on this subject for Routledge.

Writing academically about a subject as emotive and personal as death is not easy, and the content and especially the style of the book have benefited from the many suggestions offered by those who have read drafts – Clive Seale, Rod MacLeod and the anonymous Routledge reader. Any remaining awkwardnesses and infelicities are, of course, my own.

I sincerely thank Mary Verdult both for her comments on the manuscript and for enabling me to write this book in the Renaissance city of Basel – an unexpectedly apt environment, for it was near here that in 1533 the first public dissection was carried out, thus initiating medicine's reduction of the patient to an object and contributing to the 'dying' of death. And it was near here that Elisabeth Kübler-Ross grew up before migrating to the USA and redirecting our gaze to the dying person's developing psyche, thus announcing to the world that the dying patient is a subject after all and that death may be revived as a fit subject for conversation.

To study death, even in a library, is a form of participant observation in that one's friends die and sooner or later the writer too has to die. Some of the time I have thankfully been more of an observer, with my friends and myself all in good health; at other times, the phone ringing with bad news has plunged me into being more of a participant than I would wish. I have also been struck that some of the more pertinent comments have come from colleagues who themselves have a life-threatening illness or who have lost a partner or whose partner is terminally ill. The sociological becomes the personal, and the personal becomes the basis for the sociological. I thank these colleagues for sharing their insights, and dedicate the book to them.

Tony Walter
Basel, Switzerland
January 1994

Introduction

At the end of the last century, one Joseph Jacobs wrote a provocative and prophetic article titled 'The Dying of Death', in which he describes 'the practical disappearance of the thought of death as an influence directly bearing upon practical life. There are no skeletons at our feasts nowadays' (1899: 264). In 1955 Geoffrey Gorer proclaimed that death had become the taboo of the twentieth century, confirming Jacobs' prophecy. By 1979, however, Simpson wryly introduced his English language bibliography with 'Death is a very badly kept secret; such an unmentionable topic that there are over 650 books now in print asserting that we are ignoring the subject' (Simpson 1979: vii). His 1987 update adds another 1,700 books subsequently published on death and dying. As we approach the end of the present century, one might wonder whether we are witnessing a revival of death.

The announcements that death is taboo and that our society denies death continue, yet death is more and more talked of (Walter 1991a). In Britain, cancer research, help for children with leukaemia and for hospices are all successful fund raisers; 'the grief process', a phrase referring to the need to face rather than suppress grief, is now common parlance; bereaved journalists go into print to expose their feelings; do-it-yourself and humanist funerals are becoming more popular; personal and emotional stories about death, murder and disaster, along with close-up photographs of grieving men, dominate the front pages of newspapers (Littlewood *et al.*, forthcoming); even sociologists now write about the subject (Walter 1993b). In the USA – supposedly even more repressed about death than the UK – the deluge of articles, books and television documentaries is bigger still and has been going on for longer; and college courses in death and dying, virtually unknown in Britain, numbered over a thousand by 1976.

All this sounds like a society obsessed with death, not one that denies it. In some circles, not least the quality media, death and our feelings about death are no longer taboo but the new radical chic. And yet some dying people still feel isolated, many bereaved persons find themselves an embarrassment to their friends, and many funerals remain cold and impersonal.

If death is undergoing a revival, in what form is it being revived? In this book, I contend that it is increasingly being shaped by neither the dogmas of religion nor the institutional routines of medicine, but by dying, dead or bereaved individuals themselves – though often at the invitation of doctors and nurses. In a culture of individualism that values a unique life uniquely lived, the good death is now the death that we choose. The good funeral is the funeral that uniquely marks the passing of a unique individual, and psychological manuals that prescribed stages of grief for mourners to pass through are now being discarded for an awareness of the infinite individual variations in the way people grieve. As one manual puts it:

> It should be your objective as friend and supporter to help your friend let go of life *in his own way*. It may not be your way, and it may not be the way you read about in a book or magazine, but it's his way and consistent with the way he's lived his life.
>
> (Buckman 1988)

In a popular song (played sometimes at funerals), Frank Sinatra – observing that the end was near and that he faced the final curtain – reviewed his life with evident satisfaction, concluding 'I Did It My Way'. Individualism's requirement that I live my own way is increasingly being extended to a requirement that I die and mourn my own way.

This is a remarkable innovation. In all previous societies there were *shared* norms as to how to die and how to mourn. The medieval *ars moriendi* applied to all, king and slave alike (Hawkins 1990: 314); in seventeenth-century England, published deathbed accounts told Puritans the proper way to die; in the nineteenth century, magazines instructed the various social classes in the appropriate length of mourning for particular categories of loss. What we find today is not a taboo but a babel of voices proclaiming various good deaths (Kastenbaum 1988; Hawkins 1990; Williams 1990). As one clergyman put it to me, 'There is no such thing as postmodern death. Just a million and one individual deaths.'

While 'do it your own way' is a radically new instruction to dying and bereaved people and to the arrangers of funerals, it is at the same time the logical conclusion of Western individualism, which for several centuries has been moving death rituals inexorably in this direction (Gittings 1984).

In a late twentieth-century 'postmodern' culture that celebrates individuation and fragmentation in an extreme way, we are reaping the full fruit of individualism. To discover whether the fruit is sweet or bitter is one concern of this book.

Free individuals may be able to choose in the market place between different vegetables or automobiles. But detached from extended kin and community, many seem not to have made a very good job of choosing their sexual partners, compared to those societies where marriages are arranged by the family. Will they be any more successful at knowing how to die and how to grieve? Religion has lost its authority in matters of death, just as it has in that other area where our bodily nature is so central – our sexuality. With religion, community and family providing little instruction, will people know how to determine their own exit from this world? If so, what criteria will they employ? It is perhaps not surprising that many modern people want their dying, unlike their sexuality, arranged for them and not surprising that they willingly place themselves in the hands of doctors and undertakers.

And what of the body? What if I ask for life-sustaining drugs to be withdrawn when I feel my time has come, but my body refuses to give up? The course of death, like love, never runs smooth. What kind of assistance is the individual going to require?

The more significant a choice, the more likely the chooser is to first look around to see what choices others have made. How to die is certainly one choice one does not want to get wrong. Despite all the rhetoric of choice, we find hospices promoting clear notions of the good death, undertakers offering a limited range of options, and bereavement counsellors defining as 'normal' the feelings of their clients. Certain ways of dying and grieving are promoted as 'natural', 'traditional', 'psychologically healthy' and 'normal', and thus their status elevated beyond mere personal preference, but to what extent are people influenced by such promotions? To what extent is it not so much a matter of doing it my way as doing it *our* way?

The metaphor of *revival* used in the title of this book is a triple one. There is the metaphor of death as a topic of discourse having died and now being revived; the metaphor of the revival of traditional/natural ways of dying; and the metaphor of a religious revival. The religious metaphor is particularly potent. Just as religious revival breathes new life into an ossified church, so the revival of death is breathing new life into ossified institutions – notably hospitals which are now being required to treat dying patients in a more individual and personal way. As in religious revival, there is disagreement as to whether revivalists should form their own breakaway groups (hospices) or work within the old church (hospitals). Revivalists are true believers, for they *know* the right way to die and grieve. As in religious revival, they have their charismatic leaders, such as Elisabeth Kübler-Ross and Cicely Saunders. And as in religious revival, the question emerges of how charisma can be routinised: how can a vision for a few become a system for all, without the vision being lost (see Chapter 11)?

Troeltsch's (1931) original delineation of religious revival identified two forms: sectarian and mystical. There are signs of mysticism in today's revival, for it promotes the inner and unique experience of the dying and bereaved individual. Yet there is also a tendency to sectarianism: to define the experience of dying and grief, to concoct a new orthodoxy.

The revival of death is religious in more than just a metaphorical sense. In palliative care and bereavement counselling, many revivalists are themselves committed Christians who see their work as a Christian calling. Closer observation, however, suggests that their framework is more humanist than traditionally Christian. Maybe the 'revival' is not a revival of a Christian approach to death but the introduction, paradoxically in large measure by Christians, of a humanist approach (see Chapter 6)?

In addition to perusing the wide and varied literature in this area, I conducted 45 formal interviews in 1992-3 with adherents and observers of revival: nine with hospice administrators, eight with clergy and chaplains, seven with doctors (this includes repeat interviews with one hospice doctor who welcomed the probing questions of a sociologist), six with nurses, four with bereavement counsellors, three with social workers, two with leaders of bereavement self-help organisations, two with Buddhist hospice workers, two with volunteer carers, and two with members of AIDS organisations. Nine of these interviews were conducted in San Francisco, the others in the South of England. I also had many other conversations in the course of visiting establishments and in attending professional and academic conferences, and I sought out a number of academics to discuss their ongoing and at the time unpublished research. I have drawn too on the many interviews and visits to cemeteries and crematoria that formed the basis of my earlier book on funerals (Walter 1990). I received no funding or formal institutional support for the project which has been motivated mainly by my own intellectual curiosity.

OUTLINE OF THE BOOK

Chapter 1 traces the historical development of the 'dying' of death in the modern era. It highlights the contradiction between on the one hand an increasingly rational, medical, secular and bureaucratic approach which tends to depersonalise and hide death; and on the other hand the personal and private nature of loss. The inability of bureaucratic and medical discourses to articulate private pain may underlie accusations that death is 'taboo'. Chapter 2 introduces the attempt to revive death. The feelings of people who are dying or bereaved are now to be listened to and taken seriously – private feelings become part of public discourse, and a public language is to be provided for private feelings. Chapter 3 unravels two strands within the revival. A late-modern strand expertly manages and provides a language to articulate the feelings of the dying or bereaved person; a postmodern strand is more radical in placing the individual's authority over that of the expert. Chapter 4 develops three ideal types of death – traditional, modern and neo-modern – as a device for under-standing the historical development and present complexity of our death culture.

The second part of the book examines in more detail how and whether neo-modern death may be put into practice. If people who are dying and bereaved are now required to break the taboo and tell others what they feel and what they want, then someone out there must be listening – very attentively and without presuppositions. But is it possible to develop systems and organisations that can listen attentively (in the UK) to half a million dying people a year and rather more survivors?

Chapter 5 looks at the stories told by people who are dying and bereaved, and how these have been used to create one overarching meta-story which in turn influences subsequent story telling. Chapter 6 asks how systems for listening are being developed in hospital and hospice wards, and how effective they are in attending to emotional and spiritual as well as physical distress. Revivalists are committed to caring for the whole person but may have different ideas of what constitutes a person and so in Chapter 7 I examine whether it is possible for carers to 'bracket' their expectations and assumptions about the nature of persons. Chapter 8 explores this further: to what extent are hospices and bereavement groups not only settings in which patients and clients can speak and be heard, but also settings in which they learn about the good death and good grief? Chapter 9 examines limitations to the new ideal that the dying person be in control. Chapter 10 asks to whom carers should be listening anyway. Some dying patients are not able to speak, so who should be listened to in their stead – a key question in some requests for euthanasia. If funeral directors are to pay more attention to the person's wishes, then which person – the deceased or the survivors? What if the survivors are a quarrelsome bunch and cannot agree? Who counts as the chief mourner? Religious revivals can suffer from expansion that requires rational and bureaucratic organisation. In Chapter 11 I ask whether the revival of death likewise risks losing its original vision. Some in the hospice movement fear that the federal (USA) or National Health Service (UK) funding game they now have to play may subvert their mission. Chapter 12 briefly looks at the funeral: how can the personal approach of revival transform funeral ritual rather than abolish it?

The final concluding chapter raises a number of questions. Is death a universal fear that can be faced only with the traditional resources of community, religion and ritual, as many social scientists have asserted? Or is death something the postmodern person can define and face in any number of ways? Which in the long run will prove more powerful: professional expertise or the choices of dying and bereaved people themselves? Such questions are crucial not only for the future of revival but also for postmodernism. Moreover, the company in which people face death and loss is changing: what is the effect of serial monogamy, social and geographical mobility, and self-help groups on the kind of human companionship available at this most testing of times? Is it possible that the now increasing profile of death may lead to a strengthening of certain communal bonds, or will revival collapse inwards in a fit of therapeutic introspection?

At the end of each chapter I have listed further reading and some questions for class or personal use. Some of the questions have more relevance for professional carers, others for sociologists.

Part I

Doing it my way

Chapter 1

The dying of death

RATIONALISATION

For millennia, death has disrupted communities and the language of death has been the communal language of religion. In the modern era, however, the human encounter with death has been split – on the one hand into expert medical discourse and associated bureaucratic procedures, and on the other hand into an intensely personal sense of loss. This chapter describes the historical and contemporary development of this split.

From the fifteenth to the seventeenth century, a common artistic image depicted a man or woman going about their daily business but with a skeleton, personifying Death, tugging at their coat tail or tapping them on the shoulder. In the image of death and the maiden, the living embraced the skeleton. Mortal illness could strike anyone, not only in times of plague, with little warning and with death ensuing in a matter of days; death was capricious, determined only by the inscrutable will of the Lord.

This changed with the arrival in the 1680s of the mathematical notion of probability (Hacking 1975; Prior 1989; Prior and Bloor 1992). Though no one could predict exactly when the Grim Reaper would call your name, the new science of statistics made it possible to calculate the *chance* of your dying in any given year or living to a particular age. In the gaze of the statistician, death takes not individuals but populations and sub-populations. By 1837 in England, all deaths had to be registered, thus making possible the systematic compilation of mortality statistics. The image of Death tugging at the coat of a unique individual is replaced by the life table that enables actuaries to calculate pension premiums and by statistics that enable health care planners to correlate mortality with environment, nutrition, income and so forth.

The Age of Reason shifted death from the frame of religion into the frame of reason, from the frame of sin and fate to the frame of statistical probability. The job of the public official is not to pray over the corpse, but to register, categorise and sanitise it. The rise of medicine and science replaced the basic category moral/immoral with normal/abnormal and healthy/unhealthy, in death as in life – the word *normality* appearing first in 1759, and *normalised* in 1834 (Arney and Bergen 1984: 21; Canguilhem 1978: 151). Exit the good death, enter the normal death. Exit the bad death, enter the abnormal death.

Modern law cannot allow a death not to be rationalised. If there is any doubt about the circumstances or causes of death, the body becomes the property of the pathology lab or the coroner so that a post-mortem can be conducted and a cause determined, often to the considerable distress of relatives who are not able to view, let alone care for, the body (Naylor 1989: 238). In post-mortems, scientific examination of the body (often necessitating considerable mutilation) takes precedence over the personal sensibilities of survivors or (in the case of some minority religions) the requirements of religious ritual.

Statistical rationalism has now colonised even the emotions of the dying and their survivors. The basic category in the psychology of grief since the 1950s has been that of normal grief/abnormal grief. Worden, one of the authors most widely recommended on both sides of the Atlantic in the training of bereavement counsellors, makes it clear that 'normal' gets its meaning from the discourses of medicine and of statistics:

> I am using the word *normal* in both a clinical and a statistical sense. 'Clinical' defines what the clinician calls normal mourning behavior while 'statistical' refers to the frequency with which a behavior is found among a randomized bereaved population. The more frequent the behavior, the more it is defined as normal.
>
> (Worden 1991: 21)

In the seventeenth century the religious event of Death taking a soul became a medical event; in the twentieth century human emotion has been shifted into that same rational medical realm. Kübler-Ross's (1970) classification of the emotions of the dying in terms of five universal psychological stages completes the 300-year rationalisation of death. The dying join the living in being judged by those experts in normality whom Foucault has argued are major wielders of power in modern society.

> The judges of normality are present everywhere. We are in the society of the teacher-judge, the doctor-judge, the educator-judge, the social worker judge; it is on them the universal reign of the normative is based;

and each individual, wherever he may find himself, subjects to it his body, his gestures, his behaviour, his aptitudes, his achievements.

(Foucault 1977: 304)

The rationalisation of death is well illustrated in the Consumers' Association book *What To Do When Someone Dies*. This tells you nothing about what you should do to prepare the soul for the next life, nothing even about the emotions you may feel, but is entirely about the forms that have to be filled in, the bureaucratic procedures that have to be gone through in order legally to dispose of the body. If you live at the margins of society, you can get through most of life without paperwork, but you cannot get through death without paperwork (Prior 1989).

This much is all too apparent to the survivors. So much so that they willingly move from the medical arena into the arms of a funeral director to help them through the maze of bureaucracy. One book on etiquette describes how the doctor hands you over to the undertaker and: 'In this way, the person who is perfectly ignorant of the proper procedure is passed on from one authority to another and is guided throughout with valuable information' (Willoughby 1936). Bureaucratic rationality permeates behind the scenes as well. The American practice of holding the funeral in the funeral parlour began because of the organisational nightmare of transporting coffin and mourners together along the crowded highways of Los Angeles to the often distant cemetery.

A more efficient 'funeral' is held at the funeral home: the casket bathed in light, the family around it, the eulogy spoken, the casket lowered into the darkness, tears shed, and the family departing. Once in the basement, caskets can be stacked and driven, singly or in multiples, out to the appropriate cemeteries according to the work schedules of those cemeteries. Deaths and the accompanying cemetery work, formerly unpredictable, can now be brought under rational control.

(Kamerman 1988: 80)

In the UK where cremation is the norm, the scheduling of funerals to fit into a time slot available at the crematorium rather than for the convenience of mourners is another example of bureaucratic rationalisation. The rapid expansion of cremation in the mid-twentieth century was largely driven by local authorities as a way of solving their financial and administrative problems (Jupp 1993), so the actual layout of British crematoria is determined neither by the requirements of religious ritual nor by a careful study of the needs of mourners, but by ease of operation and by Department of the Environment guidelines. In some other countries, however, such as Finland and to some extent the USA, cremation developed not for reasons of rationality but to enable families to place remains in a family grave when there was no room left in the grave for a further body.

In France, the rationalisation of cemeteries goes back to the Revolution (McManners 1981); in Britain it began in earnest in 1843 with Chadwick's report and Loudon's influential treatise on cemetery management, both of which recommended that the chaos of burial in the rapidly expanding industrial towns be solved by constructing out-of-town cemeteries with rational layouts, clear numbering of graves, no re-use of graves, and (in Chadwick's report) only one grave per person (Prior 1989: ch. 5). With ownership of the new cemeteries in the hands not of the church but of municipalities and private companies, the corpse could be cared for in the efficient hands of Reason rather than in the ritual hands of Religion.

MEDICALISATION

At the late eighteenth-century deathbed the doctor took control from the dying man or woman and from the priest. Previously, doctors had seen their role as predicting the timing of death so that the dying person could organise their last hours. But then the doctor remained until the moment of death, administering opium to relieve the pain and sometimes keeping knowledge of imminent death from the patient in order to relieve suffering. Thomas Sheridan, writing in the 1760s, observed this shift and didn't like it: 'Very few now die. Physicians take care to conceal people's danger from them. So they are carried off, properly speaking, without dying; that is to say, without being sensible of it' (Porter 1989: 89).

Death ceased to be a spiritual passage, and became a natural process overseen by doctors. 'We have seen death turn from God's call into a 'natural' event and later into a "force of nature". . . . Death had paled from a metaphorical figure, and killer diseases had taken its place' (Philippe Ariès, quoted in Arney and Bergen 1984: 31). This deconstruction of death into discrete, identifiable diseases is seen by Bauman (1992) as the hallmark of death in the modern era. The human being is no longer shadowed by a single skeleton personifying Death, but by any number of germs and diseases which attack medically identifiable organs of the body.

In medical practice, these vulnerable organs have a double relationship to the corpse. It is not only that the corpse is explained by the presence of one or more failed organs, but also that in medical training the organs are identified by means of the corpse. The role of the anatomy class, in which pairs of students learn anatomy through dissecting a corpse, has been revealed in the past two decades by some of the most intriguing of sociological and historical research. Whereas in life all the doctor can witness are symptoms, under the scalpel death reveals to the student's gaze what the body is really made of. In this medical gaze, the human body becomes objectified, no longer a person but a constellation of objects to be subjected to medical scrutiny (Foucault 1973). The patient's own experience of his or her body is inferior to the objective knowledge of the doctor. Richardson (1989) has shown the extreme lengths to which unscrupulous characters (who dug up fresh corpses and even murdered unsuspecting victims) and, after 1834, even the state (which made available the bodies of paupers) would go in order to meet the insatiable demand of the anatomy schools for corpses in good condition. Though voluntary donation now meets the demand, the anatomy class remains a key part of medical training, even if it is a process that some students find distressing (Coombs and Powers 1976; Hafferty 1991). Not only are dead and dying bodies medicalised, but dead bodies enable the medicalisation of living bodies.

Death is medicalised in other ways too. The deathbed itself has moved from home to hospital, where two-thirds of Britons now draw their last breath. Cases of serious stroke and heart attacks are rushed to hospital; those with a lingering illness may spend most of their time at home, but are likely to be transferred to hospital for their last days.

Once the body has been buried or burned, medicalisation is extended to the survivors. Lindemann (1944) wrote about the 'symptomatology and management' of grief, and Engel suggested that grief is comparable to a disease and should become 'a legitimate and proper subject for study by medical scientists' (1961: 20). These two widely quoted articles reflect what was in any case happening: psychiatrists were, from the 1950s, laying successful claim to be the experts on grief, while the bereaved themselves were more likely to go and see a doctor than a priest or social worker.

Along with death's rationalisation and medicalisation went its masculinisation, for rationalist and medical discourses have, until very recently, been largely the preserve of men. It is significant that those in the 1960s who first challenged the appropriateness of these discourses for describing the dying person's experience and who began instead to pay close attention to what the dying themselves had to say, have been in large measure women – notably Cicely Saunders and Elisabeth Kübler-Ross.

SECULARISATION[1]

If medicalisation forms one side of the dying of death, the other side is secularisation. Although the oldest forms of some world religions, such as early Judaism, have not been concerned with the problem of death, it has been central to later religions, notably Buddhism and Christianity (Bowker 1991). Christianity has historically been a defence against death, offering a place in heaven for the righteous and defining death as a spiritual passage. This was a particular feature of the late Middle Ages, with fear of going to the wrong place becoming a major cause for devotion, art, prayer, and the increasing power of the church. Theologically, the Reformation rejected such trading on fear (though there have subsequently been hell-fire preachers enough who have traded in a very similar line). The paid-for prayers of the church were denounced as ineffective; all that mattered now was the faith of the person while alive and the grace of God. If the dying person was a believer, there was no need for a priest at their bedside – leaving an empty chair ready to be filled some two centuries later by the doctor. In the decades immediately after the Reformation, funerals were spartan affairs, as any prayers over the body could be interpreted as popish and even lead to the arrest of mourners. John Knox's Genevan Service Book of 1556 simply stated that

> the corps is reuerently brought to the graue, accompagnied with the congregation withe owte any further ceremonies, which beyng buriede the minister goethe to the church, if it be not farre off, and maketh some comfortable exhortation to the people, touching deathe and resurrection.
>
> (quoted in Rowell 1974: 82)

The Scottish Book of Common Order of 1564, said much the same, adding after the words concerning the minister 'if he be present and required'.

Just as the Reformed deathbed left a space to be filled later by the doctor, so the Reformed funeral left a space to be filled later by the undertaker – who first appeared in London in the 1680s. If Protestantism allowed dying to become medicalised, it allowed the funeral to become commercialised. Even before that, in the seventeenth century, mourners filled the gap left by Reformed religion with feasting, so that the funeral became more a social than a religious ritual (Gittings 1984).

Philippe Ariès' (1981) magisterial survey of Western attitudes to death is written from a largely French perspective and therefore underplays the effect of the Reformation compared with English historians such as Gittings or Americans such as Stannard (1977).[2] But Ariès does highlight another feature of secularisation, namely what he terms the shift from my death to thy death. In the high Middle Ages people were concerned with what would happen to their souls, but in the Renaissance the concern was more what would happen after death to their reputation on earth. The Renaissance man hoped that the art, architecture and literature produced or patronised by him would survive and so guarantee immortality. By the nineteenth century, however, people became concerned less with what would happen to their soul or name when they died than with how they would manage when their loved ones died. Thy death came to be feared as much as my death, bereavement as much as my own demise. In the romantic age of the holy Victorian family in which identity was increasingly found within the private family, the question became: how will I cope when death tears my family apart? 'One person is absent, and the whole world is empty' (Ariès 1981: 472).

This in turn undermined religious narratives. At the deathbed, the survivors' grief eclipsed any concern with the spiritual destination of the departing soul; the hope of an afterlife was not union with God but reunion with the beloved – still the major form of afterlife belief in Britain today (Walter 1990: ch. 21). Paradoxically it was the First World War, hell on earth, that finally killed off hell below – no field chaplain could even so much as hint that the brave lad he was burying might be going to the wrong place, and thereafter hell disappeared off the agenda in all but the most conservative of churches. And without hell, death lost any spiritual risk, and became a medical and psychological affair.[3]

All these changes are expressed in the final resting place of the earthly remains (Davies 1990: 31f). In early Christianity, believers were buried in mass graves awaiting the resurrection, with only the richest and holiest resting in individual tombs near the high altar. The Renaissance created the individual tomb that celebrated the earthly works of the male and the fertility and maternal qualities of the female. By the nineteenth century, these individual tombs began to express the grief of the survivor as well as, or instead of, the achievements of the deceased; the patriarch's tomb was adorned by his weeping spouse, symbolised by a drooping nude or less daringly by a weeping willow. By the late twentieth century it is becoming fashionable in some circles to scatter cremation ashes in a special place known only to close family. Communal resurrection has thus given way via the family tomb to private memories – a process not only of secularisation, but also of ever growing individualism and privacy.

INDIVIDUALISM

In societies where identity is bound up largely with the group, what is feared is the demise of the group. But the more individualistic a culture, the more my own personal demise becomes problematic: 'In death, we fear we will lose our "I", our "me-ness". And the stronger this idea of "I", the more distinct is the feeling of a separation from life and a fear of death' (Levine 1988: 14). This Achilles' heel of individualism has been been traced historically by Burckhardt (1960: 128–34) in his classic study of the Renaissance and by Gittings (1984) in her study of funeral customs in the early modern period, and has been noted by commentators on the present day such as Elias (1985) and Lasch in his study of narcissism in America (1978: ch. 9).[4]

In an individualistic Western culture, it is still possible to live in a settled community. I take for my measure of community how long people have lived together in the same neighbourhood.[5] All communities develop patterned ways of doing things – not least in relation to their dying, dead and bereaved – which become traditions, and out of these develop rituals. Moreover, if you live in a settled community and know every member of it, you become aware of the death not just of personal friends but of anyone in the locality who dies. You encounter death rather often, even if you live in the twentieth century with its low death rate. Leaman (1993) found that schoolchildren living in settled working-class communities in Liverpool encountered death more often than their mobile middle-class teachers; it was the teachers who were out of touch with patterned ways of handling death.

The decline of settled communities and their communal ways of death has occurred in two stages in the past two centuries. First there was the move from village life to the new industrial towns of Victorian Britain and to the booming cities of the New World. Cut off from long-established norms, people no longer knew what to do at death and all too willingly took the advice of the proliferating undertakers. Ownership of burial ground shifted substantially to (in the UK) the urban municipality and (in the USA) private enterprise (Farrell 1980: ch. 4; Sloane 1991). Now, in the late twentieth century, the automobile has made possible the professional and commercial handling of death even in remote villages. Clark's study of the once isolated Yorkshire fishing village of Staithes (1982: 134–5) notes that people are now more likely to die in hospital or nursing home far away, while the local carpenter has given way to the Co-op funeral director and final disposal of the body is often at the crematorium in the industrial town of Middlesbrough, 22 miles away.

The decline of communal rural death was not, however, the end of communal death. Many of the migrants to industrial cities created their own communities, of the kind studied by the Chicago School from the 1920s and by Young and Willmott (1957) in London's East End in the 1950s. Many of these created their own folk death cultures – I caught a glimpse of this in Bethnal Green, where in summer 1992 I found on the side of one house a memorial to those from the street killed in the First World War, still adorned with fresh flowers. The definitive embracing of privacy came with the move from inner city out to the suburbs. Without poverty to bind people together in the face of adversity, they are thrown back upon their own nuclear family and upon the services they can buy from the market and are entitled to from the welfare state. Privatisation, commercialisation and professionalisation now dominate.[6]

Possessing the body

The key to the commercialisation and professionalisation of death is the body, for power lies in the hands of whoever is in possession of the dying or dead body (Howarth, forthcoming). Relatives have to ask permission to see the dying person once he or she has entered the hospital or old persons' home. Relatives have to ask to see the body, once it is in the possession of the coroner (Awoonor-Renner 1991) or the funeral director. Funeral directors and doctors are, in Illich's (1977) phrase, 'disabling professions', removing the dying or dead body and with it the accumulated knowledge of how to care for it. For their part, families may be only too glad for the hospital to take the strain of nursing, and to have the undertaker take over after death: 'He was marvellous – he took all the pressure off. . . . All we had to do was pay the bill' (Office of Fair Trading 1989: 3.42). Those who argue that you can only regain control of dying by doing it at home, or of the funeral by disposing of the body yourself, are near the mark.

The trend towards cremation further disables mourners. Out of doors in churchyard or cemetery, mourners feel considerable freedom to do as they feel: to throw a flower on the coffin, to linger after the burial, to sit, to stand. Indoors in a crematorium, they are more clearly on someone else's territory, and rely on officials to tell them how to behave. Not that officials always find this task easy: some Anglican clergy I have talked to can find the ritual incompetence of mourners (who may not know to stand up for a hymn or what a hymn book is or that they are not supposed to chat while the service is going on) an extra stress in what is already a stressful situation. Underlying this stress in a British crematorium funeral is the uncertainty as to who really is in charge: the owners and managers of the premises are not present, while the officials who are – clergy and funeral director – are both playing away from home. In such a situation, everyone is disabled.[7]

When possession of the body is lost is important. Those dying of cancer spend most of their time at home, only being hospitalised for short periods and usually for the last period before death. So the individual and the family retain control over the months or even years of terminality, but lose control at the last moment – a loss that naturally carries over into loss of control of the corpse. In the United States things are slightly different, for hospitalisation may occur earlier or more frequently. But central to the American funeral is the wake, which the family hosts as mourners come to view the body. Even though this takes place in the funeral home, it does return some degree of management of the body to the family.[8] I surmise therefore that in the USA loss of control of the body begins at an earlier stage than in the UK, but may be partially regained after death.

Private grief

Even when the body has been disposed of, some critics (notably Gorer 1965: 64) argue that the disabling continues. Gorer claims that there are no longer rules of mourning, so neither the bereaved nor their friends and neighbours know how to relate to each other. Mutual avoidance is the solution adopted by one or both sides. Though this kind of situation has been heavily criticised by bereavement agencies, most people have will-ingly given up the older mourning etiquette and the submission to communal and often patriarchal authority that it entailed – historically, mourning has been imposed far more heavily on women than ever it has been on men. Marris's (1958: 35–41) study of widows and their families in the East End in the 1950s reveals the many ways the women of this generation chose to give up the old rituals, no longer wishing to spend long periods in widows' weeds.

Against the thesis that norms for mourning have collapsed, leaving individuals to deal with grief as they will, is the possibility that individuals have strong personal norms about the proper way to grieve, but these are not necessarily shared by their intimates (Littlewood 1992: chs 5, 6). Though this may reflect personality differences, it may also reflect differ-ent family traditions. For example, two elderly ladies in Bath, both of similar social backgrounds, were talking with me. One said that in her family women never went to the burial, the other said that in hers they always did. So Gorer may be wrong to say that there are no norms; it may be that there are too many norms, specific to family of origin, and not well enough understood by outsiders – including those marrying in.[9]

What is clear is that if the bereaved were once scrutinised for correct behaviour, there is now intense surveillance of their feelings – which previously (for women at least) had been hidden by the veil. British journalists often engage in this kind of emotional surveillance (Littlewood et al., forthcoming). Take the following biographical account, recently printed in a Sunday newspaper, of the reactions of Princess Elizabeth to the news that her father, King George VI, had died:

> Her reaction was unusual but, to those who knew her strength of spirit, perhaps not unexpected. She did not burst into tears. She did not become inconsolably grief-stricken. She did not stand staring into space, although the shock was tremendous. She went very, very pale. She became tense, strained – but very clear-sighted and very realistic. . . . She went into her room by herself. She was alone for only a short time and when she reappeared, there was no sign that she had broken down.
>
> (Hartley 1992)

A newspaper report of the funeral of 3-year-old Jonathan Ball, killed by an IRA bomb in 1993, began:

> The grief finally became too much today. Despite the barriers of dignity and pride that Wilf and Marie Ball had tried to erect around their son's senseless death, the emotions broke through. . . . Today, his mother collapsed as Jonathan's small, white coffin was taken from the family home to a waiting hearse for the short journey to the church where he was baptised. Her 58-year-old husband tried to help her to her feet. Then he too succumbed to the overwhelming sense of despair and sobbed, briefly but agonisingly, into his calloused hands.[10]

Just because there are no longer widely shared norms for grief does not mean to say that the British are not intensely interested in the grief of others. Indeed, it may be precisely because there are no shared norms that they are so interested. If it is up to me how to grieve, I had better watch others to get some ideas.

But despite all reports of mourning norms having collapsed, there does seem to be a norm, at least among the English. It is that you should feel deeply, not show your feelings, but nevertheless show that you *are* feeling. Lady Troubridge's *Book of Etiquette* (1926) provides an aristocratic exhortation to this effect back in the 1920s, and its sentiments would be echoed by many a middle- or working-class person of today.

The ladies of a bereaved family should not see callers, even intimate friends, unless they are able to control their grief. It is distressing alike to the visitor and the mourner to go through a scene of uncontrolled grief. Yet it is difficult to keep a firm hold over the emotions at such a time, and it is therefore wiser to see no one if there is a chance of breaking down. . . . Even relatives should remember that the bereaved ones will want to be by themselves, and that solitude is often the greatest solace for grief

(Troubridge 1926: 57–8)

Presumably the gentlemen of the household had enough control of their emotions not to require social isolation.

Without burdening others with your grief, you should nevertheless make clear that you are feeling, for no one wants to be seen as cold and unfeeling. *In memoriam* notices in the paper can do this effectively. Hockey gives examples from newspapers from the north east of England in the late 1970s:

No-one knows my sorrow
Few have seen me weep
I cry from a broken heart
While others are asleep.

Silent thoughts, tears unseen
Keep their memories evergreen.

A secret longing, a silent tear
Always wishing you were here.
(Hockey 1990: 48)

Behaviour at funerals must similarly hint that one is feeling, without actually displaying the feelings themselves; what is required is a stiff upper lip, but with a quiver in the voice, a sniff, a dab at an eye, to show that, really, you feel deeply. As Ariès puts it: 'Privacy is distinguished both from individualism and from the sense of community, and expresses a mode of relating to others that is quite specific and original' (1981: 610).

There may well be a two-way relation between privacy and commer-cialisation. Roberts' (1989) interviews with old people in Lancashire about life at the beginning of the century reveal that it was their increasing desire for privacy that led people to abandon the services of the local woman who used to lay out the body. They did not want her in the house doing something so intimate – better to pay the undertaker to do it as an impersonal commercial service. These new professional disposers of the dead excluded the community from participation, involving only the immediate family (Hockey 1990: 48).

Increasingly, the funeral has become a private family affair.[11] If non-family members attend, they are likely to do so not out of duty but out of personal sympathy for the family. Although the practice of publishing in the newspaper the list of those who attended still occurs in rural South Wales, it died out in Leeds back in the 1950s (Naylor 1989: 46). When in 1993 a friend of mine lost her husband, she invited mourners to fill in a card and write a personal message – not with the intention of publication but so she has a private record of her friends' own memories of her husband. Exit public duty, enter personal support.

Increasing privacy may also be seen in the evolving tradition of the funeral tea. In Clark's study of Staithes (1982), villagers would lay on a tea for the whole community. In Naylor's study of industrial Leeds the tea was for the extended family, 'no longer a gift from the deceased to the community, but . . . a de-briefing and supportive ceremony for the ber-eaved' (1989: 339). In other areas, because of the complex logistics of travel from a distant crematorium back to the home, the tea may be abandoned altogether (Jupp 1993), leaving the widow alone with just her children and a glass of sherry.

What the bereaved find helpful is not the public funeral, which can be an ordeal, but the private and more conversational rituals that take place in the following months: receiving sympathy cards, writing letters, tend-ing the grave (Bolton and Camp 1986; Clegg 1987). This hints at a recurring theme in this book: the replacement of community not by the isolated individual, but by the individual communicating with a trusted other.

Elias (1985) considers that the replacement of culturally prescribed dying by informal conversation is not easy. What he writes could equally be applied to mourning:

> The task of finding the right word and the right gesture therefore falls back on the individual. The concern to avoid socially prescribed rituals and phrases increases the demands on the individual's powers of invention and expression. This task, however, is often beyond people at the current stage of civilisation. The way people live together, which is fundamental to this stage, demands and produces a relatively high degree of reserve in expressing strong, spontaneous affects. . . . Unem-barrassed discourse with or to dying people, which they especially need, becomes difficult. It is only the institutionalised routines of hospitals that give a social framework to the situation of the dying.

These, however, are most devoid of feeling and contribute much to the isolation of the dying.

(Elias 1985: 26–7)

Many bereaved people would add that they do not even have the benefit of institutional routines. Whether Elias is right that at the present stage of civilisation we are not developing and cannot develop less formal rituals of communicating with dying and bereaved people, is a question to which I will return. But it is clear that there is something of a vacuum. Community and religion, the two underlying supports of habitual ways of dying and grieving, are in long-term decline and no longer provide unquestioned authority. We have become detraditionalised and are struggling to fill the gap.

RATIONALITY VERSUS INDIVIDUALISM

The death of the patient in the hospital, covered with tubes, is becoming a popular image, more terrifying than the skeleton of macabre rhetoric.

(Ariès 1981: 614)

Several authors nod their heads sadly at the sorry state into which modern death has got itself and look wistfully at death in previous centuries and in far-flung climes. I do not intend to do this. I am not saying that before the twentieth-century death was emotionally satisfying. An emotionally satisfying, rather than a spiritually efficacious, death is actually a twentieth-century ideal. Nor am I saying that death in the twentieth century is all bad. I would rather die in this century, with its medical help than in any previous century; it is only in this century that the poor as well as the rich get a decent funeral; and it is only in modern bureaucratic welfare states that the widow need not fear utter destitution or dependence on kin. What I *am* saying is that along with modernity's bureaucratic and medical achievements goes a painful conflict, and that this conflict is what motivates the attempt to 'revive' death in a new form.

The conflict is simply between the rational bureaucracy which has helped tame death and the ever increasing individualism of the modern era. In the seventeenth century it did not matter if clergy who said the funeral service at the graveside did not mention the deceased's name or referred to 'the corpse', for the minister was known and people not so obsessed with individual identity. But today, when the crematorium duty minister does not have the personal touch, it is an appalling final statement for someone who spent his or her life carving out a little bit of individuality from the mass society and fails those survivors who wish to hang on to some remnant of that individuality (Walter 1990: ch. 6).

This can be understood in terms of Ariès' (1981) distinction between our century's *hidden* or even *forbidden* death which is removed from the family, church and community and processed instead by impersonal functionaries; and the powerful legacy of Victorian romanticism in which the loss of the other, *thy* death, renders bereavement seemingly unbearable. Most people now die when elderly and retired, children departed and self-supporting, so that – unlike in previous centuries when many died as mothers, breadwinners and workers – the economic life of not only factories and offices but even of families can continue untouched by death (Blauner 1966). But marriages and parent–child relationships may last 40 or 50 years, so the death of a spouse or parent can be a greater emotional loss than ever it was. Death becomes socially and economically less and less relevant, but personally and emotionally more and more painful; absent in public and present in private (Mellor 1993). The modern era has to a large extent solved the economic and social problem of death, but left its members with an enlarged emotional problem. This contradiction is 'resolved' through the norm of privacy, which hides the pain of dying and grieving from public view.

Another way of articulating this is through the sociological concept of modernity (to be developed further in Chapter 3). Modernity entails a profound split between the public and the private realms, between the world of work and reason and the world of family and emotion, and this split is reflected in the modern way of death. Death has been stripped of its public spectacle and has become a private, family experience. At the same time, there are public discourses and practices relating to death – in medicine, in public health legislation, in health service planning, in actuarial practice, in life insurance premiums, in the management and maintenance of crematoria and cemeteries, and in the media. With the partial exception of the media, the public practices and discourses are impersonal and unrelated to the private experiences of individuals who are dying or bereaved. Mellor is correct to say that death in modernity is present in private, but wrong to suggest that it is absent in public. Ariès is correct to say that the pain of loss is largely hidden, but wrong if he is implying that death itself is hidden. The problem is rather that private experience and public discourse do not tally. When individuals who are dying or bereaved complain that 'death is a taboo subject', this does not mean that there are no publicly available languages for talking about death but that these languages do not make sense of the experiences and feelings of the individual and his or her friends, family and neighbours. They therefore do not know what to say or how to say it.

Revival – the critique of this modern way of death – derives from this contradiction between private experience and public discourse, and intends to abolish it. Without losing the benefits of modern medicine and the welfare state, many now feel dying, funerals and bereavement must be made more personal. The dying person must cease to be a medical embarrassment, and set his or her own agenda. The funeral must no longer be driven by commercial interests or bureaucratic convenience, and must honour the unique life of the deceased. The bereaved need not be a social embarrassment, but their grief should be acknowledged and allowed to take its natural course. Private experience must become part of public discourse.

The targets of this critique vary slightly on each side of the Atlantic. Because of their finely honed fear of law suits, American doctors are more likely to engage in unfruitful high-tech intervention so they can claim they tried everything; for the same reason, they are more likely to inform the patient of the prognosis. In Britain, our emotional reserve may make bereavement a particularly isolating and protracted experience, and it may be significant that two of the most cited critics of modern bereavement – Geoffrey Gorer and Colin Murray Parkes – are British.

In this chapter, I have outlined how dying and grief are increasingly being done 'my way' but how this very private way bears a price tag of loneliness – whether dying on my own in a side ward, or grieving on my own abandoned by friends and neighbours. In the next chapter, I will outline how the critics try to turn 'I did it my way' from pathos into triumph. Public rituals around death have withered and contracted so that, as a social event, death has 'died'; the critics would now 'revive' death, but in a transfigured form. The next chapter delineates this revived form.

FURTHER READING

Ariès, P. (1981) *The Hour of Our Death*, London, Allen Lane.
Elias, N. (1985) *The Loneliness of the Dying*, Oxford, Blackwell.
Mellor, P. (1993) 'Death in High Modernity' in D. Clark (ed.) *The Sociology of Death*, Oxford, Blackwell.
Prior, L. (1989) *The Social Organisation of Death*, Basingstoke, Macmillan.

QUESTIONS

Would you have found Victorian mourning rituals onerous or oppressive, and why? (See Morley 1971: ch. 6; Lou Taylor 1983: chs 2–6, 11.)

Do you agree that in collectively oriented societies death is less of a problem for the individual?

Is it modernity, or Anglo-Saxon reserve, that makes death embarrassing for many Britons and Americans today?

Chapter 2

The revival of death

Death in the first person

I am a student nurse. I am dying. I write this to you who are, and will become, nurses in the hope that by my sharing my feelings with you, you may someday be better able to help those who share my experience.

For me, fear is today and dying is now. You slip in and out of my room, give me medications and check my blood pressure. Is it because I am a student nurse myself, or just a human being, that I sense your fright? And your fears enhance mine. Why are you afraid? I am the one who is dying!

Death may get to be a routine to you, but it is new to me. You may not see me as unique, but I've never died before. To me, once is pretty unique! You whisper about my youth, but when one is dying, is one really so young anymore? I have lots I wish we could talk about. It really would not take much more of your time because you are in here quite a bit anyway.

If only we could be honest, both admit our fears, touch one another. If you really care, would you lose so much of your valuable professionalism if you even cried with me? Just person to person? Then, it might not be so hard to die – in a hospital – with friends close by.

(Anon 1970)

In the previous chapter I described how the rise of individualism and privacy and the erosion of community and religion led to a loss of tradition and hence to uncertainty and insecurity in the face of death, an insecurity resolved by medicine, by commercial undertakers and by bureaucratic welfare systems. As physical and financial beings people welcomed this, but as meaning-creating and self-determining individuals many felt lost. Medical discourse and bureaucratic practices failed to articulate private grief. Almost immediately, however, individuals have been attempting to regain control over the deathbed, the funeral, and their own grief, to reinsert private experience into public discourse. This chapter describes that attempt.

THE AUTHORITY OF THE SELF

First, the broader cultural context. In all areas of life as well as death, the individual is asserting his or her own authority. Old authorities – whether the church, tradition or duty – are being replaced by the authority of the individual self. Constraints are seen as undesirable, since they limit choice. The good choice is no longer the choice that is right according to external authority, but simply the choice that I have made: it is authenticated simply by me, the chooser.

This leaves the individual with a dilemma for he or she 'is free to choose among his desires, but he can never be certain that he has chosen what he needs' (Ignatieff 1990: 21). Discovering needs thus becomes the project of the individual (Walter 1985a), ensuing in a never-ending quest for the self, with seekers devouring therapies and self-help psychology books and meditative techniques without end. If once the priest told me how to live, now the therapist helps me to find my own way. The therapist also replaces the neighbour; if once I belonged to a community, now I have actively to seek my identity through expert help or through intimate friendships (Beck 1992: ch. 4; Berger *et al.* 1974; Giddens 1991, ch. 3; Giddens 1992; Rose 1989). Relationships enable me to find the real me; tradition, duty and ties of kinship obscure the real me.

As Giddens puts it, ritual is replaced by discourse. Ritualised family patterns are now deemed to destroy the self, but continuous conversation with the other (the sexual partner or if things are not going too well then a therapist or a women's or men's group) is the process through which self is discovered. Whether through talk or through more direct expression of feeling, the self must express itself. We have witnessed an expressive revolution (Martin 1981), a phenomenon of late capitalism that is in conscious reaction to the calculating utilitarianism of early and mid-capitalism (Bellah *et al.* 1985). An advanced capitalist economy has a problem of consumption: how to get its members to consume ever more when they already have all they need. The solution has been to create consumers with ever greater needs to express themselves, and who must purchase experiences and services to facilitate self-expression (Campbell 1987).

If I am to find a range of people with whom to talk, then society must become less hierarchical and more informal (Elias 1982). The child must feel free to talk with the parent, the pupil with the teacher, the patient with the nurse. The old hierarchical order, in which children were seen and not heard, in which dying patients kept quiet as starched nurses prepared the beds for matron's inspection, was not an order designed to incite discourse. It was an order designed not to promote self-discovery, but to place you unambiguously in the social hierarchy, providing you with a given identity rather than encouraging you to create your own.

How has all this affected religion? Flourishing religions today come in two varieties. Fundamentalism, which provides an external authority by which believers may live, can be very satisfying so long as believers can insulate themselves from the modern world (Bruce 1984). Second, and more important for my thesis, there is the replacement of religion by *spirituality*. If religion puts you in touch with a God out there and with meaning and mores external to the self, spirituality puts you in touch with your inner self and with the God within. Whereas the Catholic belongs to the one universal church and the Protestant chooses the church that seems right in the light of individual conscience, the New Age believer takes individualism to its ultimate conclusion, listening to an inner voice to select bits and pieces from the gamut of world religions and folklore to create a personal spirituality. The aim of spirituality is, in the title of one self-help book, to create 'a personal mythology to live by'; the distinction between the spiritual path and the path of self-discovery becomes blurred. In the words of New Age guru William Bloom, the spiritual path is 'Learning who one is. . . . Being me with more of me present. . . . Me becoming me, not me becoming something else.'[1] Clergy retrain as therapists, priests offer themselves as 'spiritual advisers'.

All this liberates the individual from external constraint and requires me to find myself, yet does it provide the conditions for this? Maybe Baudrillard is right when he says that 'we are now accelerating in the void' (1990: 4). If the self cannot exert its own authority, then normlessness is not liberation but anomie. In the next section, I will argue that the newly released authority of the individual self – with all the features described above – is what powers the current revolution in death and dying. Whether the individual self is up to the task of coping with the ultimate constraint of a failing body and with the ultimate unknown of its own demise, and what kinds of social support may enable it to do so, are questions to which we will return.

THE DYING SELF

Two significant developments in the past two decades have been in the area of palliative care and in the expanding discourse about euthanasia. 'Euthanasia' literally means good death, and advocates of euthanasia see the good death as one under the dying person's control. They argue that if a person has had enough, or has a terminal condition, or is no longer capable of interacting meaningfully with others, then that person, or those who are empowered to act on his or her behalf, should be able to end that life. The obsession of doctors with maintaining life at all costs and the dogmas of religion about life being in the gift of God rather than the possession of the individual, are rejected in favour of the authority of the dying self to determine its own end. Given the difficulty for the individual self of making such a decision when the body and maybe the mind are in disarray, it is becoming increasingly popular while in good health to make 'advance directives' or 'living wills' in which one specifies the medical circumstances in which carers have the right to withdraw life-sustaining treatment.

The modern hospice movement, universally regarded as stemming from the founding in 1967 by Dr Cicely Saunders of St. Christopher's Hospice in south London, aims to let patients define their own dying. This philosophy has now expanded beyond the hospice and is the conventional wisdom in terminal cancer care in more mainstream medical settings. As a recent article in the journal *Palliative Medicine* put it, 'the "good" death is dying the way that the individual wants' (Lichter 1991).

Both Christian and secular hospices place the patient at the forefront of their philosophy. Du Boulay's (1984) biography of Cicely Saunders reveals how for her, as a Christian, the good death is not one in which the person has made peace with their Maker, but one in which 'he was himself'. She takes as much pleasure in the atheist who might retain to the end their humour and a penchant for a dram of whisky as in the devout believer. 'We are not at all concerned that a patient or family should come to think as we do but that they should find strength in their own inner values' (Saunders 1992: 4). The aim is to let the patient 'live fully until he dies as himself' (Saunders 1965). I asked the general manager of another hospice, a convinced Christian, what it meant for his hospice to be a Christian organisation. He gave two answers, one of which was 'To start where the patient is. To start by asking him what he feels and what he thinks.' I asked the less obviously devout medical director of the same hospice what he felt about its Christian ethos, to which he replied 'It seems to me that the Christian ethic of this place means treating people as individuals.' Or as one grateful young woman dying in an American hospice put it, 'Here I am simply myself, and no one minds' (Hamilton and Reid 1980: 4). The common factor in all these statements is a returning of authority from the Church and from medicine to the dying individual.

This philosophy has been made possible by new techniques of pain control, also developed at St Christopher's. The term *terminal* care has, since the early 1980s, given way to the term *palliative* care, palliative referring to the relief of pain and/or symptoms. Whether this terminological shift represents a hasty retreat from mentioning death even in the very institution set up to enable people to confront it, or whether it is an expansion of job specification in order to legitimate claims to a new professional specialty (Ahmedzai 1993; Biswas 1993), I cannot say. It certainly does represent a concern to give hope that pain, which is what so many fear about cancer, can be controlled. And usually it can.

Hospice workers are usually opposed to euthanasia, and not only because of religious conviction. They fear that active euthanasia (taking life) would make it too easy for doctors or wearied relatives to avoid their responsibility to seek every means possible to control suffering. Passive euthanasia (withdrawing treatment when the end is near so that life is not unnecessarily prolonged), however, is very much part of the hospice philosophy. Despite the battles over euthanasia, both sides believe that the good death is one where the dying person does it their own way. One of the major arguments against active euthanasia is that it would enable relatives, insurance companies or hospitals short of beds to pressurise the patient into making a decision against their real will, 'so as not to be a nuisance and a burden' (e.g., Saunders 1992); one of the major arguments for active euthanasia is that it enables the person to make their own decision. Both sides value the autonomy of the dying person; what they disagree about is how to safeguard that autonomy.

Since the self is now required to exert authority over how it is to die, there is an emphasis on the psyche and spirit, as well as the body, of the dying person. In some formulations, death is almost defined as a psychological rather than a physical process. By far the best seller in the whole area, Kübler-Ross's *On Death and Dying* (1970), is largely about the psychological adjustments that the author claims the dying person must make; though the author subsequently emphasised spiritual processes, this never caught the popular imagination in the same way. Although there is a tension in the book between dying my own way and dying according to the author's now famous five stages, the book clearly places the self – rather than medicine or the church – centre stage. Kübler-Ross is the prophetess of the new religion of the self, the revivalist *par excellence*.

Kübler-Ross identifies the task confronting the dying self as one of 'finishing the business' – both internally, coming to terms with myself, reviewing my life and completing the last chapter of my personal biography (Marshall 1980), and externally, saying farewell to and making amends with significant people in my life. Finishing the business is important in high modernity because freely chosen relationships are becoming more important than duty-bound and given relationships (Giddens 1991, 1992), so the last days and months require considerable monitoring and repair work on those relationships if the self is to be in good enough shape to direct its final act. True to our times, the means of achieving these tasks is discourse and expressing feelings.

Telling and talking

1965 saw the publication of *Awareness of Dying*, reporting the participant observation studies of sociologists Glaser and Strauss into the organisation of dying in several San Francisco hospitals. They found various 'awareness contexts': 'closed' (where the doctor and family conspire to keep the truth from the patient), 'suspicion' (where the patient tries various tactics to extract the truth from carers unwilling to tell), 'mutual pretence' (where both sides know the patient is dying, but neither wants to upset the other by mentioning it), and 'open' (where there is open communication between the patient, the family and professional carers). This book has been widely cited as showing the desirability of open awareness, a key item in the revivalist creed.

Since then there has in fact been a major shift from believing hope may be preserved in patients by keeping them ignorant of their condition, to believing that if they are to make their own decisions about what remains of their life they must be told the truth about their condition (Williams 1989). In 1961, Oken found that only 12 per cent of the American doctors surveyed said they would usually tell patients a diagnosis of incurable cancer; in 1979, Novack *et al.*'s replication study found 98 per cent of doctors saying they usually would tell. In Britain, there has been a similar change, though not so fast and not so complete – despite more open communication overall and a general intention to tell, actual telling by British doctors is by no means universal (Seale 1991a). Doctors are often now more keen to tell the patient than are the family, and it may be difficult for the doctor to convert some families to the idea of telling.

To die my own way, in this view, *prerequisite number one*, is that my doctor should tell; *prerequisite number two* is that I should tell my carers how I want to die. Not just tell them about my plans, but talk about and express my feelings, as indicated by the revivalist testimony at the beginning of this chapter and as mandated by Kübler-Ross. This is what

Wood (1977) has aptly termed 'expressive death'. *Prerequisite number three* is that once I have begun to talk, my carers should listen and take note. It is not just that the doctor is now required to tell; the patient is now required to talk, and carers to listen (Lofland 1978).

For all this to happen, the informalisation described by Elias is necessary. It is no accident that the shift in nursing regimes from supervising and policing patients to an apparently greater equality between nurses and doctors, and between nurses and patients, historically preceded the requirement for all parties to talk about the patient's impending death. Talking about fears, anxieties and other emotions simply did not fit the old hierarchical relationship (Wouters 1990: 152). Informality, by contrast, encourages discourse (Armstrong 1987; Field 1989, ch.4) – though as Hunt's (1989) study of home-care symptom-control nurses in the south of England shows, informality need not guarantee discourse.

There is a range of reasons why revealing the diagnosis is becoming the norm (Veatch and Tai 1980). Improved health care means that many people now spend months or years dying rather than a few days (what Glaser and Strauss (1968) term a 'prolonged dying trajectory'), and it is impossible to keep the truth from them for that long; during much of that time they may in any case be in good shape and able to cope with their prognosis. Another reason is that it is now possible to soften the bitter pill of diagnosis with hope that the patient can be kept free from distressing symptoms. Yet another is that with the removal of the terminal patient to hospital, where there are considerably more carers than at home, knowing who has said what to whom becomes so complicated that telling everyone everything solves a lot of problems. And in the United States, the only way doctors can protect themselves against malpractice suits is by getting each patient to give informed consent to treatment, which of course means telling them why treatment is recommended. And there is the problem that it is (ethically if not legally) a breach of confidentiality for the doctor to withhold information from the patient but to give it to the patient's family (Field 1989: 148). Whatever the reasons for telling patients, the result is the same: they are now able to consider dying in their own way. Having broken the silence and told the patient, the doctor has created a climate of openness which may encourage the patient to continue the discourse.

Other revivalists, however, argue that some patients do not want to know, and if they are to die *their* way then this should be respected and they should not have knowledge thrust upon them. Certainly many people would like to 'go out like a light' suddenly without knowing anything about it (Williams 1990: ch. 3) – but this is not so easy if instead of a massive coronary they actually contract incurable cancer. Can their desire for ignorance be sustained over a prolonged period without compromising their professional or family carers?

THE DECEASED SELF

At a recent workshop on funerals I attended in London, the following concerns were voiced by the very wide range of participants:

- the crematorium should allow more time for each funeral;
- the funeral director should offer the family more options;
- clergy should adopt a more personal approach in the funeral itself;
- families should participate more and have more control over events;
- things would go a lot better if more of the deceased do some prior funeral planning.

Although each professional group criticised some or all of the others, their criticisms all pointed in the same direction: the deceased person should take centre stage. The funeral should reflect his or her unique life rather than the commercial, bureaucratic or religious interests of functionaries. Even if using religious language, the funeral should be what the Australians call *life centred* (Walter 1990: ch. 20). Without necessarily going to the extreme of the deceased participating through tape or video recorded messages, he or she should be present to the extent that mourners go away saying 'Jill would have approved of that service' or 'Jack would have enjoyed that.' Increasingly, people want to do the funeral in a way that honours the deceased as a unique individual, not the undertakers' way, or the crematorium's way, or the religious way.

Funerals are certainly moving in this direction. In Britain, explicitly humanist funerals which self-consciously set out to celebrate a life are still rare but increasing fast, and in many religious funerals clergy are responding to criticism and making sure they say something personal about the deceased. The Sinatra Syndrome affects the funeral, as all else.

That said, the mission of revival is to improve the lot of the dying and bereaved rather than that of the deceased. Lofland observed this in California in 1978, and the same seemed true to me in Britain in 1988 – indeed it was the very paucity of books on reforming the funeral, contrasted with the shelves and shelves on caring for the dying and on bereavement, that motivated me to write such a book myself (Walter 1990). I suspect all this reflects the privacy referred to in the previous chapter, a privacy deep within even those who would challenge it. They all want dying people to interact better with their carers and intimates, and they want the pain of those who are bereaved to be acknowledged, but they tend to assume that the public ritual of the funeral is irrelevant to the repair of private feelings and intimate relationships.

THE BEREAVED SELF

Mourning, a socially prescribed set of public behaviours, has been replaced by something called 'the grief process' – a prescribed set of inner feelings. Advice to bereaved people now stems not from the rules of social etiquette but from expert knowledge about the work that must be done by the individual psyche. Gorer's critique still applies to 90 per cent of the progressive literature on grief even today:

> Investigators tend to write as though the bereaved were completely alone, with no other occupation in life but to come to terms with and work through their grief [and] this implicit picture of the solitary [person] who has nothing to do but get over his grief has tended to dominate the literature of the last twenty years.
>
> (Gorer 1965: 150, n. 37)

Even those who decry the loss of the old mourning rituals, and it is very fashionable in bereavement counselling circles to do so, advocate not bringing them back but sharing inner feelings with one or two intimates. I quote a leaflet called 'Bereaved Parents and the Professional' produced by The Compassionate Friends, a mutual-support organisation of bereaved parents.

> Bereavement is a process that must be allowed to run its course. This takes time. Our society today has lost the mourning rituals once routinely accepted, that helped families in their sadness. We do not give time to grieve, so those involved must create emotional space and help the family when a child dies. Grieving parents need to be able to share their deep inner feeling of heartache and desolation. They need to talk constantly about their child, his life and his death.

So here we find little huddles of bereaved individuals being encouraged to share their sorrow with one another rather than be subject to rules of mourning; we find ritual replaced by discourse, mourning behaviour by expressive talk. Not only this, we also find a reinterpretation of history in which the earlier rituals, whose functions were surely numerous and whose effect on the bereaved we know not, being confidently described as 'helping families in their sadness'. The past (Hockey 1993) as well as the present (Wambach 1985) is reconstructed in terms of this inner grief process.

The growing army of counsellors and self-help bereavement groups is at pains to reveal the isolation of many bereaved people in modern society, and the friendship and the listening ear they provide are certainly valued by many of their clients and members. This creation of a small space for the intimate ritual of counselling may be all that can be attempted, for perhaps public rituals are gone for good. The sharing of loneliness may not be a cure for individualism but it can be very effective first aid. We may not be able to reconstruct community, but we can construct self-help groups and pairs of lonely individuals having heart-to-hearts.

But it is also possible that this kind of first aid is actually isolating bereaved people still further from the wider community. One criticism made to me is that a mass education campaign to teach everyone how to listen to and support bereaved individuals would be more constructive than training skilled counsellors. And I have myself been surprised how rarely bereavement counsellors have thought about the communal functions of the funeral, and how when they do they always interpret it in terms of inner psychology.

Sheila Awoonor-Renner lost her 17-year-old son in a road accident, and publicised her experience of the aftermath.[2] Instead of her grief being accepted as part of life, she described being shunted off to a special counsellor who shunted her off to a special group of bereaved people who met once a fortnight. She found people telling her that it was OK to cry, but they were not happy about her crying with them – do it by yourself, or with a special group, they said. In such cases, counselling and self-help groups collude with the private modern way of death, keeping grief conveniently out of the everyday way so that life can go on as though death did not exist.

Some bereavement agencies are explicit that healing comes from within. A counsellor at the Center for Attitudinal Healing, a respected agency in the field of loss and grief in the San Francisco Bay Area, told me: 'Each person is responsible for themselves – nobody else can provide answers for them. It's a matter of reaching the place of inner peace, and letting go of fear.' The organisation's introductory leaflet spells this out further: 'The concept of attitudinal healing is based on the belief that it is not people or things outside ourselves that cause us to be upset, it is our own thoughts and feelings.' That may sound ultra West Coast and individualistic, but the idea is present in the widely accepted notion of 'the grief process'. In so far as there is a sharing with others, it is a sharing in private of essentially private meanings. There is no shelter here under what Berger (1969) has called a communal 'sacred canopy' of meaning such as is provided by traditional religions, simply a sharing of my own way with one other who can respect that way.

Revival's attempt to bring death out of the closet, then, criticises the isolation of the dying and the bereaved and the meaninglessness of production-line funerals, and puts the dying, deceased or bereaved person at the top of the agenda. But because the concern is with individual psychology, this may entail an even profounder individualism and an even profounder cutting off of death from everyday life. To quote two analysts of the revival of death, the new cultural scripts for dying tend to be 'individualistic, varied, emergent and uncodified' (Lofland 1978, writing about California) and 'do nothing to counteract the widespread privatisation of meaning in high modernity' (Mellor 1993, writing about the UK).

While the individual is required to choose his or her own script, particular subcultures may favour particular scripts. Richardson (1984) has suggested that old people who lived through the First World War may have a different approach to their infirmity and impending mortality than those of a younger generation who care for them, while Kellehear (1990: 134–5) hints at the specific approaches of Australians who fought in the Pacific theatre in the Second World War. Kalish and Reynolds (1981) outline some ways in which ethnicity moulds approaches to death in the USA, while in my own book on funerals (Walter 1990: ch. 5) I argue that men and women tend to follow different scripts. Williams's (1990) study of older people in Aberdeen shows that even those of the same gender, age and ethnicity may be able to draw upon a number of contradictory belief systems. Add to this the fact that professionals such as doctors and funeral directors may have different views of the good death from their patients and customers (Bradbury 1993), and it becomes clear that even without any injunction to do it my way we have moved a long way from any one culturally prescribed good death:

> Perhaps one reason why dying seems so difficult today is that individuals are expected not only to confront their own death – in itself a task arduous enough – but also to *create* a death out of the fragments of ideologies and religious sentiments with which our culture provides us. In a culture that values individuality, respects relativism, and affirms plurality, this may be inevitable, but it is a problematic situation for many.
>
> (Hawkins 1990: 303–4)

MEDICINE SUBJECTIFIES THE PATIENT

One might easily jump to the conclusion that the re-entry of the person into dying, funerals and grief is the product of a consumer revolt against professionalisation and commercialisation. That may be so in certain limited areas, such as the North American memorial society movement that asserts consumer power against the funeral industry (Mitford 1963) and also the determination of persons with AIDS to die, funeralise and memorialise their own way. But what is notable overall about the revival of death is that its charismatic leaders are doctors. Elisabeth Kübler-Ross, Colin Murray Parkes and Dame Cicely Saunders are all doctors. (Dame Cicely Saunders as a qualified nurse and social worker actually retrained as a doctor in order to be taken seriously.)

Arney and Bergen (1984) have documented how the reappearance of the person in medicine generally, not just in terminal and bereavement care, developed in the 1950s prior to any consumer/patient movement. Having originally objectified the patient into a discrete set of organs and physical malfunctions, medicine reconstituted the patient into an experiencing subject, into a whole person. Wouters' (1990) analysis of Dutch nursing journals and textbooks finds the person arriving on the printed page at the same time, the 1950s. If medicine was to penetrate further into the workings of the patient, it had to penetrate the patient's mind and social relationships as well as his or her body (Armstrong 1984: 1987). Doctors know what is going on in their patients' internal organs largely by observing them and by conducting objective tests, but in order to find out about patients' psyche and relationships, there is only one way – to get them to talk, and to listen to that talk.

Arney and Bergen argue that terminal care was central to this rediscovery of the person. And again, the key text is Kübler-Ross's *On Death and Dying*, which actually got patients to speak and which has sold well over a million copies. Kübler-Ross interviewed dying patients while students watched through a one-way screen, and thus 'restaged the anatomy lesson by placing the patient, now reconstituted as an experiencing person, under the rule of the gaze' (Arney and Bergen 1984: 49). If medieval and Reformation Christians gazed upon the dying and dead person's soul, if medicine in the Age of Reason gazed upon the body and upon the corpse, whole-person medicine today gazes upon the psyche.

It is not so much that I have decided to do it my way: I am being required to.

FURTHER READING

Armstrong, D. (1987) 'Silence and Truth in Death and Dying', *Social Science and Medicine*, 24: 8, 651–7.

Arney, W.R. and Bergen, B.J. (1984) *Medicine and the Management of Living*, University of Chicago Press.

Giddens, A. (1991) *Modernity and Self-Identity*, Oxford, Polity.

Lofland, L. (1978) *The Craft of Dying: the modern face of death*, Beverly Hills, Sage.

Martin, B. (1981) *A Sociology of Contemporary Cultural Change*, Oxford, Blackwell.

Rose, N. (1989) *Governing the Soul: the shaping of the private self*, Routledge, London.

QUESTIONS

What groups do you know of that have challenged the medicalisation of death? Were they started by patients, doctors or nurses?

Assess the evidence that bereavement organisations, while offering comfort and friendship, further isolate bereaved people from the rest of society.

Think of the funerals you have attended. Did they celebrate the life of the deceased? If not, what did they do?

Would you want to know if you were dying?

Chapter 3

The two strands of revival

The modern experience is typically one in which public and private life exist in separate spheres (Berger *et al*. 1974):

Public	Private
facts	feelings/meanings
reason	emotion
science (incl. medicine)	morality
objectivity	subjectivity
work (incl. hospital)	home
production	consumer choice

In modern death the public dominates the private. The personal feelings of the patient, and indeed of medical and nursing staff, are ignored as the patient is made into an object, a case, a site of disease. Death takes place not at home but in hospital, where private experience is suppressed by institutional routines. After death, the routines of factory and office give little space to the bereaved to express how they feel or to take time off.

The revival of death challenges this exclusion of personal feeling and attempts to intertwine public discourse and private experience. Revival has two strands: in the 'postmodern' strand, private experience invades and fragments public discourse, while in a more 'late-modern' strand, expert discourse manipulates private experience. These strands exist in a tension that can either be mutually strengthening or cause friction. Each strand is often present within the same organisation or even individual.

THE LATE-MODERN REVIVAL

The *late-modern* strand replaces control through medical understanding with control through psychological understanding. Death is now controlled because experts understand the stages dying people go through and can help them reach peace and acceptance. Grief is now controlled because experts understand normal grief, and can help grieving individuals attain resolution and move back into life, bruised but not beaten and disturbing no one. Expert counsellors have mastered techniques that enable them to listen and yet remain professionally distanced from what is said. All this is a more sophisticated version of control – of others and of death – through knowledge and technique. A more sophisticated version of modernity.

The late-modern form of revival of death links private and public. Hospice and palliative care link scientifically tested techniques of pain and symptom control with a commitment to the person dying in their own way. Life-centred funerals incorporate the personal style of the deceased into the mass throughput of the modern funeral home or crematorium. In bereavement counselling, the trained professional (representing the public sphere) acknowledges and affirms the feelings of the bereaved, but in so doing protects the public from these unruly feelings.

The public sphere continues to manage the private, but more subtly. 'In this case, death means emotional processes which can be identified, controlled and managed' (Perakyla 1988: 42). 'To a great extent, the modern revival of death is only a mutation of the dying of death. It springs from the therapeutic conviction that we can master what we can touch or talk about' (Farrell 1980: 223). If modernity is characterised by the system's ability to control individual members, then the late-modern form of revival is a more sophisticated system of control.

POSTMODERN REVIVAL

The trouble with the late-modern package is that it is being rejected because it is arrogant and because research is increasingly showing that people do not die or grieve in neat stages (Chapter 5). Maybe those closest to dying and bereaved people always knew this anyway. This gives rise to a more genuinely *postmodern* strand of revival, increasingly articulated in the literature. In this view, one should not, cannot, predict or control how any individual will die or grieve:

> We should beware of promulgating a coercive orthodoxy of how to mourn. In the last analysis, an 'appropriate' mourning is one that is acceptable to or tolerated by the mourner, not one so designated by either the helping professions, significant others, or the community. Individual differences and respect for personhood must be our principal guides.
>
> (Feifel 1988: 3)

In the late-modern strand expert knowledge incorporates personal experience. The expert becomes more and more subtly powerful, influencing even how the individual feels about their own dying or loss. The postmodern strand, by contrast, places private feelings firmly onto the public agenda – in medical training, hospital routines and the media. Public discourse is thus fragmented and the authority of experts challenged.

Postmodernism is a controversial term, which I am using as a shorthand to describe certain features of contemporary society that arguably involve a moving on from modernism. Postmodernism celebrates the private, and in so doing collapses the distinction between public and private. In so far as the feelings of the dying, deceased or bereaved person become paramount, we may appropriately term this postmodern: the patient opts for the treatment that best accords with his or her values or that he or she feels most comfortable with, not the treatment that doctors believe to be most effective. Revival literature relishes examples of cancer doctors enabling their patients to make informed choices that are not the choices that the doctor would have made (e.g. Kfir and Slevin 1991: 120–1), not to mention alternative cancer treatment centres in which the person's expression of their feelings and management of their private lifestyle takes precedence over medical treatments (e.g. Brohn 1987).

In celebrating private experience, postmodernism descends directly from nineteenth-century romanticism. But romanticism was oppositional, setting emotion against reason, private against public (Jameson 1991: 4) – and in the case of death, the feelings of dying and bereaved individuals against the demands of church or society (Ariès 1981: Part IV). Postmodernism, by contrast, conflates the public and the private: the private feelings of the dying and bereaved become the concern of the professional. Even the feelings of the professional become the concern of the professional. Ariès argues that the twentieth century has witnessed a conflict between two ideal types – the romantic death of the other and the institutionalised hiding of death. Revivalists, it seems, want to institutionalise romantic death.

Romanticism and the consumer are inextricably bound up. The more we emphasise personal experience and feelings, the more business cannot but attend to satisfying consumers' inner needs, enriching their experiences, and enhancing their quality of life (Campbell 1987). Postmodernism expands romanticism into an explicit celebration of the consumer. One intellectual, facing cancer in his own family, told me 'cancer is *the* postmodern disease'. It has multiple treatments, which means that middle-class patients can gather lots of different opinions, discover the side effects of each treatment and how it impinges on their personal lifestyle, and thus choose their own personal mix of treatments.

Jencks (1986) has argued that the key to postmodernism is *double coding*. In architecture he defines this as 'the combination of modern techniques with something else (usually traditional building) in order for architecture to communicate with the public and a concerned minority, usually other architects' (1986: 14). What makes the postmodern, then, is not a rejection of the modern and of the traditional, but a mixing of them at will, without any sense of inconsistency or shame. (The modernist cannot incorporate the traditional without gross shame.)

Double coding characterises much of the revival of death. It is very clear in the Natural Death Movement (Albery *et al.* 1993), in which bits of death cultures from around the world are mixed together at will. Disillusion with the modern way of death has led to a widespread interest in death in primitive cultures (e.g. Rando 1984: 5) or at least in our grandparents' time (e.g. Kübler-Ross 1970: 5). It has become almost obligatory for revivalist writers to eulogise primitive or Victorian death, in order to highlight the dreadful taboos and depersonalisation of the modern way (Lofland 1978). Pre-technological, pre-medical death is hailed as more personal and natural, more in touch with the natural rhythms of life and death. Elements of primitive death that do *not* fit the assumption of a golden age – and there are many, such as the life-threatening self-mutilation practised by Aboriginal mourners (Durkheim 1915) – are ignored. While asserting that all primitive cultures knew how to do death better than us, postmodern revivalists actually choose just the bits of primitive death that they personally would like to embrace. And in like manner they remain free to use whatever modern medical and pharmacological techniques they feel happy with. The individual can choose his or her own mix.[1]

Double coding accurately describes much contemporary palliative and cancer care. Modern medical and palliative techniques, along with modern psychological techniques, are combined with a postmodern concept of the self-determining individual, and with traditional values, family networks, and ideas and practices from every time and place under the sun. This is particularly evident in the modern hospice, and is illustrated in the following extract from a major evaluation of American hospices. The first sentence rejects modernity and harks back to traditional community, but the second sentence praises personal autonomy – the very thing that historically has undermined traditional community:

Hospices recalled that care of the sick and dying was a valued and respected vocation prior to the advent of science and that it was provided by families, neighbours, and practitioners with little, if any, scientific expertise. It was no accident that the hospice movement arose in Western societies that were committed to individual autonomy, as opposed to the autocracy of the Eastern, socialized nations; hospice care was an expression of commitment to personal freedom rather than submission to authority, whether political or professional.

(Mor *et al.* 1988: 246)

Though certain tensions may be felt (how for example do you scientifically evaluate a traditional quality such as compassion?), the mix generally feels good to patients, staff and funders.

Another example of double coding is the chemotherapy outpatients department at one leading London hospital. As the chemotherapy cocktail is infused into them, patients are offered massage and aromatherapy, to be followed if desired by counselling and spiritual healing, not to mention help from a social worker about finance while off work. The unifying theme behind the various treatments is care for the whole person, even if chemotherapy, social work and aromatherapy each derive historically from very different presuppositions about human nature. Like postmodern buildings, this kind of mix is both becoming part of the mainstream and is consumer friendly. But like some postmodern buildings, it may also bemuse many of the working-class and ethnic minority patients, while only a few of even the white middle-class patients actually take up the more exotic treatments. And just as the design of the postmodern building, despite its eccentric appearance, has utilised the very latest computer-enhanced engineering techniques, so the precision chemotherapy dose is based on the very latest medical knowledge.

This analysis suggests that it is a fundamental mistake to see the traditional elements in the revival of death as evidence of demodernisation – as, for example, does Kearl's textbook (1989: 490). It would constitute demodernisation only if there were an institutionalised refusal of the benefits of modern medicine or of efficient modes of organisation; this there rarely is. If a few individuals choose to reject conventional medical treatment, that is simply evidence of postmodern choice.

The trouble with putting dying people in the shoes of the postmodern consumer, of course, is that they have never died before (unless they have had a prior near death experience, which some claim removes fear of the unknown), and don't necessarily know how to die or what they want (see Chapter 8). The free market theory of the sovereign consumer assumes fully informed individuals, and death is something about which we can never be anything like fully informed. This means that the truly postmodern strand, letting people do it their way, alternates with the late-modern strand, with experts and those with experience of the field letting dying and bereaved people know what is the best way or at least providing them with information so that they can make more informed choices.

SELF AND REFLEXIVITY

So the second strand of revival is postmodern, but can never be thoroughly so, as the term is understood by many scholars. There are other reasons for this too. There is not, for example, the playfulness of the postmodern building or painting, and it is difficult to see how there could be around something as serious as death.

More important is the relationship of depth and surface. The postmodern painting or building is all surface, 'surrealism without the unconscious' (Jameson 1991: 174). Persons as well as buildings are all surface: 'The postmodern individual is less a sovereign individuum and more a collection of masks, images or personae under which it can no longer be taken for granted that a single actor exists' (Shields 1991: 274). The revival of death has a much more typically modern interest in depth, in the inner reaches of the person. Edvard Munch's famous painting *The Scream* is an icon of the modern person, depicting an inner, real self, alienated from everyday roles, deeply lonely, struggling to express itself (Jameson 1991: 11). Nothing could better convey the image of the dying or grieving person that the revivalists are attempting to reach. As one bereaved woman wrote thankfully, 'I have a CRUSE counsellor coming to see me and I feel I can be myself – I can be angry, be depressed and cry.'[2] The new approach to death typically retains all the elements of the modern image of the person: a distinction between inner self and outer expression; a neo-Freudian notion of repression, indicating that there is a lot more below the surface, even in the person who denies this; the notion that dying provides a last opportunity for the person to become truly authentic, to acknowledge his or her real inner self (Becker 1973 is the classic proponent of this view). All these elements of the modern self are abandoned by postmodernists, who proclaim 'the death of the subject' – and if there is no subject, no person behind the mask, then death is not a problem. But that is not the view of the revivalists.

Buddhists, however, may be an exception. Buddhist approaches to death have been outlined by Levine (1988) and Rinpoche (1992), authors who are read and respected by many who are not themselves Buddhists. As I approach death and begin to lose my physical and mental faculties, I will naturally ask, who is this 'I'? If I can no longer work, make love, care for my children, is this still me? This is the classic problem for the modern individual facing the disintegration of his or her own body. But for Levine, the art of dying, like the art of living, is to recognise that 'I' is to be identified with neither body nor mind. The Buddhist clings to neither personal attachments nor social roles, nor even to his or her concept of self; everything changes, nothing is permanent, so the Buddhist tries to live in the present without trying to make the present permanent or to cling to past images of self. It may be misleading to describe this concept of the person as postmodern, but it does seem that Buddhism is becoming increasingly popular partly because it provides a language in which to describe and legitimate postmodern experiences of the self.

The other major way in which the revival of death cannot be truly postmodern is in its facing up to nature and to the body as a focus not of pleasure but of pain and decay. Modernity used the tools of science, technology and medicine to fight nature, and the fight against high mortality rates was an essential part of this. Postmodernity is the condition of having won the fight: nature and death are now simply outside of everyday experience (Jameson 1991: ix). Bodies appear in postmodern culture only as youthful, athletic, enticing, sexual bodies. The mid-century *dis*appearance of death from everyday life, thus heralded the possibility of postmodernism:

> There are desirable patterns of life which are held out to us in which basically we're all masters of our own time and consumers of our own pleasures; and children and old people get in the way of that, and death negates it all. I think we all want our own way a lot more than people ever used to think was possible. And anything which gets in the way is treated with cruelty.
>
> (Porter 1990: 213; *see also*
> Mellor and Shilling 1993: 412–14)

It is difficult to see how postmodern culture, a culture that celebrates freedom from natural and physical constraint, can acknowledge the continued reality of death without undermining its own existence.

Beck (1992) may have hit on a better way of conceptualising all this. Certainly, the struggle against nature was the essence of modernity. But what we are now experiencing, not only as we read Kübler-Ross or visit our aunt in the local hospice, but also as we read about global warming and breathe in our neighbour's exhaust fumes, is that the modern struggle against nature has had massive unexpected side effects that dehumanise the person and de-nature the planet. We are now in a period of what Beck terms *reflexive modernisation*, when we must use scientific techniques (monitoring the ozone hole in the Antarctic, psychoanalysing the dying) in order to solve the problems created by the solutions of science.

This is similar to Giddens' (1990) theory of reflexivity as the chief characteristic of what he calls high modernity. If Beck focuses on the use of the natural sciences to fine-tune the problems created by them in the first place, Giddens focuses on the use of the social sciences to fine-tune the problems created by modern society. Not only specialists but all of us take account of social science concepts such as 'economic recession', 'psychological repression', 'the divorce rate', as we plan our finances and our relationships. In this analysis, the revival of death may be termed reflexive. It uses the findings of sociologists Glaser and Strauss (1965) on how medical staff communicate with dying patients, of psychiatrist Kübler-Ross on the psychological processes of dying, of anthropologists on the functions of funeral ritual, of experts such as Parkes and Rando and Worden on the psychology of grief. It uses these findings in order to change the way we die and grieve and the way we relate to those who are dying and grieving. Dying and grieving can never be the same again.

So both late-modern and postmodern strands exist, as I said at the beginning of the chapter, in tension. But both are thoroughly reflexive. The way in which revivalist doctors, nurses, funeral directors and counsellors control their patients and clients all the more effectively has all the hallmarks of late modernity. The centrality of the individual, doing it their own way, concocting their own cocktail of potent but disparate ingredients with bits of modern psychology tacked onto romantic readings of primitive death, bears the hallmark of postmodernity. And the feedback into practice and experience of sociological, anthropological and especially psychological understandings bears the mark of reflexive modernity.

So is there one sociological term that can encompass these disparate themes? I propose that they all be termed *neo-modern*. *Neo* means 'new, young, revived in a new form', and the revival of death is certainly neo-modern. It is also an attempt to revive certain aspects of traditional death, so may also be termed *neo-traditional*. It might most accurately be termed *neo-modern and neo-traditional*, but that is a bit of a mouthful so I will use *neo-modern* for short. In the next chapter, I will compare and contrast traditional, modern and neo-modern death.

QUESTION

Are *late-modern* and *postmodern* appropriate sociological labels for the two strands within the revival of death?

Chapter 4

Traditional, modern and neo-modern death

In the first two chapters, I sketched traditional and modern approaches to death and the more recent 'revival of death'. In Chapter 3 I highlighted the late-modern and postmodern strands in this revival, which I collectively termed 'neo-modern'. In this chapter I will set out a schema to illustrate how each of the three cultural responses to death (traditional, modern and neo-modern) are not free floating but rooted in a particular social context and a particular bodily context, which then enable a particular structure of authority. In summary:

	Traditional	*Modern*	*Neo-modern*
Bodily context	Death quick and frequent	Death hidden	Death prolonged
Social context	Community	Public vs private	Private becomes public
Authority	Religion	Medicine	Self

IDEAL TYPES

Before setting out this schema in detail, clarification is in order. Traditional, modern and neo-modern death are what sociologists term *ideal types*. They are not ideal in the sense of desirable, but in the sense that they are ideas in the head of the sociologist. They are simplified ideas about social life that have a logical coherence but that do not exist in pure form in reality. In constructing ideal types the sociologist posits pure forms, in order to identify tensions and complexities in real life. They are like the physicists' three primary colours which rarely exist in pure form in the colours of the real world, but which are useful to the physicist in

Table 4.1 Three types of death

	Traditional	Modern	Neo-modern
Bodily context			
1 Archetypal death	Plague	Cancer/coronary	Cancer/AIDS
2 Dying trajectory	Fast	Hidden	Prolonged
3 Life expectancy	40	70	80
4 See others dying	Frequently	Rarely	Witness dying not death
5 Human condition	Living with death	Death controlled	Living with dying
6 Typical death	Child	Elderly	Elderly
7 Social birth	Follows physical birth	At physical birth	Precedes physical birth
Social death	Follows physical death	Precedes physical death	At physical death
8 Untypical death	Old (venerated)	Young (senseless)	Young (senseless)
Social context			
9 Social structure	Community	Public vs private	Private and public intertwined
10 Personhood	Belonging	Identity	Identities
Found in	Community	Family	Relationships
Death = loss of	Social position	Identity	Identities
Task post death	Reconstruct roles	Reconstruct identity	Reconstruct identities
Done through	Mourning	Grief	Grief work
Authority			
11 Authority	God/Tradition	Medical expertise	Self
	The will of God	Doctor's orders	I did it my way
Known through	Clergy (male)	Doctor (male)	Counsellor (female)
12 Institution	Church	Hospital	Home/hospice
13 Meaning	Given	Abolished (in public)	Created interpersonally
14 Religion	Given	Choice of church	Inner spirituality
Coping			
15 Courage shown in	Prayer	Silence	Talk
16 Coping strategy	Ritual	Emotional privacy	Expressing
17 Lay support	Neighbours/Kin	Nuclear family	Self-help groups
18 Surveillance by	Priest/Neighbour	Doctor/Neighbour	Counsellor
of	Soul/Behaviour	Body/Behaviour	Feelings
The journey			
19 Traveller	Soul	Body	Psyche
20 Death	Result of sin	Caused naturally	Inner journey
21 Mode of transport	Ritual action	Technology/Drugs	Talk
22 Funeral	Burial	Cremation	Life-centred
Organised by	Community	Commerce/ Municipality	Memorial society/ DIY
Values			
23 Values	Respect	Health/Privacy/ Dignity/fighting Independence	Emotion/Growth/ Choice Autonomy/Control
24 Worst sins	Unbelief	Intrusion	Isolation/Denial
25 The good death	Conscious	Unconscious/ Sudden	Aware/Precious/ My way
	Ready to meet Maker	No bother to others	Finish business

understanding the exact composition of the colours that actually exist. The aim of the sociologist is not to force complex reality into sociological pigeon-holes, but to use ideal types to identify themes and tensions in (in this case) the revival of death.

Nor are ideal types typical in the statistical sense. When I describe the neo-modern course of dying as 'prolonged' I do not mean that no one today ever dies suddenly, but that a 'prolonged' period of dying underlies many other aspects of neo-modern death. When I describe the hospice or the bereavement group as neo-modern, I am not saying that most people now die in hospices, as only about 7 per cent do (Hospice Information Service 1993b), nor that all bereaved people are in contact with a bereavement organisation (only a minority are), but that these organisational forms fit closely with other aspects of neo-modern death. The hospice, for example, is a response to there being a number of people who take a prolonged time dying.

My three ideal types are also historical types, with traditional tending to give way to modern, which in turn tends to give way to neo-modern. The bodily context (for example, the typical killer diseases) and the social context (for example, where people die) have tended to go together, creating a uniquely traditional, modern, or neo-modern package.

The bodily context and the social context, however, do not *have* to change at the same rate, so at any one time any one group can display mixtures of the three types. Within modern Western societies, medicine has created a modern or neo-modern physical context for death, but this can co-exist with a more traditional social context. Examples abound, such as remote rural areas of Britain (Clark 1982), immigrant groups in the modern city (Firth 1993a, b; Kalish and Reynolds 1981), the Irish of Belfast and Dublin (Prior 1989), each of which exhibits a modern, i.e., low, level of mortality, along with a strong sense of community and a traditional death culture. War also complicates any neat historical typology, with the two world wars still affecting the attitudes to death of many people (Blythe 1981: ch. 4; Cannadine 1981; Richardson 1984).

Table 4.1 sets out the three ideal types in more detail.

I will discuss the table, moving from the top to the bottom; in places we will revisit themes already mentioned, in others we will encounter new themes. Then I will discuss how the ideal types illuminate complexity and change in our current death culture.

BODILY CONTEXT

How a society organises itself for death depends on the characteristic form of death (Lofland 1978). Traditional death was characterised by infectious disease which could strike anyone at any time and carry people off in a matter of days. The archetypal bearer of death was the plague. With modernity, by contrast, the major infectious diseases have been beaten, so that most people die in old age. In the meantime, the less than elderly still die, and cancer in particular is feared; but diagnosis of cancer has often been hidden from patients who may therefore not know they are dying.

With neo-modern death, however, diagnoses of cancer and other life-threatening diseases are made explicit. Improved diagnosis and management of cancer and that other great killer, heart disease, means that it may take months to die even when in the terminal stage, and decades to die after first diagnosis. Medicine becomes more able to diagnose long-term life-threatening diseases that it cannot cure, HIV and some forms of cancer being the most obvious examples. Thus we find – encapsulated in the slogans 'living with cancer' and 'living with HIV' – a very prolonged and conscious dying trajectory.[1] In only a decade or two we have shifted from a society in which many members refused to contemplate their mortality or were denied the opportunity to do so, to one in which a very substantial proportion of the middle-aged and elderly know that they or close kin have a life-threatening disease which may not kill them for years but in whose shadow they must in the meantime live. Even those who do live long healthy lives are likely to know family members who are living with cancer, heart disease or HIV.

Lofland notes that in the past 'Throughout his or her life span, the average individual confronted a continuous procession of others' deaths. None the less, and rather oddly, the confrontation with his or her own death was likely to be a mere encounter' (1978: 26). Today, by contrast, Lofland observes that this is less likely to be an encounter than a prolonged affair. Clearly this is not a context in which death can easily remain hidden or 'taboo' – least of all between individual and carer. It is a new situation, which calls forth new approaches.

Typical and untypical death

We may note, though this is not so directly relevant for this present book, that the typical death is no longer that of a child but of an old person. Blauner (1966) has observed that the impact of death on society is usually reduced by reducing the social importance of those who die. In societies with high infant mortality rates, infants (Goody 1959: 136) or stillbirths (Gittings 1984: 83) do not receive full funeral rites; baptism, or some other rite of passage, marks entry to human status rather than birth itself. Social birth follows physical birth. In our own society where prospective parents assume with good reason that their child will live, social birth coincides with physical birth or even precedes it. The age at which grief is acknowledged for infant deaths is steadily falling, so that now even early terminations are acknowledged as highly traumatic and funerals are now conducted for foetuses as well as for infants (Walter 1990: ch. 25). The anti-abortion lobby's claim that life begins at conception, whether or not it is a traditional Christian view (which is debatable), surely gains any current plausibility from unprecedentedly low mortality rates among the very young.

Most of our own society's dying members are elderly, and it is no surprise that we treat them in as cavalier a fashion as our ancestors treated their infants. Thus social death of the elderly often occurs before physical death (Mulkay and Ernst 1991; Sweeting and Gilhooly 1991). Just how far we have come in only a century is shown by the advice of *The Lady* in 1899 that a woman should mourn a grandparent for 9 months but a child for only 3 months (Morley 1971: 76–7) – whereas now the loss of a child is generally considered far more traumatic than the loss of a parent, let alone of a grandparent.

It is becoming increasingly fashionable to argue that social and physical death should coincide. This is the message of both the euthanasia lobby and the hospice lobby. Both are distressed by the sight of patients so wracked by pain or so ignored by hospital or nursing home that they might as well be dead. Euthanasia would bring forward physical death so that it coincides with social death; good hospice care pushes back social death until the moment of physical death.

SOCIAL CONTEXT

Traditional death is rooted in community – in a dense network of social interaction. There are two reasons why people may find themselves within such a dense network of social interaction. One is geographical, and I referred to it in Chapter 1: people have lived in the same neighbourhood all their lives, so those they live near are those they know. Relatives also live nearby and are part of everyday life. The other reason concerns life-cycle (Blauner 1966). Over the life-cycle of any individual, there are times when he or she is more enmeshed in a network of relationships than at other times. In modern times, the young and middle-aged tend to be more socially engaged than some of the elderly, which means that death before old age is not just more tragic but also more traditional – the young person dying of cancer may not be neglected like an old person, the funeral

is much less likely to be routine and impersonal, and more people are likely
to attend. When a lot of people are affected, as with the death of a popular
political leader or in disasters such as a coal mine accident or the Hillsborough soccer stadium disaster, we may find emotions released in public
and rich funeral rituals that seem distinctly un-modern.

But most of us, most of the time, no longer live in the dense circle of
kinship and community. We live on the one hand in the world of work,
and shopping, and travel, where we deal with others on an 'affectively
neutral' basis, even if they are not strangers; and on the other in a private
family in which we invest our emotional life. There is a split between the
public and the private, as described above, and this split is nowhere more
clearly expressed than in modern death. Death is on the one hand bureau-
cratically managed by hospitals, life assurance companies and coroners;
on the other hand, the feelings of the dying and the grieving are private,
and difficult to ritualise publicly. The exclusion of personal feeling from
the public sphere can be very firm; bereaved people are allowed little or
no time off work and are expected to keep their emotions under control
(Awoonor-Renner 1991), and hospital nurses find tears are allowed only
out of sight in toilet, sluice or chaplain's office (Carmichael 1991: 87–96).

As suggested in my discussion of postmodernity in the previous
chapter, changes are occurring in the public/private split. Private experience is now publicly celebrated and managed, and this is clearly reflected
in the revival of death. Hospice nurses may feel able to cry on the ward
with patients and relatives. Also the voluntary association, developed in
modernity, is becoming a dominant form of human organisation. Information technology and mass transportation enable people to join others
with similar specific interests in different parts of the country or the world,
so that association is decreasingly with those we live near to or work with
and increasingly with those with whom we share a specific interest or
experience. Training in palliative care is offered not so much in regular
medical or nursing training as in national and often international workshops. National self-help groups of those with a specific disease now
number several hundred, while bereavement organisations are creating
groups and newsletters for members who have suffered particular kinds
of bereavement: loss by suicide, loss of a baby, loss of a sibling, loss in a
particular disaster. This kind of networking is made possible by the twin
features of postmodernism: advanced communications systems and the
celebration of inner experience.

Personhood

The three kinds of social contexts give rise to three experiences of personhood. In traditional community, I belong; if I leave, it is because I feel I don't really belong, and if I die the whole community has lost a member. In the modern family, I discover my identity; if I leave, it is because I feel I am losing my identity, and if I die my partner feels they have lost theirs. In the intimate relationships and voluntary associations of postmodernity, I develop multiple identities; if I die, it is not so clear who has lost what. Death revivalists highlight the pain of modern loss, epitomised in their favourite research subjects – the middle-aged person dying of cancer and the middle-aged widow. But the solutions offered are postmodern: the hospice as a temporary community and the bereavement group as an association of neither neighbours nor family but of otherwise unrelated widows.

After death, the task is different in the three social contexts. In the traditional context, there must be a reallocation of roles; mourning provides time out from commitments prior to reintegration of the member into a new position in the community. In the modern context, the widow or bereaved mother has not so much lost her place as her identity, a matter of supreme indifference to society. So it is the individual's task to reconstruct an identity, not through the social process of mourning but through something altogether more inner, through something now known as 'the grief process'. In the modern context, the widow is more or less left alone to do this; in the neo-modern context, she is assisted by fellow travellers, counsellors, self-help groups and books.

It might be noted here that Americans tend to construct themselves in a more modern/postmodern way, while Europeans do so in a more traditional way. An English person, for example, knows who they are, identifying a place within a certain social class where one might almost say they belong. French, Swiss and Italians more clearly embrace gender stereotypes. The American, by contrast, believes every individual must create him or herself and so has to continuously create an identity. Field and Travisano (1984) suggest that on meeting one another Americans talk so much in order for each to establish their respective identities; they also observe that it was American sociologists who developed symbolic interactionism – a sociological method of analysis in which identity is seen as constantly negotiated. The relation between these different national ways of belonging and identifying, and what happens when identity is lost through death, has yet to be researched. One might hypothesise that the widow's task of constructing a new identity for herself would be a newer experience for European than for American women.

AUTHORITY

The three forms of society rely on different concepts of authority. The habits that characterise community become traditions, and these are often given religious authority (Durkheim 1915). In modern society, authority comes not from tradition but from expertise: we do not trust the sage or priest, but the engineer and the doctor. In neo-modern society, however, we are not so sure we trust the experts, even though when technology goes wrong we look to experts to fix things (Beck 1992). We like to believe the only ultimate authority is now the individual self.

These three types of authority are expressed in three phrases that epitomise who is in control of my dying: 'the will of God', 'doctor's orders', and 'I did it my way'. Not that the will of God or my own way are likely to be known directly. God is known through the church, while I am likely to discover my way through others (such as a nurse or counsellor) trained to help the dying or bereaved self know itself.

Institution

Each form of authority has its own institutional bearer. Tradition is rooted in the church, the extended family and the village; expertise in institutions such as the hospital and in professions such as medicine; and the self is rooted in the family and in counselling. Hence the revivalist vision that if the dying person is to regain control over their own dying, they had better die at home. In the USA the hospice movement is designed primarily to facilitate home deaths, and in the UK there is also a significant focus on this. The in-patient hospice unit aims to be as little like a hospital as possible: certainly not a home, but an anti-institution designed not to mortify (Goffman 1968) but to develop the self.

Most societies have ritualised death within the context of kinship systems (Parsons and Lidz 1967: 146). This was certainly true of ancient Rome but the tradition was challenged by the early church, which relocated the dying person symbolically within the church. Just as Ferdinand Mount (1982) has argued that marriage was captured by the church and then in the past century wrested from her control so that people now feel free to organise their sexuality and their fertility without reference to religious morality, so one might argue the same has occurred with death. We think about dying and bereavement less and less in the light of religion, and more and more in the light of medicine, psychology and personal choice.

The family, however, has not necessarily regained control. Lasch (1977: ch. 5) argues that the private family, set up as a haven of personal freedom to which the members of a mass society could retreat in order to repair their selves, has been retaken by the very functionaries of that mass society: by doctors and therapists who tell us what to eat, how to make love, how to die and how to grieve. Experts tell us what to do and what not to do. In Britain, grieving people are frequently upset by the rules and regulations of ecclesiastical and municipal authorities who will not let them have the lettering, the picture, or the size of gravestone that they desire as a personal memorial to the deceased (Walter 1990: 194). The authority of the self is constantly challenged.

Meaning and religion

Meaning changes directly in relation to social structure. Traditionally, meaning is given within the community – the church is not in the business of giving meaning, but of affirming and embodying the meaning that already exists in everyday life. In the modern situation, meaning seems to evaporate in the public sphere, and is sought in the private. In the neo-modern situation, it is sought in a range of intimate relationships and voluntary associations.

In so far as religion still exists, this too moves in a similar direction. In the modern situation, self-determining individuals choose a church (or none) from a range of churches, but personal faith cannot be imposed on others. In the postmodern situation, the experiencing self discovers its God through an inner spiritual journey, drawing on beliefs and writings from a range of religions. Cicely Saunders (1992: 4), for example, encourages her patients at St Christopher's to 'find strength in their own inner values'.

COPING

As we move down the table, we move from general bodily and social contexts to the specific cultures of death and dying. How do people find the courage to face death and loss in the three cultures? Traditionally, strength is found in prayer and ritual. In modernity, especially in Anglo-Saxon and north-western European cultures, courage is found in silence – in the mid-twentieth century, the courageous person was the one who bore cancer or grief in silence. By the late twentieth century the courageous person is the one who dares to talk, though in the more postmodern strand the right to silence is also respected if that is the individual's chosen way.[2]

The modern person copes by not showing their feelings and by crying in private (Carmichael 1991). The kind neighbour makes clear he or she is available if needed, but will not pry or intrude for intruding on another's grief is the ultimate *faux pas*. And though now unfashionable to think so in revivalist circles, a lot of people get through dying and grieving this way without any problem (Wortman and Silver 1989). It can be a very functional experience. In eighteenth-century London or Paris sociability did not depend on intimacy, for people wore metaphorical masks that distinguished public and private selves. The nineteenth-century romantic cult of sincerity, by contrast, led people to fear they might reveal their innermost selves in public, which undermined public sociability (Sennett 1993). Today the cult of sincerity creates problems for dying and bereaved people: if they express their true feelings, ordinary social interaction becomes profoundly difficult, yet if they do not they are being insincere (or, in Freudian terms, repressed or denying). Keeping one's feelings to oneself and reverting to the eighteenth-century mask is perhaps the simplest way out of this dilemma.

Most revivalists would have none of this. True romantics, they see the good death as expressive death, good grief as grief expressed (Wood 1977). Some cancer therapies are based on the view that expressing your feelings may even help keep you alive: 'The appropriate expression of emotion is a way of discharging the potentially stressful effect that deep feelings can have on us. . . . Suppressed emotions can cause us a lot of physical as well as mental problems' (Brohn 1987: 121).

Support and surveillance

Lay support comes in different guises in each context. Traditionally, neighbours and extended family rally around the deathbed or the house of mourning, a practice still seen in urban Britain among West Indians, Orthodox Jews, and Hindus. The modern emphasis on the nuclear family, however, naturally places considerable obligations on those living in the home to be the main source of support. Often they are able to provide this, as illustrated by the Australian cancer sufferers studied by Kellehear (1990); sometimes they are not, as illustrated by the family conflicts over appropriate grief described by Littlewood (1992: chs 5,6). It is difficult to live with someone who is frequently expressing the full force of often irrational feelings, and support may be found less in the nuclear family than in the time-limited counselling session or support group.

Different kinds of support entail different kinds of surveillance. Traditionally, the religious community surveys the state of the soul of the dying, and the faith and orthodox belief of the bereaved. There is also a concern with correct behaviour, but today there is greater surveillance of feeling. In a group of English widows and widowers talking about their experience of the funeral,

> Some, aware of themselves as the centre of interest, felt called upon to act a part that did not fit with their genuine feelings. . . . 'It's the one day you don't care for yourself. You keep going for others.' Some wanted to cry and could not; others cried and felt they should not: 'Shoulders back, head up, mustn't let the side down.' 'I had to behave well for his sake.' It seemed that . . . behaviour was what mattered.
>
> (Collick 1986: 21)

This extract appears in a book that is recommended reading for CRUSE bereavement counsellors, and is therefore critical of this kind of funeral and suggests that feelings should be expressed. Thus the widows move from a modern funeral in which friends and relatives monitor their behaviour, to a neo-modern bereavement group in which a trained counsellor monitors their feelings.

THE JOURNEY

From ancient Egypt onwards death has been represented as a journey, but the nature of the journey has changed. For centuries the prayers of the living helped transport the soul of the dead. In the modern era, the doctor helps the dying body complete to its passage as painlessly as possible. In late-modern death, counsellors and doctors and nurses trained in psychology help the dying person to reach Kübler-Ross's final stage of 'acceptance', while other experts help bereaved people to pass through 'the grief process'. A spiritual journey became a physical one, which in turn is becoming emotional. One sees this clearly in revivalist talk about the funeral: religion is mainly a formality, the body may as well not be there, and the purpose of the event is to help move mourners on in their grief.

Traditionally, death comes through sin, through the curse – either in the biblical sense or in the sense identified by anthropologists of it being brought on by disrupted social relationships. Sin can be dealt with only by prayer, faith and ritual. In the modern type, death is patterned, subject to natural laws of causation and probability, and can be staved off only through deference to those with expert knowledge of those laws. In the neo-modern type, death becomes a journey of the self, facilitated by talking to therapists and family; if there are postmodern rituals, they are not to deal with sin or put you in touch with an external God but to put you in touch with yourself, and they are personal and interpersonal rather than communal. As one American book, *Rituals for Living and Dying*, puts it, 'Personal rituals . . . guide you toward fresh contact with the core of your being' (Feinstein and Mayo 1990: 43).

The mode of transport varies too. The soul is transported through ritual. The body is processed towards death by medical technology and pharmacology. And the psyche is moved towards acceptance (of dying) or resolution (of grief) through talk and through expressing feelings. The contrast between the traditional and postmodern modes of transport is revealed in the following radio interview in 1993 with a young Hindu widow in the English city of Leicester. She epitomises the traditional approach, whereas the interviewer's question presumes neo-modern listeners favouring the release of emotion:[3]

Widow:	On the day of the cremation, the body was brought home, the lid was open, and my children, they were only ten and eight, they did all the rituals for their father. And they did it so beautifully. Though he was only thirty-six, the vibrations were so strong, there were no tears, we just said a beautiful [voice quivers] goodbye to him.
Interviewer:	Why do you think it is so bad to show your grief a lot?
Widow:	Our scriptures say that you are holding the soul back, because it has to go on a journey, and only the prayers that the family chants will help the soul move forward. Tears will only pull him backward.

The funeral

When it comes to the funeral, the official rite of passage, we find different formats. In the West, burial has been the norm since the beginning of the Christian era. The period of decomposition in the ground, in which bodily corruption is transformed into clean white bones, models the purification of the Catholic or Orthodox soul, not to mention the grief of survivors (Danforth 1982; Hertz 1960). By denying that there was any possibility of spiritual purification after death the Reformation opened the way to cremation, but it was not for another 350 years that cremation began in earnest – when secularism meant that there was no soul to be purified anyway. But in Britain it was in fact pragmatism that drove the development of cremation (Jupp 1993); once Protestantism and secularism had made cremation possible, disposal of the body could become simply a matter of efficient waste disposal. If mourners want to focus on memories rather than on the deceased's spiritual journey, why not reduce the body to a few pounds of ashes? Neo-modern funerals go beyond pragmatism and turn private memories into public ritual in the form of a life-centred funeral that recounts and celebrates the deceased.

Who is in charge of the funeral also changes hands. Traditionally, it is the community. In the modern era, commercialisation takes over, perhaps supplemented by municipalisation. In the postmodern era, the consumer begins to take control, archetypally in the North American memorial society movement; or family and friends take control, as in the do-it-yourself funeral (Albery *et al.* 1993: ch. 6; Walter 1990: ch. 23) and in a significant number of AIDS funerals.

VALUES

Much of the above is captured in the catchwords that represent the values of each type. The traditional catchword is respect – for the deceased, for tradition, for social mores – and the archetypal sins are unbelief, and incorrect and therefore ineffective ritual. The catchwords of modern death are health, privacy, dignity, discretion, independence, and a fighting spirit, while the archetypal sins are dependence (in the dying person) and intrusion (into the feelings of the bereaved person). The catch phrases of the neo-modern death are expression of emotion, personal growth, sharing, autonomy, and informed choice, while the most heinous sins are social isolation and psychological denial.

The good death

Another way of summing this up is in images of the good death. Traditionally, the good death is an opportunity to say farewell to one's family and a preparation to meet one's Maker. In the modern era, death should be quick, unconscious or at least painless. This is charmingly expressed by one 92–year-old clergyman's widow: 'I don't dread dying in my sleep but I do dread dying any other way. Mostly for the nuisance, you know' (quoted in Saunders 1990a: 37). The postmodern good death is best done 'my own way', but there is a definite preference for a particular style: aware, pain-free, finishing my personal psychological business. The following was originally written as a deliberate caricature, but it does reveal the values of revival:

When we think of our death, we imagine ourselves surrounded by loving friends, the room filled with a serene quietude that comes from nothing more to say, all business finished; our eyes shining with love and with a whisper of profound wisdom as to the transiency of life, we settle back into the pillow, the last breath escaping like a vast 'Ahh!' as we depart gently into the light.

(Levine 1988: 8)

CONTRADICTIONS BETWEEN TYPES

The purpose of developing these three ideal types, traditional, modern and neo-modern is to illuminate the varied and often conflicting elements that make up the death culture of today. Everything in the traditional type tends to hang together; everything in the modern type tends to hang together; everything in the postmodern type tends to hang together; but there is little consistency *between* types. Since people's experience is characterised by a mixture of the three types, the schema highlights the contradictions, conflicts and uncertainties in their experience. The population cannot be neatly categorised into traditional, modern and neo-modern; rather these types help make sense of contradictory and changing ideas and practices. In generating ideal types to understand the complexity of our death culture I am following Williams (1990); and in generating types that point to varied historical sediments in the present I am following Ariès (1974, 1981), though my types are somewhat different from theirs.

The ideal types can illuminate differences, and often conflicts, between different generations within the same family. The conflict between traditional and modern is present in many immigrant families. The first generation needs to die and to mourn according to the traditions of their religion, while their children want to do the right thing by their ageing parents but don't know what the right thing is, and may have to rely on a funeral director to tell them; and they may also have more faith in the modern ways of hospitals than do the parents they are caring for.

The conflict between modern and neo-modern tends to occur more within middle-class white families. The middle classes shifted towards modern death early in this century, abandoning mourning rituals and adopting (in Britain) the stiff upper lip. The working classes did not make this shift until after the Second World War, with the redevelopment of inner-city communities, the move out to more private suburbs, and the creation of the National Health Service. It is among young to middle-aged middle-class people that the expressive revolution has taken most hold (Martin 1981); those who grew up in the hippy era now populate the senior ranks of teaching, social work, nursing and the other caring professions. They are the ones writing revivalist tracts on nursing the dying and counselling the bereaved. But those they are nursing, whether professionally or in their own family, may have a much less expressive approach to death. Elderly people may display courage through silence, and find psychobabble an acute embarrassment. Their more youthful carers can find themselves caught between a belief that the good death is the expressive death and a commitment to let the person die their own way.

This generational conflict is expressed in a leaflet prepared by the Compassionate Friends titled *To Bereaved Grandparents* (published in the UK, but written by a member of the American Compassionate Friends). It is not uncommon when a child dies for the (neo-modern) parents to grieve differently from the (modern) grandparents; their mutual incomprehension adds to the burden of grief of each. The leaflet tells grandparents that people have to grieve their own way, but then hints at the merits of the parents' expressive style over the grandparents' stoical style:

> Do not tell your bereaved child how he 'should' feel. Don't tell her to 'be brave' or 'control yourself' or 'don't cry in front of the other children'. Don't tell him to 'think of all the good memories'. Don't tell her to 'do' or 'not do' anything. Respect your child's way of handling their pain. Allow them to express their emotions and to talk and talk and talk about their child or the circumstances of his or her death. Allow them to cry, even to wail if they need to. . . . And finally, some of us, for whatever reason, are not able to be of help to our child. . . . Some of us cannot accept the fact that to grieve openly and with others is the 'right' way to do it.[4]

There may be contradictions not just between different generations of the same family, but also within the experience of any one individual or in any one death. A person may be terminally ill at home and with considerable involvement in the local community (traditional); then become isolated on transfer to hospital (modern, medicalised); and after death, the survivors are offered counselling (expressive, neo-modern).

In England, funerals tend not to reflect the new expressiveness. After an expressive death at home and before the offer of professional counselling for the survivor, the funeral is interjected as a hangover from the impersonal modern era. The funeral director is unctuous but unknown to the family and to the deceased, the clergyman conducting the funeral has learnt the deceased's name but little more, in-laws appear from nowhere and expect the stiff upper lip, and the whole procedure feels like an assembly line. No wonder it is an ordeal to be got through. In Northern Ireland and much of Wales, by contrast, the funeral is more likely to inject tradition into an otherwise modern or perhaps neo-modern death, with neighbours carrying the coffin, burial rather than cremation, the service conducted by a minister who knew the deceased even if he or she was not a churchgoer, a good turn-out, and a list of attenders published in the local paper.

Even where the social context is thoroughly modern or neo-modern, if the person dies while enmeshed in social ties – as a teenager, young mother, stalwart member of the rugby club, active member of the church, head-teacher, or young soldier – then the funeral will have many of the hallmarks of the traditional funeral, because of the number of people affected. Not only will they have lost a friend or colleague, but the institution to which they belong will have been eroded and be in need of affirmation (Walter 1990: 118–21). Schools, parenthood, the health culture of the sports club, even the military, all assume a stable and predictable future: children assume their teacher will be there throughout the school year, our massive investment in education assumes that children will live to adulthood, parents assume their children will outlive them, sports clubs assume their sport will make them healthier and live longer, the military suppress thoughts of death and encourage hopes of seeing the world and learning a trade to set the soldier up once military service is over.

The contradictions between the ideal types may be illustrated in the conflict between the modern idea of the good death as sudden and the neo-modern reality for many of a prolonged death. In such a situation, how can we invent a new way of dying when religion has lost its traditional authority to tell us how to live and modern medicine is concerned only with our body? Likewise the neo-modern project of finishing the business through talk (which presumes a lingering death), cannot be engaged in by those individuals who die suddenly and unexpectedly.

How do Hindus perform the correct traditional rituals (dying person on the floor, all the relatives around chanting) to ease the soul from the body when the dying person is in a modern hospital ward? How can traditional Hindu rites, such as the eldest son lighting the pyre and the family circling the pyre incanting the correct words, be adapted to fit the utilitarian setting of a modern Western crematorium built to dispose not of souls but of bodies? Likewise, is it possible to develop ritual (essentially rooted in religion and in community) from a psychological understanding of grief? The typology highlights also the distrust of counselling (which presumes confidentiality) in settled communities (where everyone knows and gossips about everyone else).

The contradictions between the three types can help us understand the tensions just illustrated. They generally arise when individuals did not choose the mix and find themselves in alien environments or when generations rub up against one another or when death comes not in the expected form. But mixing of ideal types can also be embraced. As I mentioned in the previous chapter, double coding – the mixing of traditional and modern elements without being concerned about contradiction – is a hallmark of both postmodernism and of the revival of death.

The mixing of elements of each type without apparent tension, however, is not restricted to revivalists. In Britain, though contradictory elements can make the funeral a stressful occasion, many people's idea of the good funeral draws on very disparate resources – traditional burial in the village churchyard, arranged through a commercial transaction with a modern funeral director, and preceded by a postmodern personalised funeral ceremony. Some clergy, especially in the Roman Catholic church, see a contradiction between a personalised eulogy and a God-focused funeral, but the average family will be very happy with this kind of mix.

So what we find is not so much three opposing death cultures, but a criss-crossing between them (Williams 1989). Revivalists, however, exaggerate the oppositions between modern (bad) and neo-modern (good) death, and between modern (bad) and traditional (good), in order to demonstrate the urgency of reform. The strategy of reformers is to simplify our picture of reality in order to galvanise us into single-minded reform. But there is a lot more overlap and ambiguity than such crusaders would have us believe – and a lot more continuity too, chiefly in the form of individualism. The aim of sociological ideal types, to reiterate what I said at the beginning of this chapter, is not to simplify reality but to illuminate its complexity.

IDEAL TYPES AND HISTORICAL CHANGE

Though each ideal type has a certain internal consistency, each is vulnerable – which is why each has a historical tendency to collapse and give way to the next type. For centuries, as Gittings (1984) and Ariès (1981) demonstrate, the community underlying traditional, religious death has been undermined by individualism. People became more concerned about being united in heaven with their loved ones than with God, and concerned about leaving behind some trace of their individual identity (illustrated by the increasing individuality of gravestones from the seventeenth to the nineteenth centuries). But all this existed within a society still based on rural community and still using the vocabulary of religion, so it is only as these have radically declined in the present century that the full effects of individualism could be seen. By the twentieth century we find only a very few burials in Britain in communal graves. Meanwhile Taylor (1983: 283) argues that women gave up submitting to the onerous demands of mourning because they were no longer willing to suppress their individuality for the sake of family reputation, preferring instead to be mistresses of their own feelings. Novelist Susan Hill (1977) speaks for millions of early twentieth-century women in her character Ruth's rejection of socially respectable mourning; far better to remain true to one's inexpressible feelings, even if they cannot be socially articulated and result in terrible isolation. People want privacy, they do not want to be buried in a communal grave, they do want to go to hospital for the best possible care, and they do not want to have to wear black.

So we find the arrival of modern death. But people have not been entirely satisfied with this either, for medicalisation and privacy entailed major psychological costs. Bearing alone the knowledge of your own cancer, unable to talk with your spouse or children about it though you suspect they know, is not easy. Nurses in wards where they do not know who has been told what find slips of the tongue a major occupational hazard. The private style of mourning cuts those who are bereaved off from social support, and though some are glad they do not have to cry in public, others are desperate for someone to cry with. So modern death is now dissolving into more open communication, more talk, more expression of feeling.

The trouble with this neo-modern solution, however, is its extreme subjectivity, its radical centring of everything on the self, which then finds itself denied the shelter of the traditional canopy of religion and the modern canopy of medicine. The neo-modern solution may be even more vulnerable than the modern, though it is too early to be sure. Despite revivalist attempts to find roots in traditional death cultures, their approach can exist only in symbiosis with modern death and its institutions. Patients can choose how to die only because they are assured of good medical care and know that there are hospitals and hospices available at a moment's notice should the home death prove too painful for them or too onerous for their family. (This is very similar to the situation of home birth.) Revivalists can talk about the need for dying or bereaved individuals to express their emotions because they have a fair idea – culled from modern psychological research – what these emotions may be.

QUESTIONS

Can you identify traditional, modern, and neo-modern elements in the norms concerning death in your own family? What tensions exist between them?

What authorities do you respect when it comes to death and dying?

Outline your own values about what makes a good funeral and the proper way to grieve.

Do we give little status to the elderly because this draws the sting of death? Or do we fear death, because of its association with old age?

Part II

Keeping on listening

'We have helped people to listen to dying people and to hear what they're saying, and the challenge for the future is to keep on listening.'
(Dame Cicely Saunders,
interview with author, 1993)

Chapter 5

Stories and meta-stories

> Grief simply does not follow any kind of ordered linear progression. If anything the experiences of grief are better characterised in terms of wave after wave of violently contradictory emotional impulses. Paradoxically, the stage/phase presentation may only ever make sense to people who have not had the experience, i.e. in all probability most young to middle-aged health care professionals.
>
> (Littlewood 1992)

> Each [person] is as unique and individual in dying as in living. Nobody dies by the book.
>
> (Churchill 1979: 33)

Six hundred thousand people die in Britain every year. They, and their survivors, all have their own stories – they are now required to speak, and we to listen. How can sense be made of this diversity? Can one meta-story be told out of all the different stories?

Telling stories is the main format for revivalist talk. The interview quote from Cicely Saunders with which Part II began emphasises the importance of listening to the dying, and continues: 'I've influenced people through telling patients' stories – this is what moves people.' Kübler-Ross also told the stories of individual patients, and that too moved people, over a million of them. Impersonal hospitals are exposed by the very personal stories of those patients who have suffered within them; heart-warming stories of home and hospice deaths inspire people to volunteer their help, give money, and set up their own local hospice. Those training to be counsellors find bereavement autobiographies of more help than psychological theories. If the message of revival is that the person is to come first, then the best medium for that message is to let the person him or herself speak, often through the mouthpiece of evangelists such as

Saunders and Kübler-Ross, or through the many printed case studies, biographies and autobiographies.

It is no coincidence that the most famous evangelists are women, for this is a feminine mode of communication, comparable to that of the early women's movement. If patriarchy (or medicine) controls through abstract systems, then liberation can come only through women (or patients) giving their own, concrete, unedited stories. Only then can the person expose the impersonal, and many dying and bereaved people (like participants in women's groups) have valued being able to tell, for the first time, their own unedited story.

But individuals cannot continue to speak unedited stories for ever. They find connections with other people's stories. They need to find connections if they are to form a radical community. They need to bring the stories together into some kind of meta-story if they are to communicate with a wider world – in our instance if they are to tell others what it is like to be bereaved, or to die in hospital, or to have AIDS. Certainly the stories relayed by Saunders and Kübler-Ross are not unedited. Meta-stories have to be constructed if the story-tellers are to lobby for change, if scarce financial resources are to be squeezed out of government, if young nurses and doctors are to be educated in what to expect when they first encounter a dying person.

Can this be done without eroding the integrity of the original stories? Many of us know someone who has beaten a hasty retreat from a first tentative foray into a women's group, men's group or bereavement group, sensing that the stories of the core members have become a new orthodoxy which no longer allow for the unique story of the new arrival. And are some meta-stories a sell-out to the requirements of a male, bureaucratic society from which funding and approval is required?

In this chapter I will start by looking in some detail at the meta-story that has been by far the most cited and the most influential. It is that woven by Kübler-Ross (1970) out of the 300 or so stories she collected from dying cancer patients in a Chicago hospital in the 1960s. It is this meta-story, more than any individual stories, that readers of her book remember.

THE FAMOUS FIVE

In *On Death and Dying* (1970), Elisabeth Kübler-Ross argues that the emotional responses of those with terminal cancer tend to follow five stages. After initial shock at the news, there is the first stage of *denial*: 'It can't be true!', 'They must have got the tests mixed up!', 'It doesn't seem real!' This is a natural defence mechanism (a concept developed by Freud to refer to the ego's defences against the sexuality of the id, but later expanded to refer to defences against any anxiety-provoking stimulus) that gives the person time to absorb the news, but with some people may last indefinitely and cause major problems for carers. Once the ego begins to accept the truth of the diagnosis, then *anger* is a natural second stage: 'Why me?', 'What did I do to deserve this?', 'Why not that grouchy old man next door who's smoked fifty a day his whole life?' When anger has been expressed, a third stage of *bargaining*, often with God, may ensue: 'Just let me live till my son's graduation in two years' time', 'I'll start going to church again if You can cure me of this.' When bargaining for a cure or for more time is manifestly not working, the person may pass quickly into the fourth stage of *depression* as the truth sinks in deeper and deeper. This may last some time, but many patients reach the final, fifth stage of *acceptance*. The patient is not so much happy as peaceful, quietly accepting what is to come, and now has little need of family and friends – which can be experienced by them as rejection if they themselves have not reached this stage.

So this is the Kübler-Ross meta-story. It is a story in a 150-year-old American romantic tradition that elevates female over male, feeling over technique, home over hospital – a story of the triumph of ordinary people and their experience, championed by a caring woman, over the depersonalisation of male technological rationality. In conflating hard data, personal involvement and a message that will save the world, Kübler-Ross has written not so much a scientific monograph offering testable hypotheses as a persuasive political/religious tract (Klass 1981). It is also true to the times in being secular. Death is portrayed not as a spiritual transition but as a return to the acceptance of infancy – a comforting message to a neurotic generation thirsting for self-help books on unconditional acceptance. (Later, Kübler-Ross did re-cast dying as a spiritual transition, and found a substantial following, but many more felt she had gone off the rails.)

Her meta-story is one many want to hear. Her message is that so long as carers do not engage in conspiracies of silence, so long as they let the patient be and express feelings, then death is not to be feared – patients will naturally progress to the final peaceful stage of acceptance. For nursing and medical students, worried about what they will find when they encounter their first dying patient, this is immensely reassuring. Although Kübler-Ross states that not everyone goes through all five stages or not in the same order, and that each person copes their own way, there is nevertheless a logic to the stages she describes. The meta-story is neat as well as hopeful – and therefore can be easily remembered for student exams. (When I ask the mature theological students I teach whether they have done anything before on death and dying, the ex-nurses and ex-social workers invariably say 'Oh, we did Kübler-Ross's five stages in college, but I don't remember much else.')

A brief survey I conducted in 1993 of basic nursing texts in my local nursing college library revealed usually a short chapter, or in the less recent books part of a chapter, on death and dying. Kübler-Ross's theory gets by far the most space in these texts, an exposition of the five stages being prefixed or suffixed by warnings against taking them as gospel. Field (1984, 1986) asked teachers in UK medical and nursing schools what reading they recommended their students on death and dying. In the nursing schools, Kübler-Ross came out top at 85 recommendations, followed by the publications of Saunders (63) and Parkes (45); in the medical schools, she came a respectable third after Hinton's *Dying* and Parkes' *Bereavement* (1986).

Kübler-Ross gives very little information about the age, gender, ethnic and class composition of her sample (Kellehear 1990: 19–22), but it seems likely that many of them had not yet reached their three-score and ten; in other words, their deaths were premature. These days, however, most people die in old age and there are good reasons why they need not go through her stages. Marshall (1986: 139–43) concludes from his studies of the elderly that as they reach old age many write the 'last chapter' of their life, through a process of reminiscing and reviewing. Most conclude that their life was pretty good, and so come to terms with their forthcoming demise; an active and contented old age may follow. Later as contemporaries die and aches and pains mount, they may actively look forward to death. In other words, the old person has reached the stage of acceptance without any shock, denial, anger, bargaining or depression, and before a terminal condition is reached. Blythe's (1981) sensitive interviews with old people in Britain paint precisely this picture. Marshall comments, 'It is often difficult for young people to believe that the vast majority of older people come to a point where death, and their own dying, makes more sense to them than continuing to live forever' (1986: 141). It is much easier for students to identify with the rather younger subjects of Kübler-Ross's research for whom a terminal diagnosis is much more of a shock (Retsinas 1988).

Going through her five stages is also impossible for those who die suddenly. What Kübler-Ross provides, therefore, is a picture that is assuring to students training for the caring professions; a picture that is easy for them to absorb; a picture that may, possibly, be true for many of those dying in hospital of cancer prior to old age (the very death her relatively young readers most fear for themselves), but is almost certainly not true of the majority of other deaths.

Kübler-Ross observes that we each die according to our own way of coping; certainly if I am spending some months dying I will continue with many of the ordinary joys and concerns of life as well as emotionally preparing for death, a point well documented by Kellehear (1990). Her book nevertheless gives the impression that dying is *the* major concern of the dying, consciously or unconsciously affecting their entire being. This may not be true for many individuals.

Aid or hindrance to listening?

The paradox of all this is that, though Kübler-Ross set out to get people to listen to dying people and her book is based on what they told her, the meta-story she develops can easily be used by readers as a way of *avoiding* listening to dying people. The stages are a lot neater than the reality of dying for many people, and it can be easier to imagine the person is going through the stages rather than to listen to what they are actually saying. It is hard to sit with a frail and confused elderly patient and really listen to what they are trying to say, and disturbing to see a young person enjoying life without apparent reference to his or her impending death; it is much easier to believe one already knows what is really going on, because one already knows the meta-story.

> Anxiety and a lack of structure among health professionals working with dying people led them to apply Kübler-Ross' findings in a particularly rigid manner, thereby giving themselves a falsely secure knowledge base. . . . The tendency towards adopting a fixed view of Kübler-Ross' work was more difficult to avoid than had been anticipated.
>
> (Kastenbaum 1975)

No one can blame Kübler-Ross herself for this. Had she written a more cautious academic monograph, few would have read it and the feelings of dying people might still be absent from the syllabi of medical and nursing schools. But her theory does seem peculiarly prone to criticism for being misused in this way, and in this section I will explore why it is that it may be a double-edged sword in the battle to get carers to listen to dying people.

Several critics note how difficult it is for practitioners to identify which stage a patient is in. Fitchett (1980) found only a quarter of health care professionals and students could agree that any one patient was in a stage of acceptance, with many (usually the more experienced workers) thinking the same patient to be in denial. Schulz and Aderman (1972) note that Kübler-Ross failed to specify assessment procedures for determining which stage a patient is in. Doctors and nurses can listen to the patient, but hear different things.

An important point must be made here. Kübler-Ross's research was based on one-to-one interviews between the patient and herself, a skilled psychiatrist. Most of those who read and apply her theory are not psychiatrists and rarely have the luxury of one-to-one interviews with their patients. Even if two psychiatrists might agree in placing a patient in the same stage (and it is by no means certain they would), doctors and nurses not trained in psychiatry are much less likely to agree. To practise as a psychoanalyst you must yourself have been analysed, in order that you may understand yourself well enough not to project your own feelings onto the patient. Without clear guidelines to carers who have not themselves been analysed, it is difficult to see how those listening to the dying can employ Kübler-Ross's essentially psychoanalytic diagnostic categories. It seems this point has been taken by Kübler-Ross, who now insists that her students go through an expensive, personally demanding self-awareness training lasting between four and seven years before they can become an EKR-approved facilitator.

The stage whose identification has caused the most confusion has been *denial*. If one assumes, as Kübler-Ross does, that death is inherently terrifying, then the news that I have a terminal illness must be met with either outright fear or denial. But some people appear to display indifference, stoicism, resignation or religious faith: do we take such displays at face value or are they really forms of denial (Marshall 1980: 64–70)? The answer depends upon your assumptions. A confident faith in the Christian resurrection is more likely to be taken at face value by a fellow believer, and more likely to be categorised as denial by a sceptic.

Many other concerns may press upon the dying person, unrelated to their coming demise: problems with the landlord, with a partner, with the children. Should the practitioner take such preoccupations at face value or categorise them as denial? More subtly, someone who is dying may deliberately get involved in other things in order to make a clear statement that there is more to life than death, and that they do not want to be seen as just a dying person any more than a mother wants to be seen as just a mother (Kellehear and Fook 1989).

I have mentioned that there can be a difference between an older generation that copes silently and stoically, and a younger generation that copes through talking and sharing feelings. When an older patient chooses to cope by means of silent stoicism, how can the younger professional observer distinguish this from psychological denial? How may those who feel deeply but privately be distinguished from those who have blocked out all feeling?

There is considerable evidence that patients deny their terminal condition in order to protect not themselves but doctors whom they sense – often accurately – to be embarrassed by their own powerlessness and failure to cure. Patients are open with doctors who want things out in the open, and silent with those who do not (Hinton 1980) – indicating how dangerous is a psychological assessment of the patient made on the basis of one encounter with one doctor. The female patient, used to a lifetime of massaging men's bruised feelings, may be particularly anxious to reassure a male doctor – and be particularly good at this (Kellehear and Fook 1989: 534). The busy doctor who has read his Kübler-Ross but who is poor at communication may incorrectly diagnose this as the patient denying *to herself* the seriousness of her condition.

Anger is another stage whose identification is highly problematic. If a patient dying in hospital is angry at the failure of treatment, the nurse may assume that the patient 'is in the anger phase'. The nurse will accept the anger and let the patient express it, in the belief that this will help the patient move on. But perhaps the anger has nothing to do with the impending death, and everything to do with poor treatment or bad communication – for which a more appropriate response would be at least an apology, and at most a review of the medical or nursing regime. By pointing to the patient's terminal condition rather than to the hospital regime as the source of anger, stage theory provides a convenient way for the nurse not to listen to the patient's real complaint.

Attempting to understand patients' emotions without taking account of the social relations in which they are enmeshed is clearly likely to lead to the opposite of understanding (Charmaz 1980: 148–55). Denial, anger, bargaining, depression, acceptance are precisely the ways people respond to incarceration in a total institution, leading to what Goffman (1968) terms mortification of the self. My normal self is in danger of dying if I am institutionalised and stripped of my everyday identities:

Dying people fear losing control over their lives. In the hospital, the staff takes over and largely dictates what the patient can and must do, when you can see them, etc. You and the dying person don't have time to adjust gradually to loss of control. At home, on the other hand, you can take a few steps at a time toward giving up control, which makes dying easier.

(Duda 1987, quoted in Albery *et al.* 1993: 93)

Kübler-Ross herself sees much merit in dying at home, yet her book interprets individual instances of anger, depression, etc. as responses to impending mortality rather than to present institutionalisation. The uncritical reader may well do likewise. Such a reader, once on the ward, will listen to patients but may not accurately hear what they are saying because everything is heard in terms of the fear of death.

There is plenty of anecdotal evidence of stage theory being used not to promote listening but to give the practitioner a premature sense of having heard all there is to be heard. One Californian bereavement counsellor told me she was very disturbed by her mother's death a couple of years ago, and once nearly thumped a colleague who commented, 'Ah, you're in the anger phase.' She didn't want to be told where she was, she felt she was being pigeon-holed, reduced to a system – though she would have been happy with a response such as 'I sense you're feeling angry', which would have given her the right to define her own emotions. Levine has similar observations to make of nurses in American hospitals:

> For some the stages of dying have been a way of not touching the living truth of death but instead disguising it in ideas and models. For many, such concepts, rather than bringing them deeper into the experience of another, have allowed a certain quality of disconnectedness with the process by concretizing the flow. How many times at nursing stations have I heard, 'He's in denial,' or 'He's in the anger stage,' 'He's hitting depression now.'

(Levine 1988: 234–5)

Whether applied to dying or bereaved persons, categories such as denial and anger have the potential to be both an aid to listening and a short-cut that cuts out true listening. The five stages are also increasingly used by individuals to describe their *own* experience of loss, and again they are a double-edged sword. They may provide a helpful framework for articulating feelings of loss, but by providing a meta-language they can also enable some individuals to intellectualise their feelings in a way that others may consider self-alienating (Hawkins 1990: 304–8).

Stage theory on the ward

In the previous section, I discussed several critiques of stage theory that indicate it can be used to hinder as well as help attending to what the patient has to say, and I gave some anecdotal evidence to this effect. Unfortunately there has been very little observational research conducted to see how *in practice* stage theory is used. Kübler-Ross is certainly there in the bookstores, on the students' book shelves and cited approvingly and at length in the textbooks, but are her stages actually used as diagnostic tools on the ward? And if so, do they help or hinder listening?

What little evidence there is is confusing. In my interviews in 1992 and 1993 with a range of palliative care workers in Britain, no interviewee spontaneously mentioned the five stages and when I mentioned them the prompt was rarely picked up. Nor do James's (1986) and Wright's (1981) participant observation studies of British hospices reveal nurses routinely using stage analysis. In Wright's study, the nurses did carefully monitor the patients' progress, employing the concept of a normal dying trajectory in order to give predictability to their work, but the markers of this process were not psychological stages but physical symptoms.

On the other hand, North American literature is full of anecdotes of the five stages being used on the ward, and Arney and Bergen (1984: 101–3) claim that they are accepted by American doctors as the ideal way to die. Kellehear and Fook (1989: 527) writing in Australia have been astonished at how often doctors, nurses and social workers apply the term denial to a wide variety of behaviours.

How can we account for these very different observations? There seem to me to be two possible explanations. One is that Kübler-Ross caught on in the USA much more readily than ever she did in the UK. Americans think more in terms of the individual and individual psychology – witness the proliferation of pop psychology books in American bookstores (often found in a section labelled 'Self', a label virtually unknown in British bookshops) and the general popularity of psychoanalysis and a myriad of other psychological therapies. People tend to die as they live, so Americans are likely to die wanting to read a pop book on psychology. Kübler-Ross provides them with precisely that. In the UK, more pragmatic, less interested in psychology, maybe she doesn't strike the same chords. It was after all a British novelist, Colin Douglas (1983), who lampooned the American obsession with placing patients in Kübler-Ross stages.

The other explanation is one not of place but of time. My British reading and data are mainly post-1980, while much of the American literature I have read and cited is pre-1980. This is in part because 'death and dying' became fashionable in the UK a decade or two after it did in the USA. Death and dying became a substantial part of British medical and nursing curricula only in the 1980s and by then criticisms of Kübler-Ross were so well established that the heyday of her influence on actual medical and nursing practice was probably waning (Corr 1991). In particular, critics pointed to the paucity of evidence that dying people tend to go through a universal set of stages (Germain 1980).

I suspect there is something in both explanations. Either way though, we still do not know whether overall the famous meta-story of the five stages has helped or hindered the process of listening.

GOOD GRIEF

The Kübler-Ross stages, developed to make sense of the experience of losing one's own life, have also been used to make sense of the experience of losing someone else.[1] The most respected authors on bereavement, Colin Murray Parkes and William Worden, employ slightly different frameworks, though both retain the idea of progressive stages.

In his classic book *Bereavement* (1972/1986), Parkes describes three stages:

> Numbness, the first stage, gives place to pining, and pining to disorganisation and despair, and it is only after the stage of disorganisation that recovery occurs. . . . There are considerable differences from one person to another as regards both the duration and the form of each stage. Nevertheless there is a common pattern whose features can be observed without difficulty in nearly every case, and this justifies our regarding grief as a distinct psychological process.
>
> (Parkes 1986: 27)

Parkes makes clear that these emotions are not constant during any one stage, for 'the most characteristic feature of grief is not prolonged depression but acute and episodic "pangs"' (1986: 60). Also, some people do not experience some feelings, such as anger or guilt. Parkes never says that you *will* feel x or y, but instead he itemises the emotions that the doctor, counsellor or friend should look out for and affirm as normal. This makes life that bit more comfortable both for the counsellor who knows what to expect and for the bereaved person who can be reassured that strange and scary feelings are actually normal. Western individualists do not want to be told what to do or feel (which is why they gave up public rules of mourning), but being thrown back on themselves is not comfortable either. Most of us need to know that what we feel is 'normal' and that what we are doing is 'OK', especially when (as often in bereavement) those feelings and behaviours are new and strange.

But at root, Parkes does have a simple meta-story: grief proceeds through pain to resolution. This story provides the basis for Parkes' concept of *normal* and *abnormal* grief: when pain is not shown in the early stages or when resolution is not attained even after years, then grief is pathological. One of Parkes' (e.g., 1990) major concerns has been to develop predictors of pathological grief, so that skilled help can be offered in such cases at an early stage. This also alerts counselling organisations to when a client needs more skilled help than can be offered by a volunteer counsellor with only a basic training.

Another text that has been very influential on counsellors is Worden's *Grief Counselling and Grief Therapy* (1983/1991). Worden presents four psychological tasks which the bereaved must accomplish – 1) accepting the reality of the loss, 2) experiencing the pain of grief, 3) adjusting to an environment without the deceased, 4) emotionally relegating the deceased and moving on with life. Worden portrays the bereaved person as an active agent with tasks to complete, rather than the passive experiencer of powerful emotions portrayed by Parkes (and Kübler-Ross). This is attractive to modern individuals who want to be in control of their own lives and who may adhere to some kind of work ethic. It is also attractive to counsellors who no longer need to sit indefinitely and powerlessly absorbing their client's pain. With Worden, they can help the client move purposefully through the tasks, both counsellor and client feeling a sense of purpose and direction.

But like Kübler-Ross and Parkes, Worden has produced a method of normalising. He gives a description of basic psychological processes which usually occur, which then becomes a prescription for what *should* occur. Norms (in the prescriptive sense) are derived not from religion or tradition, but from what is normal (in the statistical sense) – it is therefore the doctor, the psychologist and the statistician who can tell us how we ought to die and ought to grieve.

Changing paradigms

Scientific knowledge, however, is not static. In his celebrated book *The Structure of Scientific Revolutions* (1962) Thomas Kuhn has argued that scientific knowledge does not develop evenly. Knowledge makes sense only within a framework or *paradigm* and changing the paradigm is a massive upheaval, not only mentally but also because it threatens professional reputations built up by working within that paradigm. So most of the time we have what he calls 'normal science', when a basic framework (say Newtonian physics) is accepted, and experiments produce little increments in knowledge within that framework. Experiments often throw up rogue results, but if each of these were allowed to challenge the overall paradigm, science would become impossible; so such results are ignored or dismissed as due to errors in experimental procedure. But such contrary findings accumulate and sooner or later some scientists cannot but begin to notice. Eventually the whole paradigm comes into question and a brief but exciting period of 'revolutionary science' ensues. A new paradigm (say Einsteinian relativity) emerges to guide the next extended period of normal science.

The scientific study of grief has gone through just such a process. The research of Parkes and his colleagues in the 1960s and 1970s focused on premature loss of a spouse – notably in studies of 22 London widows whose husbands had been under age 65, and of 68 widows and widowers in Boston under the age of 45 (Parkes 1972/1986). This was a reasonable focus since early loss of a spouse is a particularly painful and not uncommon form of bereavement. (It is also particularly feared by the young and middle-aged who work in this field – like dying prematurely of cancer, the basis of Kübler-Ross's original research.) Parkes' paradigm was developed from such relatively youthful samples, and – as with the Kübler-Ross five stages – explicitly or implicitly generalised to the whole population.

Since then, a lot more research has been conducted into other kinds of loss – of parents, grandparents, siblings, children, and into bereavement through suicide and accident, bereavement in the elderly, bereavement in children, bereavement in men, and so forth. This was the period of 'normal science'. Not surprisingly, these studies produced a range of findings, but until the late 1980s the typical verdict was that despite the variations the basic pattern was the same. Writing for GPs, Walton, for example, observed 'The progress of grief tends to follow a definite pattern, although there is much individual variation' (1987: 872). The introduction to the second edition of Parkes' text noted with pleasure the considerable amount of research done around the world since the first edition in 1972; 'It is reassuring to find that most of the conclusions of earlier studies have now been confirmed' (1986: 15). Awareness of the variations was growing by leaps and bounds, but they were still seen as variations on a now well-established theme.

From the late 1980s, however, the still rapidly growing mound of data is being seen by some in a different light. Parkes began to emphasise that not everyone experiences numbness, pining and despair: 'Many people mature and grow in psychological stature after a bereavement. For them the death may be the end of a long period of stress, and their own mental health may subsequently improve.'[2] A major challenge came in 1989 when Wortman and Silver reviewed the literature and discerned three, not one, basic patterns of coping with loss:

1 moving over time from high to low distress;
2 never showing intense distress;
3 staying in high distress for years.

Wortman and Silver note that what they term 'clinical lore' normalises only the first pattern; it categorises the third pattern as pathological, and simply fails to recognise the existence of the second pattern. Equally challenging was Margaret Stroebe's (1992) review of the 'grief work' hypothesis – the idea that bereaved people must experience painful emotions before they can attain resolution (pattern 1 above). Though widely assumed by counsellors to be essential, she found little empirical evidence that working through grief is necessary – suppressing painful memories (pattern 2 above) can be just as effective.

One might speculate as to why the literature had previously been read in such a one-eyed way. Most of the readers are practitioners rather than academic psychologists, and it may well be that Wortman and Silver's second type rarely shows up in the offices of bereavement organisations. Type 1 might well come for help at an early stage, and it is satisfying for counsellors to see them move with time and counselling to a lower level of distress. Type 3 might also come for help, but it is disturbing for counsellors (especially unpaid counsellors) to think that some people might remain in distress for years whatever help is offered. It is therefore not surprising if counsellors and self-help bereavement organisations have normalised type 1.

Rodgers and Cowles (1991), after reviewing 401 journal articles, are highly critical of the cavalier way in which the concept of normal grief has been employed. The very elementary question of defining grief has yet to be agreed upon, let alone concepts

such as pathological grief, complicated grief, and atypical grief, which signify a variation from the normatively accepted or expected response. At present, such concepts seem to be of little value either in charac-terizing or understanding individual experiences. Authors often failed to specify what they meant by using such concepts. . . . The lack of a consensus concerning the parameters of 'normal' grief seriously jeop-ardizes attempts to discuss aberrations from the expected response.

(1991: 455)

Lister's review of studies of male grief (1991) questions Gorer's (1965)

view, ever since a conventional wisdom among psychologists of grief, that
it is healthy to relinquish normal social obligations for a definite period
(as in Victorian mourning); he points to evidence that resuming social life
as soon as possible can be equally healthy. Kavanagh (1990) comes to a
similar conclusion. Cleiren (1991: 247) identifies ways in which spousal
loss is different from other kinds of loss, suggesting that paradigms
developed from studies of middle-aged (and largely female) spousal loss
may not be typical of other kinds of loss.

Leaflets produced by bereavement organisations are quickly picking
up on this. The general drift of these leaflets seems to be away from
itemising the feelings the bereaved may experience towards emphasising
the varieties of grief. As one recent Californian leaflet says in its second
paragraph, 'In grief there are no right or wrong emotions, no timetable or
correct way to move through the pain.'[3]

It is exciting times, with postmodern accounts of the almost infinite
variability of grief competing with late-modern research that attempts to
specify in ever more detail how to predict which reaction will occur when.
Counsellors who once were convinced that it was essential that grief be
expressed are now being urged to respect each individual client's way of
coping. Having been trained in listening skills, some must be wondering
whether their overly specific model of how grief should be may have got
in the way of listening to what some clients were really trying to tell them.

Stroebe (1992) has suggested one way of holding the two perspectives
together. The concept of grief work – the painful and repeated dwelling
on the lost relationship that serves eventually to produce detachment –
originates from Freud's paper 'Mourning and Melancholia' (1984) which
was based on patients of Freud who were having difficulty letting go. It
may be a useful concept for treating such patients but, like so many
theories developed on the psychiatrist's couch, it may be of limited value
for describing a cross-section of the population. For many people, a
measure of 'denial' may be positively functional in enabling them to get
on with life, especially after very traumatic bereavements.

Stroebe's paper helps explain two things. One is the gulf between
bereavement counsellors (who generally, though not universally, advocate cathartic expression of feelings or at least talking about feelings) and
the general population (who often advocate a more stoical getting on with
life). Maybe they are both right. The trouble comes when the expres-
sive/talk model of the counsellors is advocated for an entire cross-section
of mourners – as is increasingly popular after disasters when all the
bereaved are now, in the UK, likely to be offered counselling. (Inciden-
tally, Stroebe (1992: 25) cites evidence from Holocaust survivors that not

working through the loss may be particularly functional when the loss is particularly traumatic.)

The other thing Stroebe explains is why advice given to those finding it difficult to let go of their deceased (whom counsellors see a lot of) may be counter-productive for many other mourners. In the individualistic West, psychologists generally define resolution as a relinquishing of ties with the deceased and becoming once more an autonomous and free individual. There are many cultures, however, in which the final goal is *maintenance* of ties with the deceased – for instance Japan of a generation ago (Yamamoto *et al.* 1969, 1970), the Shona of Zimbabwe (Walter 1991c),[4] or even Victorian society when diaries revealed a striving to maintain ties rather than relinquish them (Rosenblatt 1983). Even in the West, many parents who have clearly come to terms with their grief and are functioning well both physically and mentally nevertheless say that they have not lost and will never lose their emotional tie to their dead child (Stroebe 1992: 33). It may be that for many bereaved people in the West (not just those who have lost a child) their need is not to let go, for they know perfectly well that the deceased is dead; their need is to be reassured that they can keep the deceased in some compartment of their mind and heart. For them, a model in which grief results in keeping the deceased in some form (a model embraced by The Compassionate Friends, a self-help group of those who have lost a child) may be more helpful than standard Western models in which grief is resolved by an eventual letting go of the deceased and therapy is geared toward that end.

The cross-cultural evidence suggests that people in the West take longer to get over loss than do people in many other societies. The standard explanation for this among counsellors and in psychological theories is that our society does not give permission for people to grieve and to show emotion, so the necessary grief work is not done and resolution is delayed. It is just as likely, however, that a culture that elevates the autonomous individual does not give permission to *retain* the deceased and this is why people take a long time to finish grieving. Counsellors and psychologists who go on about the need to 'let go' are simply compounding this.

In the second edition of his textbook (1991), Worden has recognised this, admitting that his original formulation of the fourth task – 'withdrawing emotional energy from the deceased and reinvesting it in another relationship' – sounded too final. Now he states that

> The counsellor's task then becomes not to help the bereaved give up their relationship with the deceased, but to help them find an appropri-

ate place for the dead in their emotional lives – a place that will enable them to go on living effectively in the world.

If the very definition of resolution is being thus turned upside down, then we are indeed in a revolutionary period.[5]

STORIES AND STAGES

This chapter has discussed two competing discourses: one which emphasises the uniqueness of each person's story, the other which compiles a meta-story in terms of universal stages of adaptation. What is the relationship between the two discourses? There are two possibilities.

One is that the practitioners have imbibed stage theories, tried them on the ward and in the counselling room, and concluded – sooner or later – that they do not adequately describe the very varied human experience of loss. The other possibility is that those who have themselves been bereaved or cared for a dying person never believed in stage theories in the first place: they know that dying and grieving are too complex and contradictory to be encapsulated in neat stages. The function of stage theories, therefore, is mainly to reassure students who have yet to encounter these experiences.

There is a curious reflexive relationship in this second case between knowledge and experience, with tutors pushing a framework that does not fit their own experience and students who – on first encountering dying and grieving people – find a tension between what they have learnt and what they experience. Hafferty (1991: 23) gives an example of young medical students losing respect both for patients who did not want to know they were dying and for a hospital regime that respected the patients' wishes, as both were in the students' eyes indulging in 'denial'. In San Francisco, one hospice administrator described to me the de-socialisation that volunteers, motivated by reading Kübler-Ross and Stephen Levine, have to go through if they are to be of any use to real patients. Doubtless many tutors have shared the approach of Thomas:

> It is crucial to remember that generalisations are helpful only as a framework within which to individualise. In the final analysis, it is a *unique* individual with his or her own feelings and experience of life who has to bear a *specific* loss.
>
> (Thomas 1978; emphasis in original)

It may be crucial for the student to remember this, but apparently it is not easy. Professional listeners need some paradigm or meta-story in order to organise what they hear, but there is always the danger that after a while the paradigm ceases to be functional. Instead of organising what is heard, it filters out much of what has been said so effectively that it is simply not heard.

There are also good organisational reasons for believing in meta-stories. It is only possible to plan bereavement services and allocate scarce resources if planners have some advance notice of how grieving people are likely to behave, how many are likely to be in prolonged distress, how many need specialist counselling, and when that counselling should be completed. It is possible, though, to plan palliative care services without a meta-story about the psychology of dying – controlling pain and symptoms provides a clear goal, the dying process is more easily measured physiologically than psychologically, and so long as psychological counselling is available a unit can still successfully claim to care for the whole person. Ultimately, dying ends in death, which is physically defined; bereavement ends in resolution, which is psychologically defined. This is why bereavement services cannot do without a psychological meta-story.

FURTHER READING

Stages of dying

Charmaz, K. (1980) *The Social Reality of Death*, Reading MS, Addison-Wesley, pp. 148–55.

Germain, C. P. (1980) 'Nursing the Dying: implications of Kübler-Ross's staging theory', in Fox, R. (ed.) *The Social Meaning of Death*, Annals of the American Academy of Political and Social Science, vol. 447.

Kübler-Ross, E. (1970) *On Death and Dying*, London, Tavistock.

Grief

Parkes, C. M. (1972/1986) *Bereavement: studies of grief in adult life*, London, Tavistock.

Stroebe, M. (1992) 'Coping with Bereavement: a review of the grief work hypothesis', *Omega*, 26, 1: 19–42.

Worden, J. W. (1991) *Grief Counselling and Grief Therapy*, 2nd edn, London, Routledge.

Wortman, C. B. and Silver, R. C. (1989) 'The Myths of Coping with Loss', *Journal of Consulting and Clinical Psychology*, 57, 3: 349–57.

QUESTIONS

Consider your own experience of loss. Can you make sense of it in terms of a sequence of stages? If so, what kind of stages are they?

Whom have you heard talk of Kübler-Ross's stages or of the grief process? Have they been put forward as more or less useful concepts or as uncontestable reality?

Is it possible to experience feelings without labelling them?

Can you rescue the concept of 'denial' and give it a defined use in the nurse–patient relationship?

How do you envisage a healthy resolution of grief?

Chapter 6

Systems for listening

Care of the dying. . . includes care of the family, the mind and the spirit as well as the body.

(Cicely Saunders 1965)

One of the things we're supposed to be good at is talking to patients about their inevitable death, and I think the times we actually do that are very small.

(Hospice nurse, quoted in James 1992: 502)

I don't know what nursing is; nurses don't know what it is.

(Hospice doctor, interview 1993)

How, in practice, does the practitioner listen to each and every individual passing through a palliative care unit, funeral parlour or bereavement agency that routinely has to deal with scores or hundreds of patients or clients a year? Can *systems* be developed for something so personal? Can death be tailored according to personal preference? In this chapter I will concentrate on care of dying patients, especially in hospices, because this has been better researched than either bereavement or funeral directing.

The evidence from Naylor (1989) and Walter (1990) is that funeral directors, though personally taking pleasure in the occasional unusual funeral (not to mention subsequently describing it for public relations purposes), organise most funerals in a standardised way. Despite the rhetoric of the family being able to choose the funeral it wants, the choices offered are routinely limited to those that enable the smooth running of a complex business. I look at bereavement care in more detail in Chapter 8.

HOSPICES

Only a small minority of people die in or are cared for by hospices – in the UK in 1988, 13 per cent of cancer deaths, 7 per cent of all deaths

(Hospice Information Service 1992b) – so why do I refer so much in Part II to what goes on in hospices? The reasons are simple: hospices have been major promoters of the idea that patients should die as they choose, the vast majority of hospice patients know they are dying and have time to die their own way, and hospices (both in-patient and home care) are better resourced than most hospitals, nursing homes, old people's homes, and non-hospice-based home-care teams. The hospice is what many regard

> as the ideal form of care for sick people – individually tailored treatments and support provided in the place of patient/family choice, by a team of practitioners, specialists and volunteers, to a fully informed patient, using the full range of medical knowledge and appropriate technology and delivered in a caring and holistic manner to take account of the patient's physical, psychological, spiritual and social needs. The hospices have pioneered not only the re-placing of the patient at the centre of care, but also the necessary organizational changes.
>
> (James and Field 1992: 1368)

If patients cannot die their own way with the help of a hospice, it is highly unlikely they will be able to do it anywhere else. Any problems faced by hospices are likely to be faced *a fortiori* by other organisations. Hospices have set themselves up not only as medical and pharmacological pioneers, but also as a social experiment onto which the eyes of researchers and the public are invited. In responding to that invitation, I have found them very easy to drop in on – more so than large bureaucratic hospitals or old persons' homes whose management can often be on the defensive.

As of January 1993 (Hospice Information Service 1993a: ix; Smith *et al.* 1992), there were in the UK and Ireland 193 hospice in-patient units with 2993 beds (average of fifteen beds per unit), 400 home- care teams, 216 hospital support teams or support nurses, and 200 day hospices. Following the establishment of St Christopher's Hospice in 1967, the concept was widely discussed through the 1970s, but most of the growth in actual facilities has taken place from the 1980s (du Boulay 1984, James and Field 1992). Most of the patients have cancer, but some are suffering from AIDS-related illnesses or motor-neurone disease. Most of those cared for by a hospice die at home, supported by visiting nurses who advise on pain-control, but the person may go into a hospice in-patient unit for a week or two in order to have intractable pain or symptoms controlled, to give the family a rest, or for the final few days. Most hospices are grass-roots community initiatives, and in Britain it is government policy to fund up to 50 per cent of their costs.

The hospice idea spread across the Atlantic and hospices were founded rapidly in the United States once federal reimbursement from Medicare had been announced in 1982. American hospice (usually written in the singular, but I will henceforth use the British plural form) is more nurse-led than in the UK where doctors play a more prominent role, and is even more focused on home-care. American hospices assume intact families – whereas in the UK there are more in-patient beds to be occupied by those with no family or neighbours to care for them. The hospice has not transferred well, however, to other European nations (Palouzie 1985; Albrecht 1989).

Hospices generally have an atmosphere that is Christian, middle-class and feminine. On entering one hospice near London, I felt as I was ushered to a reproduction period armchair in the peach wall-papered and thickly carpeted waiting area that I was walking into a Laura Ashley showroom – soft, feminine, traditional and almost aristocratic, and unlike any hospital I knew of. This is no coincidence. Given that the interiors of most private homes are organised by women, if a hospice is to feel homely it must have a feminine feel – sending a clear signal that this is *not* a hospital. Some have observed that hospices are also stereotypically feminine in allowing tears but not anger. Several of the hospices I have visited have accessible and delightful gardens where patients, visitors, staff and friends mingle, refreshed by the sound of falling water or (especially in the West Coast of the USA) tinkling wind bells. Many hospices are motivated by a Christian concept of compassion, and in some of them a high proportion of the staff are committed believers.

These accounts hint at a contradiction within hospices. On the one hand they are committed to letting patients live as they wish until they die. On the other hand, hospices have a very clear idea of 'the good death' as one in which patient and family accept the terminal diagnosis and in which the actual death is peaceful and preferably in the patient's own home. These are the two classic strands that together make revival: a late-modern/neo-traditional attempt to promote a particular idea of healthy dying, and a postmodern enabling of individuals to do it their own way. I explore this tension in the hospice in more detail in Chapter 8.

There is considerable variation, however, between hospices. The two Buddhist hospices in San Francisco, for example, both of which provide a home for the indigent and homeless (who need not themselves be Buddhist), are otherwise very different. One occupies a gorgeous and immaculate Victorian mansion, grander than anything the cancer-stricken occupants of its two splendid bed sitting rooms have ever lived in while in better health; the work is done by a team of 25 volunteers, supplemented by two paid staff. The other feels more like a 1960s commune – two old houses knocked together, pleasantly shambolic and relaxed, with people wandering into the kitchen for a coke or to heat up some food, watching TV, hanging out. Eight residents with AIDS organise their own lives, assisted by 30 non-resident volunteers and a resident abbot, while skilled nurses from a home-care team visit. Unlike in the first hospice, the volunteers need not be practising Buddhists.

TEAMWORK

If palliative care is to help patients die their own way, it must develop systems for listening to each individual patient. This involves attending not only to their bodily ailments but also to their emotional, social and spiritual concerns. This is not going to happen automatically. On hearing they have a life-threatening disease, most people want to know the medical facts: how long have I to live, what symptoms will there be, how much pain? The patient wants to be reassured that pain can be controlled. Communication with the doctor or nurse starts at the medical level, and unless the doctor or nurse enquires about other levels it is likely to remain there.

Cicely Saunders trained as a social worker, nurse and doctor, and also has a deep spiritual awareness; she is therefore exceptionally well-qualified to attend to every concern of her patients. Since few practitioners can hope to be so multi-faceted, the hospice movement has developed the concept of the multi-professional team (Hull *et al.* 1989).[1] Instead of the one-woman band, we find in most hospices something more akin to a five-piece band, comprising doctors, nurses, occupational therapists, social workers and chaplains – supplemented on occasion by other consultants and para-medics such as a psychiatrist or family therapist, and a team of volunteers.

Although the manifest function of the multi-professional team is to listen to and care for the whole person, it also has other functions. Even though a doctor or doctors are on the team and carry ultimate responsibility, they have been attracted to the work in part because they prefer collaborating on relatively equal terms with other professions. Teamwork offers a measure of equality and status for nurses, social workers, and clergy – all professions otherwise struggling to find a clear identity and of lower status than medicine.

This, though, hints at a dilemma. If the aim is to care for the whole person, and team members are not clear about the specific areas of their professional competence, there is much scope for conflict and competition. This emerged in my interviews with hospice chaplains, doctors and nurses. One chaplain resented her hospice bringing in a nurse from outside to run a training course on spiritual needs without consulting her; the nurse concerned told me she feels strongly that nurses should learn about spiritual care from other nurses, not from clergy. Another chaplain said 'It took me six months to be accepted. Doctors and nurses can be very possessive: "This is *my* patient!"' Hunt's study (1989: 345) of domiciliary symptom control nurses found they never referred patients to social workers or psychiatrists.

Put simply, there are two models for organising teams. One is for each member to have a clearly defined role totally separate from the roles of others. This makes for ease of relationships within the team, but unfortunately erodes the concept of whole person care. If the patient's family problems are bundled off to the social worker, their emotional problems handled by a psychotherapist, the chaplain called every time they show spiritual distress and their drug dosage prescribed by the doctor, then the patient is not being treated as a whole person but chopped up into separate analytic bits. It is also a concept of teamwork certain to be rejected by nurses, who are left with nothing to do but basic hands-on physical care, a role which historically has justified low status and low pay. And it leaves no role at all for the nurse (such as the UK's Macmillan nurse) who visits the home not to do hands-on care but to advise on pain control and a range of emotional and social problems; their job would be better done by a team comprising GP, social worker and local clergy.

The other extreme is where every member of the team can do everything. The trouble with this is that it leaves each profession unsure whether it is really needed. Why bother with professionals at all, if anyone can give psychological counsel, if anyone can listen to spiritual concerns, if anyone can sort out family problems, and so on?

In practice, therefore, multi-professional teams aim to be somewhere between the two extremes. Each profession claims a particular competence, while accepting that preliminary work in each area can be done by most other members of the team. If everyone knows a bit about everyone else's job, this enables informed referrals to be made from one team member to another. But it certainly does not eliminate tensions, as witnessed by a flood of articles in the nursing press about the strains of multi-professional working (e.g., Adams 1990; Marshall 1991; Wattis 1990). If roles are blurred, patients may become anxious about to whom they are meant to tell what and who can help them over which problems. Confidentiality exists within the team, but patients may be unsure who is and who is not a member of the team, and thus be unsure who will pass what information on to whom. There is a danger that the patient is rendered not more but less able to regulate the flow of information and thus less able to be in charge of their own dying.

What about non-professionals? As nurses become better paid, they are being used more as ward managers, with hands-on nursing left to untrained auxiliaries – it is they who have most contact with patients, but they are rarely included in team meetings. Nor are volunteers. One hospice volunteer, a former medical researcher/administrator currently doing tasks such as hair-washing and taking patients to the lavatory, commented:

> We are tolerated. The volunteers, perhaps rightly, are at the bottom of the pecking order, sometimes it feels as though we are a cheap labour force. . . . Many volunteers have skills and experiences which are not tapped. In other words they carry out menial tasks. No attempt is made to see whether a more valuable contribution could be made by an individual.
>
> (Hoad 1991: 244–5)

Patients are unlikely to know whether information given to auxiliaries or volunteers is likely to be passed on to the rest of the team.

The rest of this chapter will explore the development of systems for listening to the patients' emotional and spiritual needs: the development of a therapeutic gaze and a spiritual gaze. This is the real testing ground for holistic care and for listening to the dying person, for two reasons. Physical pain and symptoms are generally what brings a patient to the attention of a palliative care team in the first place, so if these are dealt with, all parties may be happy. Emotional and spiritual care is an added extra, which may easily be forgotten. Second, in the historical development of any one palliative care unit, pain and symptom control are the original challenges and it may not be until some years later that systematic attention is paid to emotional and spiritual care. A new unit will always have nurses and in the UK a medical adviser, but it may be some time until social workers, chaplains, a consultant psychiatrist or family therapist are appointed, if at all. So both in the care of one patient and in the development of a unit, emotional and spiritual care are add-ons, rather than integral to care; or they may not be added on at all.

THE THERAPEUTIC GAZE

Nurse   Mrs D., could you just start by telling me what has brought you into hospital today?

Patient   Yes, I had to have my breast off about 3 years ago.

Nurse	Did you? Could you tell me why you had to have your breast off?
Patient	Oh, it was cancer.
Nurse	You were told it was cancer at the time, were you?
Patient	Yes, Mr W. told me.
Nurse	How did you feel when he told you that?
Patient	Honest to God! Smacked, totally smacked.
Nurse	How do you mean, smacked? I'm not sure what you mean.
Patient	Shocked, but I've coped with it OK until this happened.
Nurse	And what's this?
Patient	Terrible pain in my back.
Nurse	Is that what's brought you in here today?
Patient	Yes, I can hardly walk now it's got so bad. I can't sleep for the pain either.
Nurse	Oh dear, you have been having a rough time, Mrs D. Can you tell me what you think is causing the pain?
Patient	The cancer. It's come back in my bones and that's why he wants to do some X-ray treatment to relieve the pain.
Nurse	Mr W. has told you it's in your bones, has he?
Patient	Yes, love.
Nurse	What do you think about that?
Patient	Well, I'm not pleased. I was very upset when he told me as I realise that I may not get better. But if he can get rid of the pain I shall be so thankful as my grandchildren are coming from Canada for a holiday and I just want to be able to enjoy their visit and be able to go out for days with them.

(Wilkinson 1991: 681–2)[2]

This extract illustrates well the therapeutic gaze – the ability to get the patient to reveal how they feel – as exercised by a skilled nurse as she takes the nursing history of a patient just admitted to a British hospital cancer ward. As a result of this kind of communication, there is a good chance that Mrs D. may be able to die the way she chooses or, to use Saunders' phrase, to live the way she chooses until she dies. The researcher compares this style of communication (used by only ten of the 54 nurses she studied) favourably with the next communication, in which the nurse repeatedly fails to pick up cues that could lead to emotional disclosure:[3]

Nurse	Right then, I only want to ask you a few questions. No problems since we last saw you 3 months ago?

Patient	A bit tired.
Nurse	A bit tired. No diarrhoea or anything, no sickness?
Patient	No.
Nurse	Have any of your home circumstances changed? Do you still live at B?
Patient	That's right.
Nurse	And your next of kin is still your wife?
Patient	Yes.
Nurse	Do you know what you have come in for this time? Has it been fully explained?
Patient	Yes, things aren't right so I'm having some chemotherapy and a blood transfusion.
Nurse	Right, OK. Have they told you how long you will be in for?
Patient	Until Monday.

[The interview continues in this vein.]

(Wilkinson 1991: 682–3)

It is only recently that research has documented how hospice and palliative care nurses actually interact with dying patients, and (as far as I am aware) it has yet to document how chaplains, social workers and occupational therapists do. Wilkinson, in the above extracts, got cancer nurses to tape record an admission interview. Hunt (1989, 1992) got five symptom control nurses to tape record their conversations with 54 cancer patients in their own homes over a three-month period; and Lanceley (forthcoming) got seventeen hospital nurses to carry a walkman to record conversations with cancer patients. All three of these researchers are nurses concerned to find out whether the therapeutic gaze is used in practice. In addition, there are some good studies employing participant observation, notably those by James (1986, 1989, 1992) in Scotland, Hockey (1990) in England, and Perakyla (1988, 1989, 1991) in Finland. Perakyla has also collaborated with British sociologist David Silverman in doing detailed conversational analysis in an HIV clinic (e.g., Silverman 1989).

Perakyla (1988) notes four frames (Goffman 1974) in which staff interact with patients: the lay frame of ordinary actions and care, the biomedical frame of tests and medical explanations, the practical frame of getting nursing and other tasks done, and the semi-psychiatric frame, which I term the therapeutic gaze. Two or more frames may be present within any one interaction, as in the first nurse's conversation quoted above: 'Oh dear, you have been having a rough time, Mrs D. [lay frame]. . . . Can you tell me what you think is causing the pain [semi-psychiatric frame]?' It seems from all the taped and participant observation studies, however, that the therapeutic/semi-psychiatric frame is not routinely used. Why might this be?

One reason could be that patients believe doctors and nurses to be concerned with their bodies, not their emotions or souls, so do not raise emotional or spiritual issues. This is surely true in many instances but, as the first Wilkinson quote above shows, profound emotions are associated with being terminally ill and there are methods by which skilled workers can elicit these. On analysing her tapes, Lanceley (forthcoming) considered that patients often disclosed feelings and existential concerns but nurses did not respond to many of these disclosures, despite considerable training and skill. For example, one man with cancer mentioned that his wife had died of cancer two years previously, but the nurse did not pick this up. Lanceley considers that the feelings and fears of dying people can be too painful for carers to acknowledge on a continuous basis without considerable support. Ann Cartwright (1990: 21) found that nearly half of the GPs she interviewed found it difficult to handle the distress of dying patients and their families, and a third found their own emotions difficult. Silverman noted that 'one of the strategies by which professionals cope with people with HIV infection is by separating "bodies" from "minds"' (1989: 123–4). If a person is suffering, it is easier for the doctor to put a boundary around the bodily bit of suffering and relate to that, and doubtless it is likewise easier for the counsellor to relate to just the emotional bit.

Perakyla (1988: 45), however, argues that the feelings aroused in the lay frame, as one human being observes another dying, are so massive that it is easier actively to manage those feelings through the therapeutic frame, than to ignore them (Lanceley) or compartmentalise them (Silverman). Perakyla found that the therapeutic frame was employed in the hospital ward, not routinely but in order to solve the bigger problems which arose in the other frames:

> It is the problem-solving frame, which resolves the identity disturbances faced in other frames. Shifts are never made from the psychological frame to other frames in order to solve problems. The psychological frame is specially devoted to this – not for problems originally faced in psychological terms, but ones faced in practical, medical and lay terms.
>
> (Perakyla 1989: 124)

My previous chapter suggested that Kübler-Ross's stage theory is used in precisely this way, with nurses defusing complaints about treatment with comments such as 'He's in the anger phase.'

This exactly replicates my own findings some years ago in a comparable institution, namely a residential school for young offenders which was committed to treating their emotional problems. In practice, the concept of 'emotional disturbance' was not routinely applied to all the boys but only to explain particularly disturbing instances of behaviour (Walter 1977). The officials in the home towns who had sent the boys away, however, did see all the boys as at the emotionally disturbed end of the spectrum of cases *they* had to deal with. It seems that it may not be possible to see *every* member of a given population as in severe emotional distress, because this involves living in a crazy world in which no one can be expected to act rationally and predictably, but it is possible to attend to a minority believed to be emotionally disturbed. This may well also be the case when working with dying people.

Nurses themselves are torn between the desire to sit and listen to patients (either as old-style ladies with the lamp or as new-style holistic carers) and the urge to be 'getting on with the work', work meaning physical nursing tasks such as drug rounds and making beds (Clarke 1978). This urge has two sources (James 1992). One is that doing physical, achievable tasks gives nurses a sense of doing something, in contrast to the sense of inadequacy felt in listening to a hopeless story or just sitting with a dying patient. One sister on a coronary care unit said, 'We're so used to acting. To actually sit there [when someone is dying] is – you find we all start twitching around doing anything in sight' (Field 1989: 74). The other reason is that physical tasks are the only ones that are scheduled. James (1986: 472) cites the night duty procedure at the hospice she studied. From 9.15 p.m. to 7.45 a.m. there were fifteen routine physical tasks which had to be done at stated times (wash medicine glasses, empty bins, set up breakfasts, drug rounds, two-hourly turns, etc., etc.) and without which the ward could not function. Stopping to chat to patients might be encouraged, but was not mandatory in the way that physical tasks were.

Patients perceive nurses to be busy people, and may not want to bother them. A test of this are the UK's Macmillan nurses, who visit cancer patients at home to advise on problems. Despite having no hands-on nursing to do and despite spending 50 minutes or so in each home (compared to the GP's five), they can still be perceived by families as 'busy' (Hunt 1989). Cancer patients and their families raised emotional issues in interviews with researchers Young and Cullen (forthcoming) but not necessarily with the Macmillan nurse as she was perceived as too busy.

Hunt (1991a: 933–4) provides one, if minor, reason why this might be so. At one level, Macmillan nurses have nothing to do but sit and talk (and they tell their families this is what they are there for), but how are they to end an encounter? An effective and oft used way is to refer to the work ethic: 'OK, I've got lots to do so I am going to press on, love' or 'Well, I'd better be on my way' (which could easily be interpreted to mean, 'I've got lots to do').

Offering a listening ear while doing a practical task, especially if it involves physical contact such as rubbing a bottom or bathing the patient, is often hailed as the best form of holistic nursing care:

> I find that you get far more out of a patient when you're doing things with them than you do sitting down beside them on the bed and saying, well, I've got five minutes, tell me your problems. And I find you get better conversations when you're bed bathing them or something.
>
> (James 1986: 160)

Auxiliaries, cleaners and others with clear physical tasks are often best placed to offer simple human compassion as they go about their business, in Perakyla's lay rather than semi-psychiatric frame. But of course there is even less *requirement* that they do this than there is for nurses.

A range of research (e.g., Gilligan 1982) shows that women are particularly good at continuing personal conversations while simultaneously engaged in physical tasks, and most nurses and auxiliaries are women. In the hospice studied by James (1989), nurses recognised that the most emotionally sensitive care was shown to patients by the older auxiliaries who had spent half a lifetime becoming skilled in 'emotional labour' through bringing up a family. Waugh (1992: 56) likewise found that personal maturity and having gone through personal trauma of their own were important factors in enabling nurses to give patients spiritual help, while Cartwright (1990: 21) found that the doctors most likely to say they could cope with the distress of terminal patients were older doctors. Wilkinson (1991: 688) found that emotionally rich nurse–patient conversations were not correlated with post-basic training in communication skills. All this is potentially embarrassing for the nursing profession which claims a unique ability to offer holistic care based on extensive training; it would seem that experience of life is better than any formal training when it comes to teaching the skills of emotional labour.

Nurses know they should be listening to and talking with their patients, especially their dying patients, and are all too aware how patchy their attainment of this is and aware of many of the reasons given above. Most of all they are aware of the financial pressures from above to be measurably productive, and of course the productivity of sitting chatting with patients cannot be measured. But even without these external and financial pressures, in well-resourced hospices for example, there are still good emotional and organisational reasons why nurses employ the therapeutic gaze a lot less than one might have supposed.

A SPIRITUAL GAZE?

In part because of the influence of Cicely Saunders, the standard definitions of palliative care in the UK include 'physical, emotional, social and *spiritual*' care. It is only from the late 1980s, however, that the nursing press in the UK has begun to consider what 'spiritual care' might mean. In the USA, holistic care seems to be more often defined without the inclusion of the spiritual, though recent years have seen nursing publications discussing spiritual care, including the publication of a textbook on the subject (Carson 1989). If listening to patients and helping them to die in their own way involves listening to their spiritual concerns, how is this to be done – both in secular institutions and in religious foundations in which most patients are not religious?

At St Christopher's Hospice, a Christian foundation, a member of the chaplain's team aims to see each new in-patient the day after admission in order to assess them spiritually. This is the most systematic application of spiritual care I am aware of, though St Christopher's patients cared for at home are likely to be left to the hit-or-miss ministry of their local pastor; if they are not churchgoers, that probably means miss. In many other hospices and certainly in hospitals, it is very hit or miss whether in-patients are seen by a chaplain.[4] As one hospice chaplain said to me, 'A nurse walks in to a four-bedded room to attend to a patient and the other three want her too. I walk into a room to see a patient, and the other three hide under the covers!' This leaves preliminary spiritual assessment very much in the hands of nurses.

Beyond ticking church membership on a form, however, nurses can be strangely averse to enquiring about religion. 'Nurses have society's notion that spiritual beliefs are private and that as professionals they should not discuss this information. Yet nurses do not hesitate to inquire about an individual's elimination and sexual habits, which are also private matters' Carson (1989: 154). Medicine may now gaze without embarrassment into any part of the human being, even into sexuality and inner feelings (Arney and Bergen 1984: 18), but religion seems to be exempt from the medico-nursing gaze.

Most of the nurses interviewed by Harrison (1992: 82) claimed never to have thought about spiritual care before the interview. In a hospital seminar at which I presented James's (1989) findings about emotional labour in the ward, the experienced nurses present thought it undermined what nursing was all about to leave emotional care to auxiliaries, but they were content to leave spiritual care to the chaplain. Spiritual care apparently did not feature in their view of the nurse's role. The library of my local nursing college has only two or three books in the section on 'Spiritual Care', despite the growing number of post-basic training seminars on spirituality and recent articles in the nursing press. Nurses in the UK in the 1990s are not generally on the lookout for patients' spiritual needs, nor is this part of their basic understanding of the nurse's job.

What then about the patients? Do they talk of spiritual issues? Here the opinions conflict. On the one hand, many nurses – both in their role as practitioners and as researchers (e.g., Hunt 1989: 354) – do not see many patients raising spiritual questions. On the other hand, Peterson's (1985) study of a hundred elderly hospitalised Americans found three quarters who would have appreciated a nurse trying to help them relate their religious beliefs to their attitudes about their illness. Shelly (1982) suggests that patients make more reference to spiritual concerns than nurses hear. Jacik has found that 'Experience proves that in a time of need persons are eager and willing to share their spiritual concerns and discuss personal issues with anyone who can give them genuine caring, acceptance, understanding, and trust' (1989: 276–7).

The confusion as to whether patients do or do not frequently express spiritual concerns is based on confusion about what practitioners and researchers mean by the word 'spiritual'. The practitioner's understanding of the term in turn affects how the patient talks or does not talk.

Defining the spiritual

By far the most common definition in nursing practice is that which is most common in modern society, namely that spiritual equals formal religious membership and belief. When Harrison (1992: 94) and Waugh (1992: 54) asked nurses how they respond to spiritual need, the most common response was to call the chaplain. An American survey (Highfield and Cason 1983) found that, out of a wide number of behaviours identified from the pastoral literature, nurses identified as 'spiritual' only those containing direct reference to God or to particular religious beliefs. In Britain, a recent official circular 'Meeting the Spiritual Needs of Patients and Staff' (National Health Service Management Executive 1992), sets out what is required to meet the Patient's Charter in this area:

1 Provider units should decide how to meet the spiritual needs of patients and staff. Options include:
- employing suitably qualified staff to meet the spiritual needs of all patients and staff [since there is little training in this area for nurses, this will invariably be taken to mean employing chaplains];
- contracting with relevant religious or spiritual organisations to provide equivalent services on a sessional or other basis [i.e., get clergy, rabbis, etc. in from outside as part-time chaplains];
- facilitating visits to patients by their religious leaders or spiritual advisers on a voluntary basis.

2 Patients and staff should have reasonable facilities for religious observance:
- a chapel, or rooms set apart for equivalent purposes, should be provided where appropriate;
- provision for whatever accessories are required for worship, or for storing items provided by religious organisations.

In other words, the Patient's Charter is met in the spiritual area if the patient has access to ministers of religion and to a properly equipped chapel. There is no requirement for nurses or other non-ordained staff to be trained in spiritual care.

The activist nursing ethic of 'getting through the work' contrasts strongly with ministry to the dying as espoused by many clergy, namely that it is a matter of 'being with' or 'being there' rather than of doing. Spiritual pain cannot be removed with a pill or with careful nursing: 'We are not there to take away or explain, or even to understand but simply to "Watch with me", as Jesus asked' (Saunders 1988). To shift from doing to being is a substantial shift for a nurse, whereas meeting spiritual needs by *doing* something – like calling the chaplain – fits the nursing ethos. This enables the nurse both to feel she has done something and to avoid facing her own powerlessness to answer the unanswerable questions about the meaning of life that the patient may be asking (Harrison 1992: 97). Calling the chaplain fits both general cultural understandings of religion and what in the UK the patient may expect under the Patient's Charter.

The literature on spiritual care, however, has moved towards a very different definition. Spirituality is seen as a search for meaning that is engaged in by every person, whether religious, atheist, or humanist (Stoll 1989: 11). Each individual will find their own meaning, and spiritual care involves helping them in this, largely through letting them talk and sort out their own views and feelings. Cicely Saunders is particularly influential here – see for example her often-cited lecture, 'Spiritual Pain' (1988), in which she notes her indebtedness to Austrian psychiatrist Viktor Frankl's book *Man's Search for Meaning* (1987). Frankl believed that people would find inner peace and mental health when they could embrace what for them is the meaning of their lives.

Defined so broadly, however, one has to ask in what way this differs from any humanist's understanding of the human (or at least the modern) condition? Certainly we all have to make sense of life, especially perhaps in the modern era when there is a choice of ultimate meanings. Especially also as we come near to death in a detraditionalised society in which:

> the historical legacy has left us with a very unclear and contradictory set of meanings for death and dying, the individual has the enormous task of making sense of himself or herself as dying – making sense of self and making sense of dying.
>
> (Marshall 1980: 93, 107)

But why label this search 'spiritual'? Why should it be the concern of chaplains rather than therapists? Surely it is nothing more than the human search?

The simple answer is that, historically in our culture, clergy have been widely regarded as dealing in questions of meaning (which is not to say that those who are dying and bereaved need find them helpful). Few psychiatrists share Frankl's concern with meaning, and neither do social workers. So the clergy's claim to this area is in part historical.

But there is a more significant reason (Taylor 1987). Palliative care is supposed these days to be holistic, and even in a secular society we still conceive of the person as 'body, mind and spirit'. But many patients have no explicit religion so, if spiritual is not to be reduced to an option for those who are active believers (which is what generally happens in practice), it has to be defined in a much broader, secular way. Which is how many chaplains (who obviously would like to expand their influence and be able to minister to all patients, not just the elect) define it. And it is how nurses who have got interested in the area define it – if they are to care for the whole person they cannot say some patients have a spiritual dimension but not others, any more than they could say that some patients have an emotional dimension but not others. So the expanded definition gives an important role to clergy, expands the role of the nurse, and makes the religious-based hospice a pioneer in care for the whole person.

The problem with such a wide definition of spirituality, however, is that it verges on being so wide as to be meaningless. How does spiritual care differ from any general concept of care? Saunders in her classic 1988 lecture expands the definition still further, observing that even if nurses cannot sit discussing with patients the meaning of life, they can still give spiritual care:

> We can always persevere with the practical. Care for the physical needs; the time taken to elucidate a symptom, the quiet acceptance of a family's angry demands, the way nursing care is given, can carry it all and can reach the most hidden places. This may be all we can offer to inarticulate spiritual pain – it may well be enough as our patients finally face the truth on the other side of death.
>
> (Saunders 1988)

This understanding of spiritual care is certainly wide enough to allow nurses and chaplains to squabble over rights to its practice. Nurses who emphasise that spiritual care is part of the nurse's task of caring for the whole patient define it in this broad way and try to restrict chaplains and clergy to more formal religious activities, such as taking church services or praying with patients. Chaplains, however, don't usually find it satisfying to restrict their role to that of ritual specialist, claiming instead to be experts in helping patients seek meaning. The result can be disagreement as to whether it is clergy or nurses who should be developing standards of good spiritual care on the ward, running training workshops for nurses on spiritual care, and so on.

The wide definition is also very private. Patients can decide the meaning of their life to be what they like, totally detached from any public religion or philosophy. But this is precisely the character of postmodern religion – in contrast to modern religion in which the individual chooses to embrace one particular version of a historic religion (the understanding of religion held by most nurses and patients) and in contrast to traditional religion in which the person is given the community's religion. To give an extreme example, a sadist who dies relishing his acts of sadism can correctly be said to have found meaning in his life; but to call this 'spiritual' – as it seems the wide definition requires – both stretches the word as anyone commonly understands it and ignores the moral dimension of the effect of his private meaning on others.

The problem with the wide definition then is that it does not fit conventional concepts of the spiritual as having to do with God, with belief in the transcendent, and with goodness – a concept not surprisingly held by the vast majority of patients. Employed to solve the problem of how to offer holistic care in a secular setting, it finds itself up against modern common sense. Publications on how to nurse those from non-Christian religions – whom it is politically incorrect to offend and whose faith may be based not on personal choice but on the authority of doctrine – always revert to the conventional definition of religion (e.g., Charnes and Moore 1992). The concern not to offend a minority religion overwhelms the concern to push the postmodern definition devised to solve a particular institutional problem. This also suggests that the broad definition in terms of finding meaning in God, whatever you conceive him to be, or indeed in *anything*, is essentially a product of secularised Protestantism, and has to be abandoned when dealing with adherents of other religions.

How then is the plausibility of the wide definition maintained? In my interviews with nurses and chaplains the only time I found this definition unproblematic was with one chaplain who oozed peace and an indefinable spirituality from every pore in a way that might make the most unlovable feel loved and the most sceptical wonder if, just possibly, there may be a God. In other words she had charisma. Care is perceived by the patient as spiritual, I suggest, only because of the personal spirituality of the carer – or more mundanely because they are seen to be wearing a dog collar. Otherwise, care collapses into compassionate humanism (Wood 1976, 1977: ch. 6).

The quest to discover how to attend to each patient's spiritual needs and thus help him or her approach death is still in its early stages. It is not surprising if most nurses duck the issue. Those who do address it using the wide definition, however, may well be stimulated the better to listen to patients and to elicit the meaning to them of their own death.

THE NURSING PROCESS

Since the late 1970s, nursing in Britain has been committed to the nursing process. This involves attending to the patient's physical, social and psychological responses to their illness, and in each area entails four stages: assessment, planning, care, and evaluation. Evaluation then feeds back into further assessment, planning or care in an evolving process. The nursing process is an attempt to routinise care, but it is also an attempt to personalise care. Traditional nursing involved allocating tasks to nurses on the basis of their status or experience, whereas in the nursing process each patient is the special responsibility of one nurse.

In theory, the nursing process provides a perfect vehicle for ensuring that a patient's emotional and even spiritual concerns are attended to. On the basis of his interviews with nurses, Field (1989: 53–7, 60–2, 120–1) argues that the nursing process is more likely to succeed in this than is task-based nursing. The nurse gets to know his or her patient, is required to explore the whole range of the patient's concerns, write these up and devise a care plan in the light of them. It is difficult for a nurse not to get to know and even become emotionally involved with the patient. In wards where the nursing process is used, Field found nurses more likely to grieve and cry at the death of a patient and more likely to attend the funeral. With adequate support, nurses welcomed this level of involvement over the 'detached' mode many of them had been taught when in college some years before.

Although the nursing process may well enable nurses to feel more emotionally involved with their patients, observational studies suggest that nurses rarely use the nursing process to care for emotional and spiritual concerns except in the most rudimentary way. Hunt's study of Macmillan domiciliary pain control nurses observed that

> Despite the nurses' recognition of their responsibility to consider patients' non-bio-medical needs, there were no explicit methods of assessing such needs employed comparable to the well-defined assessments of bio-medical problems utilised at all first visits.
>
> (Hunt 1989: 271)

Despite their commitment to the nursing process, the nurses interviewed by Harrison (1992: 39) simply noted the patient's religious affiliation, with neither nurse nor patient wanting further probing.

Some hospices may be different. Macmillan nurses operating out of my local hospice, for example, have to fill in a nursing process form on each patient following each visit. This has a page each for physical pain, psychological, and spiritual aspects, each page having four columns: problem, goal, action, evaluation. An appendix lists four or five areas to check on each page. Looking at one nurse's notes, I found regular entries under each column, including considerable discussion of psychological and spiritual problems. The nurse found this process a useful check on whether action had been taken and its result, but found the amount of paperwork time-consuming – especially when added to all the audit forms which now have to be completed in the new contract culture. (An unpublished survey from the same hospice found Macmillan nurses spent on average only just over two hours a day with patients, the rest of the time being spent in traffic jams, waiting to see GPs, making telephone calls, writing up notes and other administrative and educational activities.)

With spiritual needs, there is a problem of confidentiality. The nursing process requires full documentation of needs, care plans, and evaluations, available to be read by any team member, but many patients and nurses regard religious discussions as private (Harrison 1992: 98–9). The only way around this is to record that the patient has spiritual concerns, but not to specify them – which undermines the nursing process, since there is then no way of specifying care plans, let alone evaluating them.

Perhaps the biggest question is the rationalism of the nursing process and whether this is compatible with the more personal languages used in emotional and spiritual care. James's (1989) article on emotional labour in a hospice reveals two different languages. There is the language of rationality that speaks of the normal and the pathological, of processes and systems; and there is the language of emotional labour, which is largely couched in the lay frame of compassion, empathy and sympathy. To write up nursing process notes, the lay frame has to be converted into the rational, and thereby destroyed.

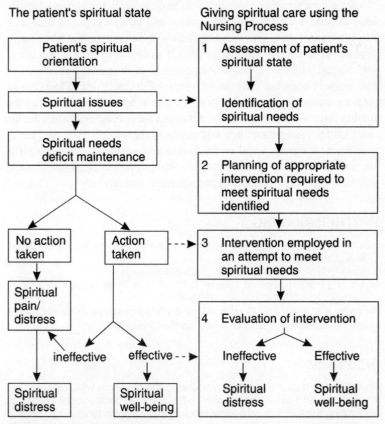

Figure 6.1 A proposed conceptual framework for giving spiritual care using the nursing process
Source: Waugh (1992)

To illustrate this see Figure 6.1, which comes from Waugh's (1992: 53) article 'Spiritual Aspects of Nursing'. The jargon ('spiritual needs deficit maintenance', etc.) is certainly not a personal language, and the objectification involved in using the word 'need' as a noun is a sure sign of rationalism (Walter 1985a). In seeing spiritual 'needs' rather like chemicals to be processed in a factory, the author goes against the whole thrust of pastoral writing in this field which emphasises that spiritual pain cannot be neatly removed as can many physical pains and that the carer's job may simply be to stay with the patient irrespective of obvious benefit (e.g., Lunn 1990). Whether spiritual care can be incorporated within the language of the nursing process in any but the most rudimentary of ways has yet to be demonstrated.

I am not aware of any research into how nurses actually turn observations and conversations into notes and if and how those notes feed back into subsequent care. Interviewing and observing nurses, the main forms of research to date, have told us little if anything about the process of note-taking, which is central to the operation of the nursing process. The translating of complex and intensely personal concerns into a few lines of notes by a nurse not trained in psychiatry or religion is a key part of the nursing process. The nurse could either put these concerns firmly on the care plan for each patient, or could objectify them into a form the patient would not recognise. Until research into note-taking is conducted, it is impossible to tell to what extent the nursing process helps, or hinders, attention to patients' emotional and spiritual needs.

FURTHER READING

Carson, V. B. (1989) *Spiritual Dimensions of Nursing Practice*, Philadelphia, W.B. Saunders.
Field, D. (1989) *Nursing the Dying*, London, Routledge.
James, N. (1989) 'Emotional Labour: skill and work in the social regulation of feelings', *Sociological Review*, 37: 15–42.
Perakyla, A. (1988) 'Four Frames of Death in Modern Hospital', in A. Gilmore and S. Gilmore (eds) *A Safer Death*, London, Plenum.

QUESTIONS

How might nurses and doctors respond to the research which shows that gender, age and parenting are more effective than professional training in generating the skills of emotional labour which are the lynchpin of holistic care?

Is there any other way of operationalising spiritual care in a secular setting, other than those documented in this chapter?

Is there an inherent contradiction between responding to a patient's emotional and religious concerns, and the rationalism of the nursing process?

Chapter 7

Expectations and assumptions

However many dying people I've known, this person is dying for the first time and I don't know what they need: everyone has different needs. You must hold your previous experience of dying patterns very lightly, so if they prove incorrect for this person then you can shift very quickly.

(Frank Ostaseski, administrator, Zen Hospice Project, San Francisco. Interview, 1992)

Central to Buddhism is the observation that things are always changing, nothing remains constant, and therefore it is pointless getting attached to particular ideas, experiences and expectations. The next moment is different from this moment, and is not conditioned by it. Zen Buddhist palliative care therefore *pays attention* to this particular person at this particular moment, and is not influenced by what came before and what the carer may expect or hope to come next. Expectations are what get in the way of listening to the person.[1]

However, if sociology has demonstrated anything over the years it is that people enter social interaction with expectations of self and other. Is it possible to suspend these expectations as I approach the bed of a dying person? And if anthropology and the history of ideas have demonstrated anything over the years, it is that we enter social interaction with basic assumptions about the nature of the world and of persons, with a worldview or *weltanschauung*. Is it possible to sit lightly to this too, to be unattached to our very assumptions about life and persons?

I mention the Buddhist philosophy not because it has been particularly influential in the revival of death – it has not, though interest in it is growing. In the UK, palliative care, the taking of funerals and bereavement counselling have been motivated to a striking extent by Christian concepts. I mention Buddhism because it highlights most acutely the difficulty for those of any religious persuasion or of none who would listen to the individual.

Though expressed in a different language, the Buddhist concept of care is similar to a Christian concept. Christians emphasise the importance of listening, of simply being *with* the patient, and root this in a theology which stresses the importance of the carer, like Christ, abandoning any pretensions to superiority and becoming one with the one cared for. And it would seem similar too to the concept of non-directive counselling.[2] *Listening, paying attention, attentive listening, compassionate attention* are terms heard time and again from Buddhist, Christian and humanist carers. All three philosophies agree that some giving up of preconceived expectations and assumptions is necessary if we are to listen to the individual and help them to die or to grieve in their way rather than our way. In this chapter, I want to say why this is so difficult – which is not to say that it is not worth trying.

MODELS OF THE GOOD DEATH

However committed to letting the patient die or the bereaved grieve their own way, most practitioners still have an idea of the good death or of good grief. This may reflect their own ethnicity, gender, social class and age: white, middle-class carers who are part of the expressive generation may well have different ambitions for dying and grieving than do those they care for. Kastenbaum (1988: 6) found that only one in twenty of the cancer patients surveyed in the American National Hospice Demonstration Study wanted to be mentally alert and in control of their own exit, though probably a much higher proportion of hospice staff held this ambition. In some British hospices, staff are acutely aware of how nice and middle class they are and how they want patients to die peacefully. It is not that easy getting rid of preconceptions and expectations.

Would-be practitioners are often motivated by personal experience with dying and bereavement, and are likely to have strong expectations, and disabusing them of these is a tricky business. Do it too radically and their motivation to care will evaporate and you risk losing your trainee; do it too gently and the expectations may persist. Caring organisations find this a particular problem with unpaid volunteers, for whom training – that is, resocialisation – is relatively brief, and who may be more difficult than paid staff subsequently to fire.

Even if practitioners abandon specific expectations of a good death for their patients or for themselves, it is doubtful that they can operate without some model of the person. In the rest of this chapter I look first at expressivism, then more briefly at some other models.

Expressivism

In Chapter 2 I discussed the expressive revolution of the 1960s and its place in general culture. Revivalists are often caught between wanting the patient or client to express their feelings, and wanting the person to die or grieve their own way. The expressive model of the person considers that emotions that are 'bottled up' and not expressed will go sour, leading to depression or various other pathologies; occasionally, the feelings cannot but burst out, as in the phrase '*overcome* with emotion'. If the dying/grieving person does not want to express their feelings or even talk about them, the expressivist finds it hard believing that their way is truly the best way.

Expressivists have steadily expanded the range of people who ought to express emotion. In the nineteenth century, it was widely believed that men were rational or at least stoical, and women were emotional. Go around any large Victorian cemetery and you will find among the statuary a fair sprinkling of grieving women but few if any grieving men. Doubtless in a patriarchal society the widow was supposed to miss her husband more than the widower his wife, and her identity was usually more bound up with family ties than was his, but the almost total absence of males shedding stone tears also suggests that men were not expected to express grief. Expressivists today are trying to change all that, and one of their main evangelistic activities is to get men to acknowledge their feelings.

Children too are now a subject of expressivist tracts. The bad old days of the mid-twentieth century, when children were not told their mother or father was dying, not allowed to attend the funeral and expected to bear their loss stoically and in silence, are systematically attacked in revivalist tracts. It is believed that children too need to explore and express their feelings; if they cannot do this directly, they can be helped to do so through drawings. Most of all, they need time from an attentive ear (Pennells and Kitchener 1990).

In the area of death and dying, there seem to be two forms of expressivism. The strong form is that it is good to *express* your feelings. The weak form, of which CRUSE bereavement counselling is a good example in the UK (see Chapter 8), focuses more on *talking about* feelings. This latter approach can induce a more detached relationship to one's own emotions – if you ask a bereaved person to talk about the funeral, they may well cry as they do so; if you ask them to talk about how they felt at the funeral, they are much less likely to cry. Identifying and talking about feelings is one step removed from directly experiencing them; giving words to sorrow is not the same as sorrow itself.

Both strong and weak forms of expressivism may be very alien to the culture from which some patients and clients come. In the UK, the respectable working class has an ordered, regular and time-conscious culture of control, in particular female control of the orderliness and cleanliness of the house (Martin 1981: ch. 4). Identity is constructed through orderly commitment to social roles rather than expressed through impulsive feeling (cf. Turner 1976), and it is only in liminal celebrations such as Wakes Week that this is reversed into immediate gratification and spontaneity. Martin notes that it is the caring professions (teaching, social work, the Church) which have embraced expressivism, much to the bemusement and (hence disadvantage) of their working-class pupils, clients and parishioners. She could easily have added to her list of expressive professions those who work in hospices and bereavement counselling. If this is middle-class work, it is not just because the staff are largely drawn from the middle class but because the required expressivism is so closely associated with the professional (in contrast to the commercial) segment of the middle class. Bringing in more black or working-class staff will not change this if they are first socialised into professional expressivism – though untrained auxiliaries from other class backgrounds could possibly change the ward atmosphere.

The commitment to expressivism could also go some way to explaining the speedy transfer of the hospice from England across the Atlantic to the even more expressivist USA, and its tardy transfer to more controlled cultures such as Germany and Switzerland. (In this light, the emigration of Kübler-Ross from German-speaking Switzerland to the USA seems symbolic.)

Martin's analysis nicely fits what is often found in British funerals. An expressivist minister who sees the funeral as an occasion for grief to be 'let out' may be at odds with a working-class congregation who find 'a contained presence may well be far more sustaining' (Davies 1990: 14–15). At other funerals, one finds clergy who have learnt that expressing emotion is a good thing but who are new to this style and not intuitively good at it. Or one may find older clergy being criticised by a younger expressivist middle-class congregation. In each case the clergy's assumptions about emotion prevent them from conducting the kind of funeral many in the congregation may want.

Although the caring professions tend to adopt an expressivist model of emotion,[3] social scientists and philosophers are by no means agreed on an adequate theory of emotion. Against the expressivists are ranged the social constructionists (see Harre 1986 and Stroebe and Stroebe 1987: 26–33 for useful introductions to the debate) who argue that in any situation only a particular range of emotions is socially approved. When we talk in everyday language of *showing emotion*, the expressivist interprets 'show' to mean 'reveal what is within', whereas the constructionist interprets 'show' to mean 'display to others and to oneself' a socially approved image of self. In this view, the problem for the bereaved in modern society is not that they live in a repressed culture that forbids the natural expression of grief, but that they live in a society that is thoroughly confused about the social rules for the display of grief. In this constructionist view, the task of revival – despite the rhetoric – is not to give the bereaved permission to express their emotions but to prescribe a simpler and less ambiguous set of legitimate emotions.

In their pure forms, both expressivist and constructionist theories display a lack of respect for the modern person. Both suggest that people do not know what's going on inside them. Expressivists assume that most of us most of the time are thoroughly denying and repressing our 'true' feelings and therefore don't understand ourselves anything like as well as do expressivist professional carers. Constructionists assume we have responsibility for initiating emotional displays, but because of our culture's idea of emotions being physical things inside the body which can boil over, most of us most of the time deny we are responsible for our emotions: we believe emotion to be beyond reason and beyond choice. We therefore don't understand ourselves anything like as well as the constructionist does. Both expressivist and constructionist theories, therefore, provide a poor base for any form of care that really wants to take the person's experience and view of themselves seriously.

Many mid-century middle-class and respectable working-class people have actually held a composite model, namely that feelings exist within the body (expressivism) but the person is able to obey social rules of politeness as to when to reveal them to others (constructionism). They are not so much repressing emotion as choosing not to display it in certain (usually public) settings, and in so doing are showing self-determination, self-awareness, a concern for others and a concern to keep the public order intact. When the feelings are sexual, they call it decency. When the feelings are of grief (for one's own coming demise or for the loss of another), they call it courage. This is not, however, a style approved of by out-and-out expressivists.

In sum, simple expressivism can conflict with respecting the individual, allowing them self-determination and dying/grieving in their own way. But combined with a constructionist model, with respect for social mores and with respect for the individual's right to self-determination, expressivism can certainly help people die and grieve in their own way and perhaps even help them find what that way might be.

Natural death

Expressivists see society as either repressing or allowing the expression of inner feeling. The good society is one that allows expression, the bad society is one that does not – and modern society is an example of the bad. Expressivists do not see feelings as actively shaped by society, or not at least by modern society. They do sometimes talk of a more positive role for society – in primitive societies whose rituals not only allow but also positively shape and teach the expression of personal feeling.

Allied with this is the idea of natural death. This is the idea that death has become distorted and dehumanised by modern technological and bureaucratic institutions, notably hospital medicine, and that once removed from such 'artificial' settings people may die a more peaceful and natural death. The main ways of achieving this are to die at home, and eschew heroic medical efforts to keep the body alive when it is ready to die. Funerals are best kept out of the hands of commercial funeral directors and done by family and friends. And there is also, of course, a natural process – the grief process – which, once social embarrassment and taboos are removed, will run its natural course. Societies that live close to nature are more in tune with this natural way of death, so advocates of natural death read the anthropological literature as demonstrating that all primitive societies organise death in an 'accepting' way that is very different from the denials and taboos that prevail in modern society. Although most explicit in the publications of the Natural Death Centre (Albery *et al.* 1993), many of these ideas are common to a wide range of revivalists.

This vision of the good death being natural has considerable attractions. It implies that attaining the good death is relatively easy – all you have to do is absent yourself from alienating modern institutions and you can let nature and the family take over. Get a nurse to teach your family basic nursing skills, and you can die at home; learn how to make your own coffin, and you need not pay an undertaker.

Another attraction is that the idea of natural death means that no one need worry about the future of revival. Because the good death is natural, its merits are obvious once people detach themselves from modern ways of thinking; once people have witnessed a natural death they will not want to go back to modern technological death. This means that revival cannot but succeed, because revival is not about inventing a new – and hence disputable – way of death, but about getting in touch with a universally valid natural way.

Unfortunately, the idea of natural death carries a price. The idea arose out of people's very real anxieties about modern technological death and commercial funerals and out of the desire to find a better way, but as with all back-to-nature movements there is a danger of authoritarianism. Once a particular style of dying has been proclaimed 'natural', then anyone advocating other styles and certainly anyone arguing that there is some merit in technology and/or commerce is unlikely to be listened to. So far, the natural death movement has not displayed such authoritarianism; it has simply ignored those who want a technological/commercial way of death for themselves, with the result that natural death caters to a specific and relatively small market. The idea of natural death is therefore an effective way of listening to some people, but cannot possibly form the basis for listening to everyone. Some people want heroic medicine to try everything possible before letting their spouse die; many people feel the way to respect the dead is to pay a lot of money to a funeral director who can organise a really good send-off.[4]

Shrinking versus stretching

'That a sense of well-being has become the end, rather than a by-product of striving after some superior communal end, announces a fundamental change of focus in the entire cast of our culture.' So Philip Rieff observed at the end of his book *The Triumph of the Therapeutic* (1966: 261). Most therapies look within the self to enable it to adjust and to feel happier. The aim is subjective well-being (Rieff 1966), psychological survival (Lasch 1985), being able to shape one's own life (Rose 1989), but beyond the well-being of the inner self there is, as Rieff says, no superior communal end, or as Bellah *et al.* (1985) described middle America, no sense of the common good to which the individual is committed beyond the shared good of personal freedom. Therapy therefore deepens an individualistic culture's focus on the self, a shrinking within – it is perhaps no co-incidence, as Frankl once observed, that psychiatrists are nicknamed 'shrinks'. The prospect of death would appear to challenge a life devoted to personal happiness and well-being – so how is a life of therapy not to end in despair?

This hints at why Frankl's 'logotherapy' (1987) is often incorporated into palliative care. From the Greek 'logos' ('word' or 'meaning'), it refers not to a therapy that seeks happiness within but to one that enables the patient to find the meaning of their life. Meaning is found not inside but

outside oneself: in one's family, in a religious faith, in a political commitment. Frankl's aim is not to shrink, but to stretch, the person, to get them
to look not within, but without. The patient's gaze changes direction.
Frankl is detraditionalised and modern in that he gives authority to the self
to choose its own commitments (cf. Bellah *et al.* 1985), but these commitments induce an outward gaze, so Frankl's therapy does not lapse into the
narcissism (Lasch 1978) to which many other therapies are prone. We may
also note that if that for which one has lived (family, church, political
party) can continue, then death is not so threatening.

One may therefore identify two kinds of good death. There is the good
death of the therapists, with the person experiencing death as the final
stage of personal growth (Kübler-Ross 1975), with death as the culmina-
tion of the self-aware human being, and with practitioners focusing on the
person's feelings. There is also Frankl's good death, with the person
organising practical affairs for the sake of family survivors or for the sake
of those who have to carry on the cause (political, ecological, or whatever),
saying farewells to those they love, or preparing to meet their Maker –
with professional carers helping them to focus on these external projects.
If there is a difference between the therapeutic gaze and the so-called
spiritual gaze (Chapter 6), then it may be this: that one requires the patient
to gaze within, the other to gaze without. Clearly the gaze employed
shapes any attempt to help the patient to 'be themselves' as they encounter
death.

Kellehear's (1990) survey of Australians dying at home of cancer
found most of them were gazing outward as they organised their practical
affairs for the sake of the surviving family. Bellah *et al.*'s (1985) percep-
tive analysis suggests that Americans *are* committed to people and causes
outside of themselves, but because of their individualism they have no
language in which to describe these commitments. Bellah's middle
Americans, then, might at the last find a carer in the Frankl/Saunders
mould who helps them find a language and put their external affairs in
order more help than a therapist who merely reinforces what had been the
problem all along, namely an individualism unable to gaze anywhere other
than within. Maybe this is why the hospice staff in Britain I have talked
with are more indebted to Frankl than to Kübler-Ross.

The passive versus the active person

The medical model tends to see the conscious self as the bemused and
powerless observer of a body that has been invaded by foreign organisms.
Cancer, for example, is perceived as an invading army to be repulsed by

the weapons of radiotherapy and chemotherapy, the patient's body being but the field of battle. Likewise, stage theories of the psychology of dying tend to portray the person as passively moving through a natural process over which they have precious little control (other than to block its natural course).

Some disagree that the person is, or need be, so passive. The method of American physician Carl Simonton (discussed in Kalish 1980: 272–4) requires cancer patients to accept responsibility for the disease. If they have caused their cancer, then they have the power to cure it – through positive thinking such as visualising healthy cells attacking and destroying the cancerous cells. In Britain, the Bristol Cancer Help Centre also emphasises the power of both body and mind to fight the invading cancer, the centre seeing itself not as treating patients but as educating people for self-care (Brohn 1987). Though some rapprochement between passive and active models of the person is now to be found, with active models being seen not as alternative but as complementary (e.g., chemotherapy *plus* visualisation), clearly the implications of each model cannot but remain quite different.

Thomas Attig (1990, 1991) has likewise criticised the passivity implied in most stage theories of grieving. Grief is an emotion, the passionate desire for the impossible – the return of the deceased – and when obsessed with this desire the person is indeed incapacitated, for the desire is unrealisable. But griev*ing* is an active process of moving through and beyond grief, with the person being confronted by challenges to which they can choose how to respond. It is a process of actively relearning the world, rediscovering physical surroundings and relationships with others – including God and the deceased. The best known activist model of grief is William Worden's (1991: ch. 5) theory of tasks that the bereaved must accomplish. Nor does research which shows that individuals confront death with the same coping mechanisms they have used throughout life imply an inexorable and universal process called 'dying' or 'grief'. And my discussion above of the mix of expressive and constructionist models found in common beliefs about the need to control one's grief in public likewise implies an active view of the grieving person, able to make choices.

DOES THE PERSON DIE WHEN THE BODY DIES?

I discussed earlier the concept of social death, namely that the social person need not die at the same time as the physical body (Mulkay and Ernst 1991). In geriatric and psychiatric institutions, the person may die socially years before the body dies physically. But there are many cultures and many people who believe that the person continues in some form long after physical death, perhaps for ever. What one believes on this matter can profoundly affect how one interprets both research data and the statements of the dying and bereaved and indeed how one approaches one's own death and grief.

Take dying of a broken heart. It is well documented that widows and widowers are more likely to die in the first year of their widowhood than if they not been bereaved (Parkes 1986: ch. 2). Rees and Lutkins (1967), for example, found that the death rate of widowed persons was 12.2 per cent compared with 1.2 per cent in a control group of the same age, sex and stress factors; the widowed are particularly likely to die of heart failure (Parkes 1986: 36–7), and researchers attribute this to the pain and stress of loss. The perspective of the widowed, however, may be rather different. Young and Cullen (forthcoming) found several of the elderly cancer patients they interviewed still mourning spouse or children, and actively looking forward to joining them. Their own death, far from a psychologically or physiologically determined reaction to the stress of loss, was positively looked forward to. Young and Cullen comment that, 'A death may well cause another; a death can also cancel another.' If you don't believe there is an afterlife (and such a belief is routinely excluded from the bio-physical frame of medicine), then you see one death causing another. If on the other hand you do believe in an afterlife (as do many of the elderly), then you see one death cancelling another. If you keep an open mind, as good sociologists and carers should, then you can simply listen to the patient and hear what they think.

Another phenomenon which can be interpreted variously depending on your model of the person after death is awareness of the dead by survivors. This is very common among not only the recently bereaved, as demonstrated by Welsh general practitioner Rees (1971), but also among many other people, as demonstrated by folklorist Bennett (1987) in her interviews with middle-aged English women. Bennett considers awareness of the dead to be related to the family-centredness of her women, many of whom had lost an important relative often years or decades before. For them, living in the presence of the dead is not a 'phase' they go through in the early stages of bereavement, but more like a final resolution of bereavement (see Chapter 5 of this book and Walter 1991c). Several experts (doctors, psychologists, sociologists) accept that such experiences occur in bereavement, and may even give them some function within the grief process, but cannot accept that the person has really seen the deceased, labelling the experiences as 'hallucinations' (Rees 1971;

Parkes 1986: 70; Cleiren 1991: 129), 'loss of contact with reality' (Marris 1958: 21–2), 'illusions', or 'an inability to surrender the past' (Marris 1974: 25, 26).

In complete contrast, some individuals and cultures actively discourage any contact with the dead (such as the condemnation by many clergy of spiritualism) or provide rituals to keep the dead away (such as placing a heavy stone on the grave), while others (such as spiritualism) *promote* contact with the dead and provide rituals to foster this. All these recognise that the dead do indeed have some real (i.e. not hallucinatory) presence, the difference between them being what rules govern the relations between them and the living. Yamamoto *et al.* (1969) interviewed Japanese widows who had recently (12–76 days before) lost their husbands through auto accidents:

> The family altar would be your 'hot line'. As such you could immedi-ately ring the bell, light incense, and talk over the current crisis with one whom you have loved and cherished. . . . As one widow said, 'When I look at his smiling face, I feel he is alive, but then I look at the urn and know he is dead.'
>
> (1969: 1663–4)

The last sentence fits the experience of the women interviewed by Bennett: they enjoy the contact, which feels like neither a dream nor a hallucination, yet at another level they know that the person, physically, is dead. This experience has been dramatised particularly well in the movie *Truly, Madly, Deeply*, in which a young woman, Nina, finds her recently de-ceased lover returning to share her flat with her. The film portrays him naturalistically (no unreal shades of blue or ghostly music) and he seems much more real than does Nina when she is talking about her feelings to her therapist – a nice reversal of the psychiatrist's version of reality. Yet at the same time she knows he is dead.

Bereavement autobiographies (surveyed by Holloway 1990) frequently refer to experiences of the deceased. Liz McNeill Taylor (1983: 12, 20), for example, derived great comfort from the nearness of her husband: 'I often feel your presence so powerfully. The only moments of happiness I have experienced in the past few months have been those when I felt you were near.' Yet she lives in a secular society in which the dead are not meant to be present, and may well have read psychological literature labelling these experiences as hallucinatory, so what is a source of comfort also has to be justified by her: 'I always find myself foolishly smiling when I feel that you are around. Am I madder or more sane than our many friends who would laugh to read this?' (Actually if Bennett's sample is at all typical, many of Taylor's friends will have had similar experiences, though like her will rarely mention them to others.)

In conclusion, if one is really to listen to the dying and bereaved, the Buddhists are right: one must sit *very* lightly to presuppositions (about the existence of an afterlife, or the meaning of life, or what emotions are like, or what is natural) which we normally take for granted in everyday life and which in some other situations we passionately defend. The nearer practitioners get to this, the more we may label them not only as Buddhist, Christian or humanist but also as postmodern: they shelve their expert understanding (along with all 'meta-narratives') in order to take this one individual seriously. The more, by contrast, that practitioners are wedded to particular models (that people need to express their feelings, that a peaceful death is natural, that experiences of the dead are psychologically functional but ontologically unreal), the more we may label them late-modern, in that they are attempting to label and control the experience of the dying or bereaved person within a late-modern worldview. Perhaps the really important difference is not between different models of the person, but between those who are and those who are not prepared to hold their models lightly.

FURTHER READING

Albery, N., Elliot, G. and Elliot, J. (eds) (1993) *The Natural Death Handbook*, London, Virgin.

Attig, T. (1991) 'The Importance of Conceiving of Grief as an Active Process', *Death Studies*, 15: 385–93.

Bennett, G. (1987) *Traditions of Belief: women, folklore and the supernatural today*, London, Penguin.

Frankl, V. (1987) *Man's Search for Meaning*, London, Hodder & Stoughton.

Mulkay, M. and Ernst, J. (1991) 'The Changing Profile of Social Death', *Archives Europ. Sociol.*, 23: 172–96.

QUESTIONS

Expressive theory: emotional release allows us to restructure our thinking. If we can release our emotions, we will be clearer thinking. Cognitive theory: our thoughts cause our emotions. If we can change the way we think, we can change the way we feel (Burnard 1988). Which theory would you argue for, and why?

'The concept of natural death is politically brilliant but intellectually dishonest.' Discuss.

Assess Frankl's view that reaching out toward meaning is usually more helpful for the anxious than delving inward toward understanding of inner psychology.

Chapter 8

The listening community or the defining community?

Give sorrow words: the grief that does not speak
Whispers the o'er fraught heart, and bids it break.
> (*Macbeth* IV. iii)

This leaflet is about grief and describes some of the
feelings that people have.
> (CRUSE introductory leaflet:
> *After the Death of Someone Very Close*)

In this chapter, I will explore how dying and bereaved people seek guidance and affirmation from others in revivalist settings – both from other dying and bereaved people, and from staff. What scripts are offered and what scripts are learnt in these settings? Hospices and bereavement groups portray themselves as communities that listen, but to what extent are they also communities that define? I do not consider self-help groups for those with fatal illnesses; they might well generate very different, more activist, models.

The expressivist model of emotion assumes that painful feelings are physical sensations within the individual, which can be relieved to some extent by sharing them with others. But this process is more interpersonal than this simple account suggests, for my expressions feed into how you experience your feelings. To express my feelings in a group that accepts my form of expression is to legitimate that form of expression for other members of the group. To talk about my feelings in a group involves putting those feelings into words, and if the group accepts the validity of my words then this is to teach other members of the group that their feelings too may accurately be described by those kinds of words. Having a feeling is not separate from the label I give it; the labels I use to tell you about my feelings add to your stock of labels, and hence may modify how you experience your own feelings in future. Groups that encourage the expression of feelings inevitably help to define for members what is appropriate feeling.

This process happens whether or not group members are actively seeking new meanings, words and forms of expression for their feelings. It seems very likely that in our society many dying and bereaved individuals *are* actively seeking guidance. In most sections of modern society (some religious and ethnic minorities being among the exceptions), there is a marked lack of direction as to how to die and how to mourn. Why might this be?

Most of us get to adulthood without witnessing another member of the household die, still less die in our presence, so the dying role is not one we learn as part of our upbringing. Neither do we learn grief through observation of other family members – for either they too have lost no one close, or if they have they keep their grief to themselves. Even when later in our adult life kin do die, they are likely to do so out of sight in a hospital or nursing home.

While our first-hand learning about dying and grieving may be non-existent, our second-hand learning is almost too much, too various and often unrelated to our own lives. We watch thousands of movie deaths in various stylised forms; we watch the consequences of even more deaths on the news and see people grieving from Northern Ireland to South Africa to wherever the latest bomb or earthquake has struck. We pick up odd comments from friends, doctors and nurses about our aunt having had 'a good death'. And in the past few years, we are likely to have seen TV documentaries going backstage in the funeral parlour, revealing a beautiful death through euthanasia, pondering the state of our cemeteries, praising the work of hospices, or telling us it is good to express grief. The news media are increasingly focusing on the emotions of ordinary people following extraordinary death through accident or disaster (Littlewood *et al.*, forthcoming). In the meantime, over a million people have bought Kübler-Ross's *On Death and Dying*, not to mention read an article on Shamanistic death rituals in a New Age magazine or on Jewish mourning in a women's magazine. From this worldwide postmodern supermarket, what are we to make of our own death when it looms over the horizon? We know far too much for our own good about how people die and grieve the world over, and far too little about how they do so in our own family and our own culture. If ever there were a state of anomie, or normlessness, this is it.

People dying and grieving within this normative vacuum might not necessarily welcome being told they should do it their own way. Revivalists seek authority in the needs of the dying individual. 'The question is, however, how do the dying know what their needs are? From whom or where do they get their information? Does one suddenly become enlightened by becoming a dying person?' (Wood 1977: 83–4).

Clearly not. One would therefore expect many dying and bereaved people to look around to see what others are doing and feeling. Revivalists go out of their way to provide models and/or reassurance. Every bereavement leaflet I have seen that starts by saying there is no 'right' way to grieve, then goes on to reassure me that a particular set of feelings and experiences (anger, depression, sensing the presence of the deceased, etc.) are normal and not a sign that I am going mad.

This anxious looking around to see what others are up to is characteristic of a modern or postmodern society in which the self has final authority. The United States was the prototype of this kind of society, as the French traveller Alexis de Tocqueville (1969) so pertinently observed over a hundred and fifty years ago. He

> described the American insistence that one always rely on one's own judgment, rather than on received authority, in forming one's opinions and that one stand by one's own opinions. . . . When one can no longer rely on tradition or authority, one inevitably looks to others for confirmation of one's judgments. Refusal to accept established opinion and anxious conformity to the opinions of one's peers turn out to be two sides of the same coin.
>
> (Bellah *et al.* 1985: 147–8)

That American teenagers are world-famous both for their protestations of independence and individuality, and their slavish conformity to peer group norms is well known. Dying and bereaved persons are placed by revivalists in not so dissimilar a position: facing an anxious time of status passage, they are required to do it their own way, to trust their own feelings, yet at the same time thankfully find themselves within a community such as a hospice or bereavement group providing rather clear norms as to how they might behave and feel. Their gratitude is beyond measure.

In pop psychology, the modern individual's need for affirmation and unconditional acceptance is usually ascribed to inconsistent affection in early childhood. A sociological explanation, however, might observe that the need for affirmation is endemic in a society that requires the self to choose its own destiny. The great majority of us do not have the inner conviction of, say, an Abraham Lincoln, so we need affirmation from others for what we have chosen. The more the authority of the self is proclaimed, and the USA is the most extreme example, the more people's need for affirmation reaches epidemic proportions.[1]

LEARNING FROM OTHERS IN THE SAME BOAT

Other dying patients

The patient in a palliative care unit has not died before, but is surrounded by others who are dying and will watch them with considerable interest. In his participant observation study, Buckingham *et al.* (1976: 1214) found support from other patients who reassured him that pain control and various treatments were better than he feared, that 'Doctors are 80 per cent wrong you know', and that if you know nothing about death then there's nothing to be afraid of.

Those dying at home may attend an outpatient clinic or day centre. One hospice day care leader told me:

'I'm fascinated by the relations between the patients in my group. They help each other. Some who are dependent actually do things for others in the group. It boosts confidence for them to get out of the home. They see other patients feeling what they feel. They say they'd never put up with that kind of thing at home, and give others the courage to renegotiate roles with their carers – dependency on the carer is a major problem, you know. Families tend to molly-coddle cancer patients, and it's difficult to break free of that.'

This is a good example of a staff member who definitely approves of what her patients learn from each other, and goes out of her way to encourage displays of independence and competence among them – like many nurses, she believes that patients should be up and out of bed and doing things as much as possible for themselves.

Patients learn from each other not only about dying, but also about the moment of death – a moment that many fear. Honeybun *et al.* (1992) interviewed patients in one hospice, comparing those who had shared a room with someone who had died in the room, and those who had not. Those who had recently witnessed a death tended to rate this as comforting – to see someone die of the cancer that you yourself are suffering from and will die of shortly, can remove the fear of the unknown. The researchers note that the more distressing deaths may have been removed to a single room, but that does not undermine the finding that patients take considerable note of other deaths. (It also provides an example of reflexivity: on reading this study, ward managers may reorganise their beds in order to manipulate what patients observe.)

The quiet slipping into a coma and then into death that the cancer patient may witness is not likely to be witnessed by inmates of a coronary care unit (Field 1989: 73–4, 85). They may well witness a fellow patient suddenly go into arrest, precipitating an attempt at resuscitation that involves staff assaulting the patient's chest with a violence sufficient to break ribs – the very opposite of 'slipping away'. Coronary care nurses have told me that patients may turn the other way, cover themselves with their sheets, or anxiously enquire later whether that is what will happen to them.

It has often been observed that you only die once, and therefore cannot know in advance what it will be like. But this has been challenged by those who have claimed to have had a near-death experience (NDE). Over the past twenty years, these have been widely reported and recorded – modern resuscitation techniques now bring more people back from the dead, and a few well-publicised books have encouraged people to talk about experiences they would otherwise have kept to themselves. The result is a substantial pile of evidence that at/around/after death there is frequently experienced: a) an out-of-body experience in which consciousness looks down upon the dead body; and b) a speedy movement often through a tunnel towards a light (which is turned back from and the journey back to earth made only with considerable reluctance). (Grey 1985, Moody 1975, and Ring 1980 are key texts. Wilson 1987: chs 8 and 9 gives a reasoned appraisal.)

Kübler-Ross (1991) and her colleagues gathered information on 20,000 NDEs and found that everyone had a lovely time, feeling unconditionally loved and experiencing themselves as a complete and unemaciated body, which is why so few wanted to return to earth. Those who have had such experiences say they are no longer afraid of death, while some of those who have read about such experiences also report reduced fear.

To what extent these publications have excluded accounts of negative experiences is not clear. Some argue that frightening near-death experiences do occur, if rarely, while Rawlings (1979) argues that they are as common as good ones but are so traumatic that they are repressed from recall. Most researchers disagree, holding that the bad trip really is a rare experience. The NDE is, however, a minority experience, with only one in ten of those who have been resuscitated having any recollection of what happened while they were dead (Kübler-Ross 1991).

Nor is it clear to what extent the content of an NDE is a result of learning – from religious images of the afterlife, or even from NDE publicity. All I am noting here is that an increasing number of individuals gain comfort from their own or others' NDEs, and claim to face their own forthcoming death with greater equanimity. Whether or not NDEs are a product of learning, people certainly learn from NDEs.

Pathography

A significant way in which people today can witness the dying and grieving of others is through what Hawkins (1990) has termed 'pathography' – published personal accounts of death or bereavement. Bereavement pathographies are usually autobiographical. They may be a personal diary originally never intended to be seen by others, or an account written later at the suggestion of friends, or a fictional account within a novel. I am indebted to Holloway's (1990) useful survey. There are also numerous case studies which appear within, and in some instances dominate, popular psychology books on death and bereavement.

Puritans in the seventeenth century devoured deathbed accounts, which Houlbrooke (1993) suggests took an idealised form. Puritans knew that at the last they should die in calm assurance of salvation as one of the elect, but must have been anxious that delirium, bad thoughts or bad dreams might wreck the pious performance. Hence published post-mortem accounts affirmed that indeed the dying person took an active part in their last hours, confessing the faith and reassuring all around them. The Puritan death was difficult yet crucial to achieve, so the idealised account was a fine way the family could honour the deceased's name.

Pathographies today are written for different reasons, but they are no less idealised and no less motivated by anxiety. Consider the final sentence of an extract (in Hamilton and Reid 1980: 6) from 'Lilian Preston Dies of Cancer', a case study of a 28 year old whose metastasised cancer was discovered on removal of her uterus: 'She closes her eyes and lies very still, smiling slightly, pregnant with her own death, pondering her memories, biding her time.' Whatever else this sentence does, it instructs readers in the hospice ideal of peaceful conscious dying and reassures them that they need not fear the disease so often feared.

If anxiety about pain motivates some readers of deathbed pathography, a more generalised anxiety may motivate readers of bereavement pathography. Liz McNeill Taylor (1983) reveals this as the reason for publishing her own autobiography:

> The progress of widowhood can be best compared to wandering in a maze with no map to guide you . . . what can help in tackling the maze is to be forewarned about some of the stranger manifestations that grief can bring. . . . One of the purposes in writing this book has been to attempt to chart some of the danger points along the way.
>
> (1983: 49, 159)

One counsellor (Holloway 1990) reports that a client jumped at the chance to read books by other women who had been through similar grief, and she read three books which she said put into words much of what she had been feeling. One book which I gave her to read, which was more of an analytical description of bereavement, she claimed to have been of no help whatsoever.... She confessed to having raced to the end of the Jill Truman book to see how she was coping with her grief when years rather than months had elapsed, hoping to receive some encouragement that the passage of time would dull the pain.

(1990: 23)

Unlike Puritan accounts, modern pathographies do not give just one idealised image. 'The sheer variety of models formulated for the good death in these narratives suggests that there is no one emergent art of dying' (Hawkins 1990: 303). This verdict is supported by Holloway who recommends that bereavement counsellors become familiar with a range of pathographies so they can recommend the book(s) a particular client can identify with. Holloway's aim as a counsellor is not to instruct clients on how to grieve, but to recommend a book which will validate their particular experiences and feelings.

Having noted the variety, however, we should also note the constancies, which form both the strength and the weakness of pathography. It tends to be written by middle-class, white females. Since readers tend to share these characteristics, the chances of their identifying with the story are high – and in publishing terms this is a strength. Pathographies rely on readers identifying; without this, they will not find these books helpful. One GP in a working-class London practice mentioned to me that the typical published complaint of the widow not being asked out by friends since she no longer has a partner rings no bells with her patients because in their working-class culture women go out, if at all, with other women and not with their husbands. In pathography, a culturally specific experience of grief or dying is presented not as cultural, but on the one hand as personal, and on the other hand (if the reader identifies) it is experienced as universal. Reading pathography both affirms the bereaved reader's experience, and – in implying the universality of that experience – misleads.

For readers who are counsellors or other carers, however, the effect may be the opposite. Holloway recommends bereavement counsellors read pathography because it can give them a wider understanding of the range of personal responses to grief and enables them to understand clients who may have different personalities from their own. I suspect that many bereavement counsellors prefer reading pathography to psychological texts. There is a real sense here in which the expert is learning from the client.

Yet there is also a sense in which pathography is in turn influenced by expert knowledge. The concern of pathography to normalise the feelings of the reader is a standard counselling technique. Wambach (1985: 208) notes that bereavement autobiographies may use concepts like 'the grief process' and 'grief work' which derive from psychology, while Holloway (1990: 23) found that 'without exception the books ended on some note of hope, some kind of positive resolution of grief, a word of cautious encouragement.' We surely see here not just the commercial interest of publishers (dismal books don't sell), but also the influence of the expert notion of 'resolution' as the 'natural' end of grief.

One particular form of pathography is books for bereaved children, which in fictional form explore death and the child's response – often through the vehicle of animals (*Emma's Cat Dies, Dusty Was My Friend, My Grandpa Died Today*, etc.). Greenall (1988) has surveyed eleven of these, all but two of which were published after 1982, and found that the only values promoted in every book were those of expressing sadness and of sharing memories: two revivalist values *par excellence*. The move to end the protection of children from death is well and truly under way.

One rather different form of pathography is particularly popular in modern Britain. Though, as mentioned above, media accounts of death and disaster from around the world must add to the Babel tower of confusion as to what constitutes the good death, there are particular British deaths that prompt detailed press reporting. I mentioned in an earlier chapter the highly personal coverage of the death of Princess Elizabeth's father, the King, in 1952; the death of Princess Diana's father while she was skiing in Switzerland likewise provoked detailed coverage of the emotional responses of herself, Charles and the boys. Reporting (2 March 1993) the funeral of murdered Liverpool toddler James Bulger, both *The Times* and the *Daily Telegraph* printed a picture of a policeman dabbing at a tear, while the *Guardian* mentioned that 'James's uncle read from the first letter of St John and stumbled a little.' In these reports, contra all the other forms of pathography, we find eulogised in the daily press *modern* grief: stoical, but with just a hint of the agony hidden within. More recently, however, there has been a tendency for newspaper front pages to carry photographs of very explicitly weeping men (for example, ex-soccer player George Best crying on the death of manager Sir Matt Busby), and this may possibly represent a popularisation of the expressive form of neo-modern death (Littlewood *et al.* forthcoming).

The bereavement group

Bereavement groups are of two kinds. There are self-help groups consisting solely of bereaved people, of which examples in the UK are The Compassionate Friends (for bereaved parents) and The National Association of Widows, and in the USA the Widow-to-Widow Project. And there are groups facilitated by a trained counsellor, of which those run by CRUSE – Bereavement Care and St Christopher's Hospice are examples. As in bereavement pathography, the

> first aim is to normalise grief and make it feel safer. Grief can be frightening and overwhelming, especially in isolation. A group gives an opportunity for members to express and test out their anxieties – such anxieties as the fear that they are going mad can be greatly relieved by knowing that others have similar experiences.
>
> (Broadbent *et al*. 1990: 14, describing
> the St Christopher's groups)

Participants can find it helpful to see others who are further along the path of grief, one example of which can give more hope that they too will eventually pull through than any amount of encouragement to that effect from counsellors or comforters who are not themselves bereaved. Groups often comprise those who have suffered the same kind of bereavement (loss of a spouse, loss of a child, loss through the same disaster), thus amplifying the 'hope effect'.

It is difficult to know exactly what goes on in these groups because of the paucity of published accounts, even fewer of which have any pretensions to objectivity. I rely mainly on Wambach's (1985) observations in a group for widows in Phoenix, Arizona, on Broadbent *et al*.'s (1990) account of the St Christopher's groups, and on comments from a counsellor who has advised one self-help organisation.

Groups can function to timetable grief:

> Typical first statements widows would hear at widow's groups were 'Have you heard about the grief process?' and 'There's such a thing as a grief process, you know'.... Both widows and professionals took it seriously, and there was much concern if a widow was not moving 'through grief' as expected.
>
> (Wambach 1985: 204)

One of the three issues that the St Christopher's groups address is beginning 'to let go and make some new adjustment to a new life' (Broadbent *et al*. 1990: 15). We have already noted that expert literature on bereavement on the one hand says it takes as long as it takes, but on the other hand is prone to suggest roughly how long is normal (usually one to two years). In groups facilitated by professionals whose time is precious, there are good organisational reasons for aiming at resolution or at least progress within a specified time – otherwise the facilitators will be so tied up with old groups they will be unavailable to facilitate new ones. Thus in the Arizona group:

> A widow was welcome to attend the meeting until she was past her grief. The board stipulated that time to be about one year following the death of her spouse. She was definitely encouraged to 'move on' at eighteen months.
>
> (Wambach 1985: 205)

At St Christopher's, group meetings are held weekly for ten weeks, and

> There will, of course, be great variations within any group, but it is hoped that with the planned ending of the sessions many members will then be enabled to move forward on their own.
>
> (Broadbent 1990: 16)

Wambach observed in the Arizona group that the grief process could be construed in this sense as a timetable, but that it was also construed as a guide, providing markers that enable a widow to monitor her progress without specifying that by time x she should be at point y. It may be that the grief process is more likely to be used as a guide in self-run, self-help groups where there need be no pressure ever to leave the group. As The Compassionate Friends say, 'Once a bereaved parent, always a bereaved parent.'

Indeed, trained bereavement counsellors may criticise self-help groups for precisely this reason. With no pressure to leave, the longest-standing member may well end up as the group leader; unfortunately, that person may have been in the group for so long because they have had, in the jargon, an abnormal grief reaction and be the least competent to lead the others. Professional counsellors also point out that self-help groups are self-selected which, as with bereavement pathography, magnifies both their usefulness for those who fit in and their uselessness for those who do not. Critics argue that self-help groups should have a professional consultant to advise on such issues.

Nor may professional critics approve of the norms implicitly but powerfully set up within such groups. One described to me a group in which a newly bereaved parent talked glowingly of the treatment she had received from the hospital; while a group member who had lost her child ten years ago 'in the bad old days', instead of saying 'I'm glad you had a good experience, but unfortunately that's not the experience of some of us in the past', expressed great bitterness towards her and immediately launched, yet again, into her own story. Freedom to tell one's own story in such groups may be freedom only for some.

In reply to such critics, self-help groups are suspicious of counsellors who have not themselves experienced their client's particular form of loss; groups believe the person best qualified to understand and help is another bereaved person. Clearly, the surveillance of grief that goes on in bereavement groups is an exercise of power, whether exercised unconsciously by self-help members or consciously by a professional facilitator, and far from uncontentious. Bereaved and dying people may or may not find others in the same boat better than professionals at listening and affirming.

LEARNING FROM THE PROFESSIONALS

If dying people learn informally by observing other dying people, and if bereaved people learn from each other, what do they learn from the professionals? I will look now at the hospice and at bereavement counselling.

The hospice smile

Hospices see their calling as not only to care for patients but also to educate doctors and nurses outside the hospice. In this section I want to examine an educational role not so often admitted, namely educating the patient. Despite the rhetoric of enabling patients to 'be themselves', there is overwhelming evidence that hospices also actively *teach* patients the craft of dying. As one social worker with knowledge of a London hospice put it to me, 'Hospice staff are missionaries who see their mission as enabling people to die a certain version of the good death.' Their converts are not only doctors and nurses, but patients themselves.

Hunt's (1992: 1298) tape recordings of interactions between pain-control nurses and their patients revealed that:

The elements of the 'scripts' for a 'good death' presented implicitly or explicitly by the nurses included the following:

1 physical symptoms controlled;
2 patients and relatives openly accept cancer diagnosis and prognosis;
3 presentation of hope and desire to live;

4   keeping mobile and 'fighting back';
5   enjoyment of life;
6   a peaceful death at home.

I want briefly to explore the norms of peacefulness (6) and hope (3). Most of my data comes from in-patient units, simply because there are more observers around to document what goes on there, but their observations tally well with Hunt's tapes of the hospice ideal as propagated inside the patient's own home.

Peacefulness

Visitors to hospices are often struck by the peaceful atmosphere, but not all are at ease in such an atmosphere. 'I have a penetrating laugh, and when I visit the hospice I am very wary of laughing there, as it somehow doesn't feel appropriate', one psychologist told me. 'It's very difficult to refuse or query treatment in our hospice, because the hospice is above criticism; the result is that patients are over-drugged in order to render them peaceful,' said a social worker. Even full-time staff may feel that the peaceful ethos may conflict with the commitment to patients being themselves and especially with their expressing anger (one of the essential Kübler-Ross stages, remember). One hospice medical director told me:

> 'Our ethos is chronic niceness. If we allow a patient to be angry, they end up feeling they shouldn't have done it. Our favourites are those who get on with our style, who don't upset the apple cart; they are the ones who become in-patients. I wanted an anger room, with cushions to bash, but that's not to be. In so many hospices there are pink pastels everywhere – we had an artist wanting to paint us a mural, so she was asked to do something nice with floating angels! I do wonder whether coldly painted hospital wards may be easier places for patients to say what they really feel?'

On the subject of paintings, St Christopher's is unusual in being decorated with the paintings, expressionist and by no means always peaceful, of its founder's husband.

Nor is an anger room (even if seriously ill patients could get to it) going to change the atmosphere of a hospice, since it would merely enable anger to be vented out of the way of other patients and would provide an even more effective way of maintaining in public 'the hospice smile'. The desire not to upset other patients is a very real one in a community such as a hospice or hospital. Firth (1993a) provides an example, not from a hospice but from a maternity unit:

A Sikh nurse described another woman who had a stillbirth in the maternity unit and the English nurse thought she was being very extreme because she was expressing her grief very loudly. A couple of her relatives and her mother-in-law were also wailing and 'making a scene' in a way which would be regarded as quite normal and the 'done thing' in a village setting at home but was regarded as abnormal here. The nurses, not surprisingly perhaps, kept telling them to 'keep your voices down' but the Sikh nurse said they needed to get it out of their system and work it out.

(1993a: 31)

One doctor is acutely aware of the tension between patient autonomy and living in his Christian hospice:

'Nurses talk a lot about autonomy, but there's precious little of it in a hospice. One patient said she'd only come in if she were allowed to sleep in a chair, and the nurses found all sorts of rationalisations why not – risk of pressure sores, and so on. And there was a real rumpus when there was a gay patient, and his partner came in and sat by his bed holding his hand. Another patient, who'd been a nurse, decided to test this autonomy thing and sat on the main stairs stark naked, with the visitors coming past, to see what would happen!'

Despite the hospice's determination to be more like home than hospital, in respect of patient autonomy it remains – ultimately – more like hospital. Perhaps it is only at home, where there are no other patients to take into account, let alone professional norms, that patients can be truly themselves, though even there they have to take into account other family members.

A hospice is a temporary commune. Back in the sixties, communes devoted to letting members 'do their own thing' ended up either developing group norms for behaviour, or falling apart. Or to use the analogy of the prison, the hospice is a 'society of captives' in which each captive has to cope not only with institutionalisation but specifically with living cheek by jowl with some rather unpleasant personalities (Sykes 1965). In any terminal care setting, the patient has to live alongside other dying people who may, if there is any truth at all in the Kübler-Ross meta-story, be angry or depressed; it will be no surprise if, simply for the sake of the other patients, anger or depression may be hidden or discouraged.

So far, I have concentrated on the control of anger; let us now consider how hospices manage depression.

Hope work

Perakyla's (1991) participant observation study of a Finnish leukaemia ward revealed the routine operation of what he calls hope work. Leukaemia is a disease in which the prognosis is often not good, but it is also one in which (largely because of the side effects of treatment) patients oscillate between feeling very ill and feeling a lot better. It is always possible, therefore, for doctors to put a bright face on things for the patient: 'You'll feel better in a few days', 'Once we've got through this treatment, you should have a lot more strength.' By revealing the doctor's ability to predict a better future, this kind of hope work also functions to legitimate the medical frame and the authority of the doctor. Tape recordings of nurse–patient interactions in an English oncology unit reveal the same process (Lanceley, forthcoming). On those occasions that nurses acknowledged a patient's sadness, they often ended the interaction with a 'clinical booster': either putting a brighter side to things, or returning to the paramount reality of practical work, 'OK, let's get on the with the blanket bath now.' These research findings are complemented by frequent criticisms of nurses for 'jollying patients along'. When I mentioned these findings to a group of experienced nurses, they all defended the practice of hope work, saying things like 'Often the nurse *is* aware of ways the patient is likely to feel better in a few days – you mustn't destroy hope.'

What happens, though, when terminality is accepted? Is this the end of all hope? A central tenet of hospice practice is that you never tell a patient 'There's nothing more we can do.' You never say this not only because it is demoralising, but because it is not true. As a hospice chaplain put it to me,

'Not all deaths are easy. It can be invasive, it can be degrading, revolting, to die of a disease where your innards are eaten away and you smell and you know you smell. But we can always do something. If the patient is worried about his dignity and asks 'Will I dribble?' we can say 'Yes, but we will wipe your mouth.' I explain the care we will take of them if they should become unconscious. The key is to acknowledge the awfulness, to be realistic, and then to say that even then we will still be able to do something.'

Palliative medicine is premised on hope work, on the commitment that there is always something the team can do. It literally teaches hope (which is why, see Chapter 10, it is against active euthanasia).

Patients and relatives collude in much of this, for they too – even outside of medical settings – also engage in hope work. Young and Cullen's (forthcoming) study of cancer patients dying at home found many of them seeking signs of hope, if not of a cure then a remission: 'I walked to the corner today', 'I'm putting on weight', 'Had a drink in the pub today'. Even when such activities were no longer possible, patients still made great efforts to get to the loo by themselves, or pottered around the house, to prove to themselves they still had some life left. In and out of hospice or hospital, 'courage is the response that is admired. It appears to make life easier for everyone'. (Carmichael 1991: 88).[2]

One hospital nurse put her finger on what may be the key to all this. She said to me, 'You *have* to end on a bright note if you are to get on with the next task.' That very day I had written in my own diary about a friend with cancer:

> Yesterday, she was finding the prospect of going on very hard and wanted to die; I deliberately didn't try to find reasons for her to live (though there are many), but just listened and accepted. But it has had an effect on me today, which would have been much easier to get through had I persuaded myself that I had persuaded her to feel OK.

If I find it that hard bearing another's burden for just one day, how much more difficult must it be for a nurse to carry a whole ward's, day in day out? Or for the dying themselves? Hope work is done for everyone's sake. A nurse-turned-sociologist told me, 'It's all about sustaining the moral order. To live in a social world without hope, without a future, is difficult.' We all jolly each other, and ourselves, along.

Bereavement counselling

As with pathography and bereavement groups, one-to-one bereavement counselling aims to normalise feelings. Before it can do that, it must lay them bare and give shape to them.

> It is a counsellor's task to help a client give words to his sorrow. . . . There is a special quality of reflective silence. . . which can enable the griever to find his own words. This silence . . . tells [the bereaved] that you know they must struggle to find their own words for their sorrow. As you listen and give attention they will begin to trust you not to rush

in with the useless platitude or controlling question and will be able to risk sharing more of their feelings with you.

(Lendrum and Syme 1992: 83)

This is how the authors of a textbook on bereavement counselling see the skill of 'active listening'. However, they soon make it clear that the counsellor is not silent throughout the counselling session, for another skill to be employed is that of 'reflecting experience', or 'restating in your words the literal meaning, as you understand it, of what your client has just said . . . both at the level of the content and of the feelings expressed' (1992: 88–9). They give a hypothetical example:

Susan: My husband was a fine man. His sudden death was a great shock. I still miss him terribly.

Counsellor: Your husband's unexpected death really shook you to the core. You miss him terribly.

(Lendrum and Syme 1992: 89)

Susan's first sentence, couched as an objective statement about her husband, is ignored – though presumably could have been recast in subjective terms, such as, 'You feel your husband was wonderful.' Her second sentence is rewritten to emphasise that the death shook *Susan* rather than family and friends in general. And her final sentence, a direct expression of feeling, is repeated verbatim. The authors continue:

In these examples the clients have all been able to express fairly clearly what they were feeling using the feeling-words themselves. People are not always so articulate, lucid or helpful and it is sometimes up to the counsellor to find the 'feeling-word' which expresses the sense of what is being communicated. Having one's feelings understood, accepted and tentatively put into words can be a very affirming experience. . . . In order to feel at home in the language of feelings, you need a large range of feeling-words at your disposal.

(1992: 90)

The authors then supply an initial list: angry, sad, furious, anxious, frightened, resentful, hopeless, fearful, frustrated, warm, tense, terrified, annoyed, cross, exciting, loving, desperate, hating, cold, icy, etc.

There is a translation going on here, out of the languages of religion, of family ritual, of duty, of finance, of practicality, into the language of feeling. Every statement of the client that is not couched in the language of subjective feeling is systematically translated into it and, if not capable of translation, ignored. If traditional mourning rituals converted feelings into socially prescribed behaviour, then bereavement counselling does the opposite: it translates behaviour into feelings. It would be too strong, possibly, to say that the counsellor *defines* the feelings for the client, for the conversation is two-way and the pregnant silences allow the client to correct the counsellor's definitions. Rather it is a translation, or in the words of Hockey – an anthropologist who also trained as a CRUSE bereavement counsellor – an interpreting and editing:

> The accurate clarification and summarising of extended, repetitive and often emotional speech are important dimensions of the counsellor's technique. . . . In describing their experience of grief, bereaved people are subjecting their own intense, inchoate emotion and their extensive painful memories to processes of selection and ordering. What emerges are external verbal forms which the counsellor in turn seeks to edit or clarify. The product is an account, existing outside of themselves, which the bereaved person then submits to further processes of inter-pretation.
>
> (1986: 215, 334)

Whatever some counsellors might say about their words being simply a summary, this is clearly not the case. If clients find it helpful, it is because something *new* has been added, usually a language which can be used in future to label and interpret feelings. This may not help clients to control the feelings, but being able to give them a label can reduce panic at feeling the feelings. Counselling provides clients with a discourse they them-selves can employ to make sense of their response to loss, and many are immensely grateful for this. This kind of therapy does not manipulate a passive client; it is instead the very epitome of late-modern reflexive ordering of one's own biography and inner life (Giddens 1991: 167–9).

FURTHER READING

Hawkins, A. H. (1990) 'Constructing Death: three pathographies about dying', *Omega*, 22, 4: 301–17.

Holloway, J. (1990) 'Bereavement Literature: a valuable resource for the bereaved and those who counsel them', *Contact: Interdisciplinary Journal of Pastoral Studies*, 3: 17–26.

Perakyla, A. (1991) 'Hope Work in the Care of Seriously Ill Patients', *Qualitative Health Research*, 2, 4: 407–33.

Wambach, J.A. (1985) 'The Grief Process as a Social Construct', *Omega*, 16, 3: 201–11.

QUESTIONS

Find an example of pathography (e.g., an autobiographical account of bereavement, a children's book on bereavement, or a fictional account of a death). What model of the good death or of good grief does it portray? Who are the readers, and how is this model likely to relate to their own experience and models?

Should hospices, bereavement groups and funeral directors be explicit that they are in the business of *teaching* their patients/clients how to die/grieve? What would be the effects of such an admission?

Chapter 9

Gaining control, losing control

Clergyman: 'I wanted a job where I couldn't touch the bottom.'
Dying person: 'Dying is that sort of job too.'

(Adapted from Mayne 1989)

'Doing it my way' implies my being in control. Unfortunately, death is not so amenable to being controlled: I may want to die my way, but my dying body may not cooperate. In this chapter, I explore the relationship between control and dependency.

THE DYING PERSON

To die your own way involves two tasks. The first is to assert and to continue to assert your right to self-determination *vis-à-vis* your carers. The second is to come to terms with the lack of self-determination imposed by a deteriorating body and the dependency on carers this will almost certainly entail. In other words, the dying person needs to be able both to assert control and to accept dependency, and it is the unpredictability of this mixture of control and dependency that makes each death unique. Total control, or total dependence, would make any one death predictable.

Increasing numbers of the dying will be very frail and very old, and most of the very old are women. After a lifetime of deference to professionals, and for many women a lifetime of chosen self-abnegation in favour of others and an unwillingness to be a bother, compounded by steadily reducing status in old age, the signs do not look good for the right to self-determination of dying elderly women. Hospices which have pioneered the patient's right to autonomy have younger than average patients who are more likely to have close kin to care for and support them, and it is yet to be demonstrated that this philosophy will transfer easily to settings in which the isolated elderly die (Seale 1991b).

Miles and August (1990) have analysed judges' arguments in American right-to-die cases involving incompetent adult patients (most of whom had once been competent but failed to leave a written directive). Women's preferences were either not considered by the courts, subjected to a higher burden of proof, or rejected entirely. The courts viewed earlier statements of very ill, incompetent male patients as rational, but saw women's remarks as unreflective, emotional or immature. Even though it goes right to the heart of the feminist agenda, the right to self-determination of the dying has yet to become a concern of the feminist movement (Logue 1991), presumably because feminism is about defending one's own rights and few modern feminists have as yet joined the ranks of the elderly.

If struggling to retain control *vis-à-vis* courts and doctors is a public battle for some, struggling to retain control *vis-à-vis* one's deteriorating body is a more personal and often private battle. As one hospice doctor told me:

'There's a lot of talk of dignity in the wards these days. But there's no dignity in dying: you can't have your bottom wiped with dignity. You can't either enter or exit this life in a dignified way, or not at least in a society like ours that doesn't allow dependence. Only patients themselves can allow dignity to be conferred and they have to work at it: by humour, by patience, by silence.'

They may have to struggle against being infantilised, for the last time they were fed and the last time they were put in nappies was when they were little infants.

. . . Last scene of all
That ends this strange eventful history,
Is second childishness, and mere oblivion,
Sans teeth, sans eyes, sans taste, sans every thing.
                    (Shakespeare, *As You Like It*, II.vii)

Beyond such necessary infantilisation, nurses may raise the pitch of their voice and address patients as children, or call them by their first name even in a culture where this is not the norm among relative strangers. And when were they last pampered by women in a female-run home-like place, but when as little children they were sick? If hospitals institutionalise and depersonalise, the womb-like comfort of the hospice is more likely to infantilise.

It is possible that infantilisation may help the person come to terms with death, a kind of preparation for a return to the identity-less being of the womb. Having to give up one power after another, having to hand one responsibility after another to others, the patient may begin to come to terms with that absolute loss of power that is death. That coming to terms may be with the rage of a Dylan Thomas, but it is a coming-to-terms none the less, in one's own way. But to continue with the illusion of control may paradoxically be the one way to ensure that one will *not* die one's own way, but the pathetic way of a body out of control and a mind that cannot accept this.[1]

This is most likely to happen with those who had most control through-out life – because of their male gender (Myerhoff 1979), their affluence or the good fortune of a healthy body. And those who have made a career of caring for others may find it 'hard to be the wounded Jew when, by nature, [they] would rather be the good Samaritan' (Saunders 1990a: 10). Macho men, ever-competent mothers – these have a hard lesson to learn, as one dying man wrote:

> Pride went before
> – I fell –
> Pride went
> (Quoted in Saunders
> 1990a: 12)

It may be those who have had a tough life, or who have had few sustaining relationships, or who in old age have lost most of their sustaining relation-ships, who find it easiest to let go of life (Young and Cullen, forthcoming).

The hospice response to all this is twofold: to give patients as much control as possible, while helping them to come to terms with dependency. Doctors and nurses tend to talk about the former, chaplains about the latter.

Saunders' seminal innovation in pain control, which created modern palliative medicine, rested on one core insight: that if the patient is dying, then dependency on morphine or other addictive drugs does not matter. Instead, therefore, of the medical regime limiting the taking of addictive painkillers to prescribed intervals, patients themselves can choose to take the drugs as and when they want. They then need never be in pain should they so choose – but they can also choose to be in pain, if that makes them more alert for a specific occasion, knowing they can always control it if it gets too much. Self-control of medication reduces anxiety (will I be in unbearable pain before the next drug round, will I be too dopey to talk with my grandchildren when they visit?), and reduced anxiety in turn leads to reduced physical pain. Further, addiction occurs only when the patient learns that another shot will ease the agony of withdrawal symptoms, as in the old days when the morphine wore off before the next drug round; but if the patient never experiences withdrawal symptoms, the craving for the drug doesn't materialise, so the patient never develops a fear of addiction, reducing anxiety still further. A benign circle is set up, whose centre is the patient in control of his or her own medication.

If doctors return control of medication to the patient, nurses are instrumental in discouraging the dependency of languishing in bed and giving up. Noyes and Clancy (1983) have observed that 'dependency is encouraged in the sick role whereas independence within the limits of an individual's declining resources is encouraged in the dying role.' Nurses may give medical reasons for encouraging the patient to get up and about, such as the danger of muscle weakness or fluid in the lungs, but there is also the belief that active patients are more in charge of their own lives. Nurses cajole patients out of bed and dissuade family carers from being over-protective.

Christian clergy, by contrast, are bearers of a tradition founded by one who gave up control in order to be done to death. A contemporary English theologian, W. H. Vanstone (1982) has reflected on the symbolism of the phrase 'done to' in the death of Christ: if Jesus displayed his humanness through a life of brilliant teaching and control over the forces of nature, then what of the total loss of control he experienced from the time he was betrayed until his death a few hours later? Was he any less human because he was no longer in control? Vanstone concludes that dependency, 'being done to', entails not a loss of but a different kind of humanity, a kind of humanity that a society premised on the work ethic has lost touch with. Clergy in touch with this kind of theology become experts in the meaning of dependency and, while not wanting to induce it, can counsel those who find their body makes them dependent upon carers. Clergy also ritualise dependency through the holy communion, in which people are empowered through the paradoxical symbolism of the infantile dependency of being fed – with bread literally put in their mouths, a cup literally given to their lips. The idea here is not to encourage dependency, but to recognise it as the inevitable other side of the coin of being human (Reed 1978).

Buddhism's transcendence of suffering through the elimination of desire also seems particularly well suited to helping people to come to terms with dependency. Judaism too has long contemplated the meaning of suffering, and Saunders has clearly been influenced in her thinking by Jewish patients and theologians. All this is of course theoretical. I know of no research investigating what religious personnel actually do with dying patients, still less whether clergy help them find meaning in dependency, and how.

Can meaning be found in dependency outside of a religious tradition? Marshall's (1980) study of a Canadian old persons' home suggests that meaning is constructed in everyday conversation, and there is no reason why meaning need be provided by religion. Indeed, he sees the fatalism of his more religious subjects as conflicting with the self-determination of North American culture, and therefore handicapping. Speaking in part as a sociologist, but in part it seems also as a humanist, he says

> Human beings are creatures who attempt to negotiate with others, or struggle with them, in pursuit of a life after their own fashion. This pursuit extends to the final chapters of the autobiography, and, indeed, I have suggested that in the final stages of life control becomes more important than in the early stages.
>
> Control over one's death and dying is probably more important in today's world than it was formerly; at the same time, control is more difficult to sustain because the course of dying now takes longer than in earlier eras, because the dying person is likely to be old and older people are relatively powerless and control few resources, and because ageing and dying is a status passage that usually brings the individual into contact with bureaucratic institutions that have a force of their own.
>
> (1980: 159)

This is surely true, but by focusing on social and ignoring bodily causes of loss of control, Marshall's sociology seems strangely disembodied, with little philosophically to offer the person whose dependency is induced more by a failing body than by an ageist, sexist society. If someone is tired and weak and wants to leave decisions to others, should they not be allowed this? This is a lesson some in the hospice movement, committed to patient self-determination, have had to learn through experience (Wilkes 1991).

More helpful here is Becker's book *The Denial of Death* (1973), a maverick reinterpretation of Freud that has achieved some popularity; it refers to religious traditions but works essentially within a humanist frame. He argues that the foundation of personality development is indeed fear of the body, but this is the fear not of sexuality (as Freud would have it) but of mortality. The recognition in later life that one is dependent upon a body that will eventually deteriorate and die is traumatic and yet the key to developing a more whole personality. Coming to terms with physical dependency is an important process, which a psychotherapist would be as competent as a priest in helping the person to unravel – perhaps better.[2]

THE PROFESSIONAL CARER

If loss of control is an issue for some dying people, it is also an issue for their professional carers. It has often been said that doctors abandoned the dying because they exposed the doctor's powerlessness, but that does not seem to fit the experience at least of medics working with cancer patients. In fact, on the contrary, as one cancer specialist writes, 'In many ways the treatment of a woman with advanced breast cancer can be very rewarding because most of the symptomatic problems are amenable to control, at least in the short run' (Baum 1988: 106). Baum contrasts this with earlier phases of breast cancer, when giving a prognosis more definite than in terms of statistical probability is impossible: there is built-in uncertainty. In other words, he has more of a sense of control when the patient is terminal than when she was potentially curable. A general practitioner told me much the same, when I asked him how he found working with dying patients: 'Satisfying. You see, you no longer have diagnostic uncertainty, we know now how to control pain, and that frees me to minister to the person.' Much of the time most doctors do not really know what is wrong with their patients and terminality changes that. Nurses too may enjoy nursing the dying because, as one coronary care nurse said 'they can do less and less for themselves, so your basic nursing comes in, which is nice because that's what you're trained to do. The actual basic thing, looking after people' (Field 1989: 87). The nurse is more in control than in some other settings where basic nursing skills are less valued.

Perakyla (1991: 428–9) wondered what would happen to hope work once the leukaemia patients he studied became terminal. What he found, at least among and between staff, was the dismantling of hope. Medical and nursing staff find an unexpected death disturbing, so by predicting the death they affirm that even if they cannot beat nature, they can at least understand her. In this way, death does not undermine the doctor's cognitive control.

At a weekly hospice staff meeting I attended, the major theme in the discussion of patient management was control: of symptoms, of pain, of emotions, of family relationships. Controlling such things was satisfying; not knowing what was going on was frustrating but typically turned into the challenge to understand what was going on and how to control it. The doctor introduced some patients for discussion:

Mr L. Still very anxious, flat emotionally, not making any headway. We asked his wife to stay away for three days and they were both delighted, but when she came back to see him she wanted to continue to come. He's concerned about being very weak, though he's not actually that weak. I'm really not quite sure what's going on.

Jack is back. The problem is that we don't know what to do with him, as he's not dying. He's let go, and is a delight, but he could live another six weeks.

There's a lady in village X who suddenly went out of pain control on Tuesday, and I'm not sure why. I'm going to see her this afternoon.

Doctors who passionately care for the well-being of the dying find patients who are not amenable to medical control draining. These cases constitute the research challenges that enable such doctors to claim palliative medicine as a valid medical speciality. At the time of writing, for example, pain has been largely controlled, and palliative specialists are increasingly having referred to them patients with difficult-to-control symptoms, such as breathlessness, which currently form the clinical and the research challenge.

If the satisfaction of palliative care lies in control, how does this fit with the commitment to let the patient die *their* way? Sometimes not very well. What the patient wants may be difficult for the doctor to arrange, as a hospice doctor told me:

'We have this gentleman in the unit who wants to die, but he is in discomfort and wants that relieved in the meantime. But he enquired whether the treatment – increasing his haemoglobin level – would prolong his life, to which the answer was 'probably'. So a compromise was reached. But I don't find this satisfying, because there is an effective way of removing the discomfort.'

Also the primary concern of doctors and nurses to keep the body in good shape may conflict with other desires of the patient:

Peter stopped wanting to eat or drink when he had pneumonia. The hospice tried to bully him into eating which upset him. Once he was home, I would ensure that something that he could manage was always available, but didn't make an issue of eating or drinking. Hence, I think that the actual cause of death was kidney failure. But it meant he didn't need to pass urine very often, and he could have a bit if he wanted. On Christmas Day he managed two sips of whisky!

(From a letter to The Natural Death Centre,
printed in Albery *et al.* 1993: 107)

Again, it is religious specialists who articulate a philosophy that accepts the carer's inability to control another person's dying. In one book on multi-professional teamwork, the chapter on the chaplain's role is titled 'On Having No Answer' and explores this theme of the carer's powerlessness (Lunn 1990). Elsewhere a Buddhist writes 'How can we . . . let go our need to control [death] as we have tried to control life? . . . We cannot die another's death any more than we can lead their life' (Ostaseski 1990: 11). Participant observer Hockey (1990: 182–3) writes perceptively of the conflict between *care*, grounded philosophically and historically in the West in the Christian commitment to love unconditionally, and *control*, grounded in a post-medieval and scientific view of the natural world. The 'care' of the elderly and dying in institutions exists in an uneasy tension between the two.

The funeral

Being in control is at the heart of job satisfaction in any profession: knowledge and experience provide control over events that the untrained lack. This is as evident after death as before. Funeral directors certainly want to be in control, as witnessed by their self-elevation from *undertakers*, who undertook to supply you with a coffin and hearse and whatever else you might require, to *funeral directors* who take charge of the whole show. Despite claiming to offer customers choice, the one customer many British funeral directors do not like is the do-it-yourselfer who wants to buy just a coffin rather than the whole package. Jane Spottiswoode's (1991) account of her struggle to purchase a coffin in which she and her friends could bury her husband reveals how threatening funeral directors perceived this request. A few years later in 1993, funeral directors in Plymouth were most upset when the city council published a short leaflet explaining how families could use the city's cemeteries and crematoria for DIY funerals, even though only a tiny handful of families would be thinking of taking such a line of action. When discussing DIY funerals with Mrs Spottiswoode and myself on BBC television at this time, the public relations man for the National Association of Funeral Directors explained that funeral directors do not like doing less than the complete funeral, because it is not clear who is in charge.[3]

Once the funeral party has entered the crematorium chapel for the service, funeral directors can be ill at ease – they are no longer in charge since they are on foreign territory and have handed over control to a minister of religion in whose competence they may not have total faith. By the same token, crematorium managers like to control events once the party is on their territory. The mechanically operated exit of the coffin, typical in the UK and its former colonies, tells the party that the funeral is over and it is time to leave – thus guaranteeing an empty chapel for the next party, which is a major concern of the crematorium manager. As with the funeral director, losing control over the flow can cause chaos on a busy day with several funerals scheduled in close succession. One New Zealand funeral director has followed American practice and installed a cremator in his own funeral parlour, rejecting mechanical removal of the coffin from view because he wants to return control to the family. He told me: 'The closing curtain or exiting coffin tells the mourners when to leave, but in my chapel they spend as long or as little as *they* decide.' His evident pride on taking this attitude indicates that he considers himself exceptional in giving up a measure of control.

The bereavement counsellor

Those caring for the dying may be able to exert considerable control over pain and symptoms, and may be able to exert cognitive control by predicting the imminence of death, though this control has to exist in tension with vulnerability and powerlessness. The bereavement counsellor, however, experiences only powerlessness – *if* the theory on which their counselling is based is that grief is a natural process that must take its course and whose timing cannot be predicted. The non-directive counsellor simply has to listen and absorb the pain. One CRUSE counselling co-ordinator told me: 'The other person is in pain, and you want to ease that pain, but you can't. You just have to be with them in it.' Hockey (1990: 181) describes her first visit as a CRUSE counsellor and her panic when the elderly widowed client clearly expected her to *do* something; she had to remember her training, resist the temptation to give advice, and enter the powerlessness of listening: 'I felt I must seem so much younger than she was – and so evidently not in possession of any profound resolution to her misery.' No wonder that, by contrast, Worden's task-centred counselling (1991) is attractive not only for clients but also for counsellors who want to feel they can touch the bottom.

But the trained listener is not as vulnerable as may at first sight appear, for listening is itself a technique counsellors use for coping with their own vulnerability. By not intervening with advice, by limiting expressions of sympathy and strictly controlling the timing of visits, the counsellor is not behaving as an ordinary friend and thereby limits the pain of personal involvement. But by listening at length, the counsellor also avoids the detachment of a doctor or financial adviser, a detachment which in its own way can impose psychological penalties on such professionals. Active listening is a half-way house which may well be more comfortable – it acknowledges the client's pain yet keeps the counsellor at one remove from it.

Wood's study of the clergy in death-related situations is instructive here. The clergy want to show compassion, but how do they do this, especially with non-churchgoers and in secular settings? On the west coast of the United States where counselling is common, they adopt well-known counselling techniques:

> encouraging the person to express feelings, reflecting statements back to them, being nonjudgmental, and listening. These techniques have become part of our everyday, getting through-the-world routine. They are ways of making predictable those situations in which we usually experience unease. They give us a way to structure our concern; a sort of 'how-to-do-it' formula for when we want to help, but don't know what to do.
>
> (Wood 1976: 137–8)

Having interviewed only the ministers, Wood is not in a position to know whether this technique is helpful for the patients, but it is clearly helpful in getting the minister through a difficult encounter (1977: 137–41). If it gets ministers through such encounters, it surely gets professional counsellors through.

Skilled listeners can also experience a considerable measure of control as they use techniques in order to get the client to speak, to find their own language of feelings, and generally be 'midwives' of the grief process. From a Foucauldian perspective (e.g., Arney and Bergen 1984: ch. 8; May 1992; Silverman 1987: ch.6), one might explore the power the counsellor thereby has over the client. Such analyses have been conducted mainly in team situations in hospitals and clinics where the patient is not sure who is monitoring what, situations which were never explicitly announced as involving the surveillance of inner feeling, and situations which the client cannot easily leave. I suspect the power of the counsellor over the bereaved client is considerably less: the client has entered counselling willingly, is aware that it will involve considerable self-revelation, and is free to terminate counselling at any time. But we do not know, because the process (in contrast to the outcome – Parkes 1980) of bereavement counselling has barely been researched.

FURTHER READING

Lunn, L. (1990) 'Having No Answer', in C. Saunders (ed.) *Hospice and Palliative Care: an interdisciplinary approach*, London, Edward Arnold.

Saunders, C. (1990a) *Beyond the Horizon: a search for meaning in suffering*, London, Darton, Longman Todd.

Vanstone, W.H. (1982) *The Stature of Waiting*, London, Darton, Longman Todd.

QUESTIONS

Medicine, sociology and feminism all aim to give humans more control over their bodies and lives. Medicine has often been criticised for being unable to cope with the 'failure' that death represents. Can sociology and/or feminism can be criticised on the same grounds?

How have others you know of (or you yourself) coped with bodily-imposed dependency? Have the main resources been religion, a secular philosophy, or micro-interactional strategies such as humour and silence?

In the light of this chapter, outline the limits to 'doing it my way' when it comes to dying.

If you have ever been in counselling (as either counsellor or client), analyse the counsellor–client power relationship. Is this likely to be any different in bereavement counselling?

Chapter 10

Which person?

The revival of death is committed to listening to the dying, their families, the deceased, and to survivors. But is it possible to listen equally attentively to each individual? What happens when more than one person is eligible to be listened to and they want different things? In short, which person is being, and should be, listened to?

The first question – who is being listened to – involves a question of equity. Clearly the distribution of attentiveness is not equal. Palliative care is available for many cancer patients, but if you are one of the elderly frail or are suffering from a stroke, it is much less likely that your carers will be so attentive. Even if you have cancer, your chances of finding a local and well resourced hospice or palliative care team will depend increasingly, as finances get tighter, on whether you live in an affluent area in which costs can be underwritten by effective charitable fundraising and by large pools of volunteers (Clark 1993a: 174). The tenacious roots of hospices in local communities worry national and regional health care planners who are concerned that all should have equal access to services.

Although palliative care is available for patients with AIDS, some services are restricted to cancer patients; Carlisle (1992) has suggested that in the UK doctors are falsely confirming cancer in AIDS patients in order to qualify them for Marie Curie home nursing support. Against this, the huge sums available in the UK for care of those with AIDS and the political effectiveness in the USA of the gay lobby have led to a massive concern to listen to and accommodate the psycho-social needs of people with AIDS. But as with cancer, there are wide variations. The person with AIDS is more likely to find attentive care in London or San Francisco than in a rural area where sympathy, solidarity and support may all be thin on the ground.

After death, mourners will find some funeral directors more willing to provide a personally tailored funeral than others (though you will be lucky to know in advance who these are), and the chances of being listened to by an attentive bereavement counsellor are considerably higher if the deceased died in a hospice such as St Christopher's with a well developed counselling programme than if they expired in a hospital or old persons' home.

In this chapter, however, I will not dwell on the question of equity across a range of deaths, important though it is, but on the question of who, in any one death, should be – and is – listened to.

THE DYING VERSUS THE SURVIVORS

A common situation nowadays is that the doctor knows that most dying people can bear the truth, but the relatives of this particular dying person insist that she or he could not. They know the person best – but the doctor knows more about how most people respond to such news and knows that relatives can project their own fears onto the patient. There is some evidence that the old tendency to tell no one has been replaced by an equally crass tendency to tell everyone.

Hospices claim to have pioneered the concept of the family, rather than the individual, as the unit of care. (In the UK, general practitioners might claim they pioneered this, but that is another matter.) This is necessary if lines of communication between different family members and professional carers are to remain clear. Another justification for seeing the family as the unit of care is that the patient may be far more concerned to ensure the well-being of survivors than worried about their own death, while other family members may be far more concerned that the patient does not suffer than about their own impending loss. Listening to the patient has to include considering the well-being of the family; and listening to the family has to involve considering the well-being of the patient.

That hospice teams actually do pay attention to other family members in their own right, rather than as carers of the patient, is as yet unproven. Audits of the quality of care may ask the next of kin as a surrogate for the patient, if the patient is unconscious or dead, but rarely ask kin what they themselves felt about the care. Likewise, Hunt's (1991b) tape recordings of domiciliary visits by pain-control nurses revealed that when carers themselves attempted to act as clients, by describing their own symptoms or difficulties, the nurses discouraged this, responding only by offering support and encouragement so that the carer would continue their caring and thus keep the patient at home. On the other hand, the fact that many hospices have inaugurated bereavement services indicates that they have developed relationships with families and are concerned for them after death.

Even when there is a real attempt to listen to kin as well as to the patient, it may not be clear who to listen to (Hunt 1991b). Where a dying man has remarried and has children by an earlier marriage, and the children and the new wife have never got on, they are hardly likely to agree over terminal care. Whose views take precedence – a wife of only eighteen months, or children of 45 years? Likewise when a young homosexual is dying there may be conflict over the relative rights of lover and parents to be listened to.

A final factor that affects whether professionals pay more attention to the dying or to the survivors is whether or not they believe in an afterlife, and what preparations, if any, need to be made for the transition. In an earlier paper (Walter 1993a), I have argued that Protestants have for a century or so seen the transition to heaven as virtually automatic and in the past generation Catholics have paid less attention to the last rites, so that preparation for the afterlife has virtually gone off the Christian agenda. Death ceases to be a transition, and has become loss – both for the patient and for survivors. This is in sharp contrast to Hindu deathbed rituals, which must be performed correctly if the soul is to be released easily. In particular, the tears of survivors who find it hard to let go of the dying or dead person are believed to hold back the soul, something being rediscovered in New Age approaches to death. In this view the grief of survivors can wait, for they have months and years ahead in which to express it; of paramount importance now is that the survivors assist the release of the soul.

EUTHANASIA

Euthanasia may be *voluntary* or *involuntary*, depending on whether the person's consent has been given; and *active* or *passive*, depending on whether active steps to end life have to be taken, or whether simply withdrawing treatment is sufficient to let a terminal disease take its natural course. The hospice movement often practises passive euthanasia in the last hours or days, but is strongly against active euthanasia.

Euthanasia has become an issue because there are more people to listen to. In earlier years when people died at home and a wife asked the family doctor if he could give her husband something 'to hurry him along, I can't bear seeing him like this', and when the doctor agreed, this would be a private matter between her and the doctor. Or the doctor might hasten the death by a few hours without even telling the family. But today such a decision usually involves many more people, not all of whom may agree. It is in this new context that euthanasia has become a matter for public debate for several reasons.

First, three quarters of us now die in hospitals and other institutions. That means that there are many other nursing and medical staff to witness the event, one of whom may blow the whistle. Such was the case in Britain in 1992 when a nurse reported rheumatologist Dr Nigel Cox for 'hurrying along' a woman in severe pain – he was consequently brought to court and the case hit the headlines, generating a national debate about euthanasia. Second, institutionalised patients may feel life to be worthless not because of their disease but because of their social death in an institution, or others may feel their life to be worthless – hence generating requests for euthanasia, requests that are likely to involve a number of people. Third, the revivalist commitment to listening to the dying person means that a request from him or her for euthanasia has to be taken seriously; doctors cannot just ignore it as against their professional ethics, and have to explore the matter with the patient and family.

Let us consider what should, given the revivalist agenda, be the simplest case: when the dying person asks to be killed – voluntary, active euthanasia. Even those committed to letting people die their own way may have problems with such a request, for some of the following reasons.

First, listening to a dying person is a continuous process, so any one request must be considered in context. There may be times when a person wants to die, and times when the same person is thoroughly enjoying life. A passing remark such as 'Oh, just put me out of my misery' is unlikely to be a serious request for euthanasia. And as discussed previously, people who may have valued being in control all their lives may, as their body begins to limit them, yet discover a new way of being that does not require being in charge, or working, or caring for others – some may discover, for the first time in their life, the pleasure of being cared *for*.

Even living wills and advance directives – where the person requests specified forms of euthanasia should specified conditions be met in future – are not entirely trustworthy, as they assume that the views of the writer will remain constant. This is often not the case. 'Life frequently becomes very precious even though severely limited; the human will to live is frequently stronger in limited health than when taken for granted in normal health' (Crowther 1993). Becker (1973), Kübler-Ross (1975) and Vanstone (1982) all concur that the dependency of terminal illness may prove a key time of personal and/or spiritual growth, and there is no way that carers can predict whether this will or will not happen and whether the person's attitude will change.

Second, although this particular patient may genuinely and consistently want euthanasia for themselves, there may be a problem if they want a doctor (rather than kin or themselves) to perform it. One hospice doctor told me she would be worried that future patients might never again be able to trust that this injection or drug is not the final one, motivated by financial gain or family pressure or by a casual remark by the patient intended to be taken in jest. She felt that the doctor has to consider not only individual ethics but also institutional ethics. This does not seem to me an argument against euthanasia as such, but *involuntary* euthanasia.

Third, it is not just the doctor who should think about future generations. It can be hard enough for many families to commit an elderly relative to an institution – the family may feel guilty and the old person feel betrayed. There is empirical evidence that survivors who are not spouses are more likely than spouses to think that they should have died earlier, and of course the very old are less likely to have a spouse (Seale and Addington-Hall, forthcoming a). Children, other relatives and officials are more likely than spouses to find caring a burden, and are less likely to have such close emotional ties as would a spouse. The very elderly are also more likely to say that they want to die sooner rather than later. With their number increasing fast, an increasingly common scenario could be the very old spouse-less person agreeing to euthanasia but with the degree to which that agreement is wholehearted being unclear. Semi-voluntary euthanasia might then become almost expected. So the problem is that the right of an individual today to ask someone else to hasten their death may conflict with the future right of all others to refuse euthanasia.

In this context, fasting to death (Albery *et al.* 1993: 24–5) seems a constructive solution, since it involves nobody else's action other than the agreement of carers not to forcibly feed the faster. The patient dies their own way, others have to listen and cooperate, but responsibility is entirely the patient's, and there are no knock-on effects for future family relationships or doctor–patient relationships. Fasting disentangles individual ethics from institutional ethics. Though cases of fasting to death rarely hit the headlines, there is evidence that a considerable number of elderly people may quietly give up and 'decide' to lose their appetite and stop eating.[1]

A fourth point is that professionals in palliative medicine may not be convinced that all forms of pain and symptom control have been tried – they believe there is always something they can do. In the Dr Cox case, the *British Medical Journal*[2] carried a considerable correspondence from specialists in palliative care who berated Dr Cox, not a specialist in pain control himself, for not consulting those who were. Such specialists would readily have advised him that his approach to controlling the patient's pain had been seriously flawed. The case worried specialists in palliative medicine, only recently recognised in the UK as a medical specialty, because it revealed how far they still had to go to be recognised as specialists available to be consulted by any doctor.

It seems to me from these and other arguments that legalising euthanasia should only begin to be debated in a country where palliative medicine is highly developed and widely disseminated across the whole range of doctors; and where the principle of listening to dying persons is established across the entire range of institutions (including old persons' homes and geriatric wards, where in the UK it has hardly begun). What seems to be happening is the opposite. The Western country where euthanasia has been nearest to getting on the statute book has been The Netherlands, where palliative medicine is not well developed.

The aim of this short section has not been to give a balanced or complete discussion of euthanasia – books have been written on that – but simply to explore the most obvious instance where those committed to listening to patients and enabling them to die their own way appear to go back on their word.

Doctors in the hospice movement (Saunders 1992) and a British Medical Association working party (1988) consider that in practice this is not an issue. They claim that when the patient is fully informed about pain and symptom control and is listened to over a period of time, especially in a hospice setting, requests for active euthanasia disappear to almost nil. This may be their experience, but Seale and Addington-Hall (forthcoming, b) asked two large representative samples of kin after the death whether they felt it would have been better had the person died earlier, and whether the patient had ever expressed a desire to die sooner or had requested euthanasia. They found that kin of those who had received hospice care were *more* likely to say it would have been better had the person died earlier.

Seale and Addington-Hall's discussion of this important finding goes to the very heart of this book. Though effective pain control may reduce requests for euthanasia, this may be counteracted by a hospice environment in which patients are encouraged to act as autonomous individuals. The fear of dependency is a major reason for requesting euthanasia (Seale and Addington-Hall 1994), and dependency is especially feared when people value autonomy. Autonomy is not a value as well-rooted in British as in American culture, especially in female working-class subcultures which often include a large dose of fatalism ('putting up' with things, 'not wanting to be a bother'). The hospice is an institution that actively promotes the individual's right to self-determination, which (if embraced) could exacerbate some patients' fear of dependency and hence their desire for euthanasia.

Another factor mentioned by Seale and Addington-Hall (1994) is the hospice's encouraging its patients to express their fears. Expressivism asserts this to be cathartic and to reduce fear, but for some people bringing fears to the surface can cause them to brood on them all the more and possibly to consider solutions such as euthanasia that they had not hitherto dared imagine. In so far as they have learnt (maybe from auxiliaries or from other patients) that the hospice is against active euthanasia, they may not voice such thoughts to more senior staff – which could explain why hospice doctors report so few requests for euthanasia. Hospice doctors may be listening, but patients may refrain from speaking because they know the hospice party line. Or it may be that they do tell the doctor, but hospice doctors are prone to see each request as an exception and do not add them up into a pattern.

Before moving on, one final observation. The abortion debate, currently very much alive in the USA, is like the euthanasia debate in that both sides are committed to respect for the person, but disagree substantially over *which* person is to be heard. Those in favour of liberal abortion legislation point to the right of the woman to have control over her own body, and not to be dictated to by medics and lawyers. Those against point to the right of the unborn child not to be dictated to by the convenience of the mother, and the duty of doctors to protect an embryo that cannot speak for itself. 'Listening to the person' does not solve ethical dilemmas – it makes them more complex.

THE FUNERAL

Clergy and undertakers tell me that 'Funerals are for the living' and that 'The funeral's purpose is to help the grief process.' But ask people why they attended a particular funeral and they reply, 'in order to pay my last respects'; in other words, they have come for the sake of the deceased. Or they may say they have come to support the next of kin. Ask next of kin and they are likely to say that it's an ordeal they have to go through for the sake of everyone else, because holding a funeral is the done thing. Hindus will say they are there to release the soul of the deceased, traditional Catholics that they are there to say a mass for the deceased. Apart from some members of the 'expressive' caring professions, no attenders say they are there to help their own grief process. It is a matter of religion, of the socially done thing and ultimately of human decency (Walter 1990: ch. 11).

Let us, however, put ourselves in the shoes of the minister or undertaker who operates on the working principle that the funeral is to help the grieving. And this minister or undertaker is a revivalist, who is really committed to listening to the grieving and giving them what they want. Who should he or she listen to? Who is the chief mourner?

Just as children may disagree with each other as to whether a frail parent should have yet another high-tech operation to keep them alive in a semi-vegetable state, so they may not agree as to what is an appropriate funeral. Dad, born a Catholic but for many years an explicit atheist, has been cared for over the final years by a daughter who is a devout Catholic: should the funeral be Catholic or secular? Thirty-three-year-old David dies of AIDS, and his parents only learn of his condition, indeed only learn that he is gay, days before his death. Losing an adult child is one of the most traumatic of bereavements and his parents want to arrange the funeral; David's lover, whom the parents have not met, has already set arrangements in motion. Who should the undertaker listen to? With serial monogamy and homosexual marriages expanding the range of family forms in the postmodern era, traditional rules for determining 'next of kin' and 'chief mourner' may no longer work.

I will not pursue further this issue of who to listen to in arranging a funeral, as I have considered it at length elsewhere (Walter 1990, especially chs 10, 11). Let us look instead to the days and months beyond the funeral, when the same question of 'who are the bereaved?' can continue to cause confusion and contention within a family.

WHO ARE 'THE BEREAVED'?

Definitions are being expanded so that 'the bereaved' are perceived as potentially more than just the next of kin. The following are recent titles from the American journals *Omega* and *Death Studies*: 'The Forgotten Grievers: grandparents' reactions to the death of grandchildren' (Ponzett and Johnson 1991), 'Grief and Bereavement in Mental Retardation: a need for a new understanding' (Wadsworth and Harper 1991), 'Close Friends as Survivors: bereavement patterns in a "hidden" population' (Sklar and Hartley 1990). The modern era has constructed bereavement as the experience of the lover and/or of the next of kin (Ariès 1981), but in the more fluid relationships of the postmodern era bereavement is being reconstructed as something that anyone can lay claim to. In the Victorian era, there were clear rules as to how long each member of the family had to mourn for particular categories of relative. In the twentieth century, the rules of social mourning have been replaced by the psychological require- ments of 'the grief process' and it has tacitly been assumed that grief is the experience only of next of kin. But this leaves other kin and friends with neither the old fashioned social mourning rituals, nor the new fangled 'grief process'. They have been left out. Now they too are claiming the right to grieve, and experts are reconstructing them as potential grievers.

Though the old mourning rules clearly specified the behaviour and relative loss of each family member, the new grief process does not. This is because it is a psychological concept, referring to something within the individual. If in the mid-twentieth century the grief process affected only the next of kin, now it can affect anyone – but this individualistic concept provides no rules specifying whose grief is the most important, no rules specifying who is to mourn and who is to support those who mourn.

Littlewood (1992), on the basis of both a literature survey and her own research, analyses intra-family disputes over the position of chief mourner, disputes which are serious because they can further deplete the range of informal support available to those who grieve. In her own research, disputes frequently involved:

1   brothers and/or sisters following the death of a single or sole surviving parent;
2   adult children and a dead parent's second or subsequent partner;
3   parents and partners following the death of an adult child.

(1992: 115)

Disputants regularly alleged that the claimant to the role of chief mourner had no right to the position because they had been less than caring toward the person who had died, or because they had somehow been responsible for the death. For example:

> She'd got a cheek. She hadn't been near him [her father] for years and then she just moved back and thought she could take over – it was like the return of the prodigal for me Dad – he thought the sun shone out of her. After he died the rest of the family were saying 'Poor ——'. I never went near her and haven't been since, if she was so bloody fond of him it's a pity she didn't do more for him when he was alive.

(Ibid.: 116)

When the deceased had remarried, adult children found that 'the repre- sentation of their dead parent offered by their step-parent often bore little resemblance to their own image of their parent which was usually formed when the original family was intact' (Ibid.: 117).

Problems between partner and parents can be particularly acute when an adult child dies, and not only when the adult child was homosexual:

> Many parents of adult children strongly believed that their dead child's partner should be supportive towards them. Furthermore, widows and widowers often reported that their dead partner's parents were making unreasonable demands upon them. in short, there seemed to be genuine social confusion regarding appropriate expectations in these instances.
>
> (Ibid. 1992: 118)

Clearly grief is not only a psychological process within the individual, but carries with it expectations of behaviour (expressive and/or supportive) for both self and others. However 'natural' the grief process is construed to be, this does not guarantee consensus as to who should 'naturally' engage in supportive behaviour.

Even if it is accepted that the other has the right to grieve, there can be considerable dispute over the right *way* to grieve.

> Mrs Patterson, a younger woman bereaved of her small daughter and determinedly tough-minded about the future, describes conflict with her mother: she said there was a brick wall between her and her mother, no communication. The problem wasn't going to go away, she said – she'd have to find a way of resolving it. She complained that her mother was such a wet blanket, that she ate little, wore the same clothes every day, never saw her friends. Mrs P. said she wanted support from her mother, wanted her mother to say how good the child's life had been – even if it was short. Instead her mother would just look downcast, sigh, and talk of 'Poor Helen'. Mrs P. wondered why her mother hadn't had a breakdown.
>
> (Hockey 1986: 325)

The literature of organisations such as The Compassionate Friends is full of stories where husbands and wives grieve for a child in mutually incomprehensible ways (usually, she wanting to cry and talk, he going off for long walks by himself and not wanting to talk), or where parent and child grieve in very different ways, or parent and grandparent. Sometimes this literature recommends one style (*always* the female, talking, expressing style):

> It is much more helpful for both women and men to talk and cry rather than bottle up their feelings. It is very common however for couples to

grieve differently and at a different pace. One partner may cope by wanting to talk endlessly while the other tries to escape into work.

(O'Toole n.d.)

Increasingly, however, this kind of literature is refusing to label any way as better or best, and pleading for mutual understanding of each other's style and acceptance that perhaps the other cannot support you as you might wish.

Displaying emotion can be particularly contentious. I have already observed how difficult is the English presentation of the grieving self: being composed, yet with just enough of a hint at the pain within. Often the presentation is not successful: 'Many people were particularly hurt to find that their efforts to control the expression of emotion in public, which were considerable, were sometimes interpreted by other people as insensitivity or lack of caring' (Littlewood 1992: 120–1). Or others may consider that too much rather than too little emotion has been displayed: 'He [husband] said, "Come on now, pull yourself together; you've done really well so far, don't break down now." I couldn't even cry at home after that' (Ibid.: 120).

How long grief should last is yet another matter on which there may be little consensus within a family and which has to be interpersonally negotiated without any clear rules other than generalising from one's own experience:

> My family were very nice for about six weeks – very understanding but I was terrible for months afterwards, I used to forget things – I was living in another world, it takes me a long time to get over things. Anyway, in the end they just lost patience. My husband was really nasty about it, he said: 'For God's sake woman, what's the matter with you, I was never like that when my mother died – it's been *months*.'
>
> (Ibid.: 87)

Even if grief is an inner psychological process, it is manifested in behaviour which others have to live with: grief therefore is also inevitably an interpersonal negotiation.

Listening to bereaved individuals and giving them permission to grieve their own way may be relatively simple in the isolation of the one-to-one counselling session. Outside of that in the conflicts of family life things are more complex; a few therapists are beginning to recognise this and are developing models for intervening in families rather than for counselling individuals (e.g. Bloch 1991; Detmer and Lamberti 1991). What is required, however, is not just models of family dynamics that counsellors can use, but a more social understanding of grief that can be popularly appropriated. Grief is manifestly interpersonally negotiated, but because it is widely believed now to be a natural process that must run its course within each individual, there are no rules by which to negotiate. The result is anomie and yet further pain. Now that social mourning is a thing of the past, we are not left with a psychological process playing out its natural course within the grieving individual; nor are we left with a postmodern choice for each individual to grieve as he or she will. What we are left with is the potential for confusion and conflict. The need for a more sociological understanding of grief is, in some families, desperate.

FURTHER READING

Glover, J. (1988) *Causing Deaths and Saving Lives*, London, Penguin.
Littlewood, J. (1992) *Aspects of Grief*, London, Tavistock/Routledge: ch. 6.
Saunders, C. (1992) 'Voluntary Euthanasia', *Palliative Medicine*, 6: 1–5.

QUESTIONS

This chapter outlines some arguments against active voluntary euthanasia; how might these arguments be countered?

What do you think is the purpose of a funeral, and why?

What family conflicts over grief have you experienced or witnessed?

Chapter 11

Routinisation

This book is about the revival of death as a fit topic of conversation in home, hospital and society at large. My term 'revival' deliberately suggests something akin to a religious revival. But religious revivals rarely last long, their fire sooner or later burning itself out. A useful framework for analysing this has been provided by the sociologist Max Weber, in his concept of the routinisation of charisma (Bendix 1966). Weber's framework has been brilliantly applied to the hospice movement by James and Field (1992) in an argument which directly addresses the question of whether hospices and similar institutions can not only listen to patients but *keep on listening*. Much of this chapter will be spent summarising James and Field's argument.

Similar, though less Weberian, discussions of the routinisation of hospices may be found in some American publications: Abel (1986), Mor *et al.* (1988: ch. 11), Paradis and Cummings (1986) and, more passionately, Stoddard (1989). Seale (1989), a British sociologist, valuably surveys what is empirically known about what happens in hospices, and reminds us how limited that knowledge is. James and Field therefore have identified the pressures towards change, but how far hospices have succumbed to (or embraced) them is something on which the jury is still open.

Revivals are started by individuals with the personal charisma to lead into the promised land those whose needs are no longer met by traditional institutional religion. But if the revival flourishes and grows, certainly by the time the founder dies, the new movement must be organised on a more systematic and less personal basis if it is not to fragment. New traditions and/or rational bureaucratic procedures must begin to take over from personal knowledge and loyalty. The revival begins to become routine, looking more and more like that which it replaced. Many organisations, not only religious ones, alternate in this way between charismatic revival and routinisation through bureaucracy. James and Field argue that this process describes the modern hospice movement, and the positive reception of their article within the movement suggests that its members are all too aware of the danger of routinisation eroding the hospice ideal. We got a taste of this in the previous chapter, on audit.

If ever there were a charismatic leader, it is Cicely Saunders, a doctor who led her disciples out of the old 'church' of the National Health Service and into the new radical community she founded at St Christopher's. Her long-term aim was to provide an alternative model that would eventually become mainstream and change practice within the NHS. Like a new sect, the hospice movement had clear and simple goals, and is (or was) defined in opposition to the impersonality of hospital care. Hospice leaders know where they are heading, and they know they are right. Saunders' personal drive was religious not only in the metaphorical but also in the literal sense, as she was and is driven by a deep Christian commitment.

Like a sect, each hospice has strict admission criteria, admitting only (or mainly) cancer patients (who know they are dying) and who are not too old (and therefore not too passive and fatalistic); this maximises the chances of patients being able and willing to die their own way and thus maintains the purity of hospice ideology (Seale 1991b). Driven by grass roots commitment, hospices are still springing up all over the place, to the considerable annoyance of regional health planners and the proliferation of short workshops set up by local hospices here, there and everywhere is typical of how sects train new members. Hospices may be the only sects to have royal patronage, but in most other respects they look very sect-like. Meanwhile, the USA has its own prophetess in Elisabeth Kübler-Ross, though her prophetic career has taken a different path, resisting routinisation at the cost of increasing marginalisation for herself and her disciples (Klass and Hutch 1985).

BUREAUCRATISATION

Pressures toward bureaucratisation, however, are mounting. Following Andreski (1984), James and Field identify five features of bureaucracy, each of which they claim are beginning to show up in some, if not all, hospices.

1   *The strict division of spheres of authority determined by general rules, laws and regulations.* Organisations such as, in the USA, the National Hospice Organisation and in the UK the National Council for Hospice and Specialist Palliative Care Services (note the jargon and formality

creeping back), represent hospices to government, providing clear lines of authority and communication.

2 *Hierarchy of offices and the channelling of communication through proper hierarchical channels (i.e., strict division of labour).* Doctors and nurses who once spent time chatting with patients at the bedside may now find themselves under pressure to stay in their offices scanning the latest audit results on the computer, running a tutorial for placement students, or discussing estimates for the new building project. As financial constraints bite and the labour of trained staff becomes relatively more expensive, chatting to patients is done by lowly assistants and volunteers. At my own local hospice, the female and devoutly Christian nurse who deliberately sidestepped the male medical hierarchy to found the hospice fifteen years ago has been succeeded by a medical director and a business manager (both male). Personal and spiritual commitment is replaced by professional hierarchy, even if the informality of first names prevails and morale remains high.

3 *The work of the official requires training.* Training courses abound; palliative care is no more a hobby for the enthusiast or a calling for the devoted, but a medical specialty requiring training. Even volunteers must be trained.

4 *Separation of official activities from private affairs.* Though many hospice staff still go the extra mile, this is no longer required, indeed is discouraged for fear of burnout, so there is no shame in working nine to five; the worker is free to develop a home life protected from the unscheduled demands of the dying. The calling becomes a profession becomes a job.

5 *Duties are discharged in accordance with rules.* Hospice staff who once would do anything for anyone now find themselves offered contracts with job descriptions. To gain an NHS contract or (in the USA) federal funding, a hospice must specify in great detail not only its objectives but also how it intends to attain them.

None of this is to imply that hospices do not retain a distinctive ethos. It is simply to observe the possible tendencies towards routinisation to be found in any young, vibrant, growing organisation.

PROFESSIONALISATION

Hospice care is being re-professionalised. The authority of the medical specialist, challenged by early hospice rhetoric and by the concept of the multi-professional team, is once more acknowledged. This may be simply a recognition that the early rhetoric never did describe reality, as one non-medical member of the St Christopher's team told me (by no means resentfully) in 1993:

'This is a medical institution, and the hierarchy is medical. Who gets the most pay? The longest sabbaticals? That's OK if you're not pretending otherwise, but we *were*. . . . The multi-disciplinary concept has been disclosed as the great pretender. Of course, I am included in ward rounds, which would not be the case in a hospital, but I am *invited* by the senior doctor to speak, and am *thanked* afterwards. This may be politeness, but it also reveals who has the power.'

But it is more than the exposure of rhetoric. In the late 1980s, the Royal College of Physicians (note, this is the college of *hospital* specialists, not the Royal College of General Practitioners who care for patients at home) recognised palliative medicine as a specialty. No sooner did doctors see a sphere of influence springing up outside their control than they colonised it, and indeed many hospice nurses welcomed the better informed medical advice that the colonisers offered. This new medical specialism must prove itself, and restricting its members to relieving the pain of those near death – the terminally ill – seems too small a challenge. One senior hospice nurse (Biswas 1993) argues that palliative medics are busily expanding their empire from pain control to symptom control, hence the shift in name from terminal to palliative care and the expansion of concern from the final few days and weeks to the long-term relief of pain and symptoms. She is worried: 'The hospice movement put death on the agenda, but palliative care has the capacity to relegate it to the sidelines.' She cites a related factor. Whereas nurses can shift from one specialism to another, doctors cannot, so a bright young doctor specialising in palliative medicine will be trapped there for the next 30 years and will want continual stimulation and challenge *within this specialty*. This could prove to be a fount of creativity or a dilution of terminal care's original goal. Kearney, one of these new 'consultants in palliative medicine', is also worried (1992). The drive to research symptomatology in order to maintain the specialism's status focuses on a narrow medical, i.e., physical, under-standing of symptoms – despite the evidence that there is a major subjective component in most symptoms.

The presence of a large number of volunteers is cited by some hospices as a guard against bureaucratisation, for without vested interests in careers, salaries, employment and status, they can be a constant irritant keeping a hospice true to its own goals (Mor *et al.* 1988: ch. 10). My local hospice, for example, uses a large number of volunteers, and not just for jobs such as driving patients to day care that are similar to jobs done by hospital volunteers. Each shift in the in-patient unit includes a skilled volunteer nurse, usually a retired trained nurse or an experienced ex-nursing auxiliary. On the other hand, there is evidence that where there is money available volunteers may be promoted to salaried posts or have them specially created (Mor *et al.* 1988: x), or they may be kept below their level of competence in order to reduce the threat to salaried staff (Hoad 1991).

FINANCE

Hospices that started with locally raised donations and a lot of unpaid labour cannot continue on that basis if they are reliably to provide a consistent level of service, still less if they are to expand that service. They need government funding. Whereas a local hospice wants to offer a Rolls Royce service to local people, regional health service managers have to look at the wider regional picture and allocate scarce resources among all the various sectors, each of which is clamouring for a better share of the cake. Mental health practitioners, paediatricians, geriatricians, health educators, etc. are all pushing for more resources, so the hospice has to demonstrate its value against some pretty stiff competition. Like any other health facility, the hospice is caught between a clinical world concerned to meet the needs of patients, and a financial world concerned to distribute the limited resources a society can provide for health care (Torrens 1986).

In both the USA and the UK, value for money has to be demonstrated, though the mechanisms are somewhat different. In the USA, federal funding via Medicare was made available through the Tax Equity and Fiscal Responsibility Act of 1982 (clearly we are here in the linguistic world not of the patient but of the economist), which was pushed through on a groundswell of support. The subsequent legislative details were shaped by the National Hospice Study which showed that, even if a new millenium had not been ushered in as some hospice proponents had believed, hospices were at least either comparable to or somewhat better than conventional care in terms of both quality and cost (Mor *et al.* 1988). The legislation made funding dependent on hospices demonstrating the right balance of in-patient and home care, with not too many patients staying too long, and the right balance of volunteers. To survive, the American hospice has had to change from caring flexibly for all who come its way, to framing its objectives to meet the Medicare requirements. If managers do not replace visionaries, the money will run out. As well as moulding the nature of care, Medicare also moulds the standard of care, encouraging hospices to provide home care to those 'whose care needs can be predicted to remain low . . . families with physical, emotional and financial resources' (Lynn 1985: 220).

In the UK, hospices now find themselves having to operate within the new contract culture. To gain NHS funding, any medical facility has to sign a contract with a health authority to provide a certain standard of care, which it must demonstrate it is either achieving or capable of achieving. Unfortunately it is easier to demonstrate effective pain control, high bed occupancy and financial cost per patient than to demonstrate real attentiveness to patient's wishes, and there is a danger that the contract culture will undermine those aspects of the personal quality of care that cannot easily be measured. To this vexed question I will now turn.

AUDIT

Audit is a growing aspect of hospice life, and it has two motives. One is the need to demonstrate that organisation and clinical practice meet the standards set by the NHS, without which funds will not be forthcoming. The other motive is an 'in-house' desire to monitor and improve practices, especially innovative practices on which many hospices pride themselves.

Audit faces a major methodological challenge. What really matters is what the patient thinks of the care given. A major aim of palliative care is to listen to the patient, but how may the auditor discover whether this is happening? There are four possibilities (Higginson 1993; Goddard 1993). The most obvious is to ask patients themselves, but many of them are very weak and tired, and they cannot be asked at a later stage because by then they may be dead. The second way is to ask the relatives, but there may be a poor correlation between what they say and what patients feel. A third way is to get hospice staff to make their own assessments, but this reinstates the old paternalism by which doctors and nurses presume to know what patients want. A fourth way is to bring in an external assessor, but the presence of outsiders asking searching questions can easily disturb a developing trust between staff, patient and family. The current trend is to develop methodologies in which even very sick patients can rate their own pain, symptoms, quality of care and so forth, without involving them in too much effort or the nurse who has to administer the audit in too much time.

Though simply talking with and listening to patients was what originally inspired women like Kübler-Ross and Saunders, when it comes to audit there has been a tendency to audit only that which is measurable, and to employ quantitative methodologies even when these are not appropriate. The patient's own story disappears in a welter of figures. Physical care is easier to measure than emotional and spiritual care and there are real worries that audit will erode the commitment to holistic care that is the hallmark of palliative care. Even when attempts are made to measure 'quality of life', bizarre results can be thrown up – such as the severely dependent patient with uncontrollable symptoms who scores zero on the quality-of-life scale but is known to staff to show an indomitable spirit and humour that has inspired them all. As one hospice doctor observed, 'How much easier is it to audit pain, waiting times for admission or the completeness of case-notes in a thousand patients than, say, the 'dignity' of a single death?' (Ahmedzai 1993: 147).

Are there other kinds of methodologies which could be used? The key sociological studies of the 1960s that challenged the institutional care of elderly and dying people used participant observation (e.g., Glaser and Strauss 1965, Goffman 1968, Sudnow 1967). Video recordings are used in the training of doctors and nurses, and personal tape recorders carried by nurses are being used in some research (e.g. Hunt 1989, Lanceley, forthcoming, Wilkinson 1991). But such observational methods are hardly ever used in audit, though they could be very powerful tools for monitoring the process of care. For staff, simply to watch themselves on the playback or to read about themselves in the participant observation report, reveals to them how they actually relate to patients, which in turn prompts them to ask whether this is how they really want to relate. To witness on video or tape expressions of fear or anxiety being ignored by staff, or to witness 'hope work' (Chapter 8) in operation, can be very challenging (Lanceley, forthcoming). The tape or video feeds back information on the process of care more directly and provocatively than any other methodology. Such qualitative methodologies could be used creatively in partnership with appropriate quantitative methodologies.

In the meantime, those who work in palliative care are all too aware that audit could be a useful servant, or could turn into a tyrannical master that begins to dictate hospice goals.

CONTINUITY OF MISSION

James and Field (1992) agree with Saunders that the success of the hospice movement has been due to its clear goal of caring for a small number of terminally ill cancer patients. This has enabled hospice teams to develop pain control techniques to a previously undreamed of level of sophistication, and to care for the whole family. But with success has gone diversification: more care in more ways to more people suffering from more diseases, so that each individual hospice may begin to lose a sense of direction and certainly has to face the question of how to allocate its scarce resources.

But diversification also results from the missionary vision of the hospice. The setting up of hospices outside of the NHS was intended by Saunders to demonstrate a quality of care that would eventually change standards within the NHS. To this end, she and her disciples have displayed a missionary zeal to teach the message to doctors and nurses within the NHS – and the best way to teach is to bring them into the hospice for a while, to work and to see for themselves. As the missionary programme gained ground, it became fashionable for ambitious young doctors and nurses to spend a few months working in a hospice. At any one time, therefore, a good proportion of the staff caring for patients are not committed first generation revivalists, but staff passing through on their way up the ladder. And what few first generation revivalists there are, are spending a lot of their time teaching and supervising the interns – not to mention showing around numerous miscellaneous visitors such as the author of this book! The hospice movement's commitment to research also adds to the range of personnel hanging around the place, and adds another path away from direct patient-care for those very members of staff most committed to the hospice idea. Exit the original vision of the highly trained and committed nurse or doctor sitting by the bedside caring for the whole patient.

This is one scenario, but the extent to which it is happening is not clear. Staff who come for training can provide fresh ideas and give a lot of themselves without being there long enough to suffer burnout. And the commitment to research can generate a questioning climate which counteracts institutional complacency.

REPLACING THE FOUNDER

Some related factors, not discussed by James and Field, also promote the routinisation of hospice. My impression is that hospices are becoming less distinctively female institutions, as male managers and doctors become more prominent. It is by no means insignificant that many of the early hospice founders were female, apparently more able than many men to see through the depersonalisation involved in careerist high tech medicine. And since the charismatic leader relies on neither traditional nor rational authority (both of which are stacked in favour of males) but on personal charisma, her gender is no handicap. Subsequent bureaucratisation of a female-led revival typically involves the reasserting of male authority, and hospices are no exception, even if the males involved are gentle and caring.

There is also the question of the handover of authority by the ageing leader. Saunders, now retired yet retaining a very keen interest in developments in palliative care, has nevertheless institutionalised means for her work to continue. This is less sure with Kübler-Ross. Klass and Hutch, writing a few years ago on 'Elisabeth Kübler-Ross as a Religious Leader', observed that her presence was always necessary for the success of her Shanti Nilaya organisation's *'Life, Death and Transition'* workshops, and that 'she has given no rules, rituals, guidelines, or passed on authority for leadership to others' (1985: 107–8). By 1992, when I began receiving the *Shanti Nilaya UK Newsletter*, her actual presence was not required but her imprimatur still was: 'Before any workshop is initiated – LTD, Training or Intensive – Elisabeth's approval must be obtained. Elisabeth will herself select the facilitators, although she will try to give consideration to particular requests.'[1] And each edition of the newsletter begins with 'Elisabeth's Letter' from her rural farmhouse, usually mixing personal news of life on the farm with news of her activities for the organisation, comments on the state of the world, and divers exhortations. One recent letter referred to her stocking up her cellar in case of ecological disaster (so that she has no unfinished business, whatever form the end may take), went on to mourn the death of her St Bernard dog and concluded with news of her recent travels and workshops worldwide. The reader's presumed interest in Elisabeth's personal manifestation of the ecological, holistic good life clearly indicates her continuing centrality.

Whereas Saunders has produced a new generation of doctors and other practitioners whose authority is based on widely recognised training, Kübler-Ross seems to be producing a leadership of 'bishops' who have been personally ordained by the original apostle, St Elisabeth, or by those who have been ordained by her. These are two of the classic ways Weber described of replacing charismatic leadership. The mode of succession initiated by Saunders, a very widely read woman who has certainly considered this issue, is likely to be more effective than that of Kübler-Ross's global yet personal vision.

SECULARISATION

Those hospices that were originally motivated by explicitly Christian compassion are inherently vulnerable to secularisation, for two reasons.

First, Christian hospice founders are motivated by their Christian faith to listen to the patient as an individual, but so too are caring humanists

(Chapter 6). There is nothing about listening that *requires* religious conviction. Because of the commitment to high standards, it is important to appoint new staff on the basis of qualifications and competence rather than personal devoutness. So long as there are lots of qualified applicants, this circle can be squared, but this is by no means always possible; staff are therefore appointed who are equally committed to caring for the individual patient/family, but whose motive is no longer religious.

Second, success in getting 'spiritual' added to the holistic creed of 'physical, social and psychological' care has institutionalised the spiritual dimension. All staff and all patients have, and are to attend to, spiritual concerns – at least in theory. This inevitably leads to the secularisation of the definition of the spiritual to refer to anyone's search for meaning (Chapter 6), whether or not expressed in conventional religious terms. A good counsellor can facilitate this search as well as, possibly better than, a devout member of staff whose own belief system may get in the way of the patient's. At my local hospice, there is now more talk of spirituality, but fewer prayer meetings.

TRADITIONALISM

The sociology of religion is replete with accounts of sects that had their heyday in the nineteenth century, and then for fear of losing the original vision refused to change or develop. As contexts and needs change, this kind of sect changeth not, getting ever older and smaller in membership, attracting only those who want to live in the past, until eventually only two or three old ladies come to a Sunday service whose content has remained unchanged for a century. Some in the hospice movement observe disturbing signs of this 'dodo' phenomenon. Having exerted superhuman efforts to establish and raise funds for an inpatient unit, the faithful become committed to preserving what they have so sacrificially created.

Bricks and mortar are the biggest snare and temptation, literally embodying in concrete the original vision. Home-care services are more able to bend flexibly with changing times, but by the same token are less capable of generating donations and volunteers. Shanti, the huge support organisation for those with AIDS in the San Francisco area (no relation to Kübler-Ross's Shanti Nilaya), recently received a huge federal grant and used it deliberately to resist ossification through bricks and mortar. They decided to add to their services a 65-bed facility (which by hospice standards is big), but instead of building they rented a hotel. And over the past four years, though every other aspect of Shanti has grown (it has, for

example, four thousand volunteers), permanent staff numbers have remained at around 60 to 70. Shanti seems to understand that concrete and
salaries are the biggest threat to the life of revival.

In conclusion, I have concentrated on the routinisation of hospices
because this has been so well analysed by James and Field, but similar
processes are naturally observable in other parts of the revival. Bereavement organisations have not gone so far down this road, mainly because
it is more difficult to raise funds for the bereaved than for the dying. In
the UK, The Compassionate Friends (TCF) and CRUSE – Bereavement
Care would make an instructive comparative study. TCF has remained
remarkably true to its original vision of 'an international organisation of
bereaved parents offering friendship and understanding to other bereaved
parents'. In the UK at least, all positions of responsibility are held by
bereaved parents, the remit has not been widened to include other groups
of bereaved people, and the membership and leadership is still over-
whelmingly female. That is not to say it is not aware of the fragility of this
status quo. One prominent TCF member told me she worries that there are
lots of bereaved parents out there who do not know of TCF and that
perhaps hiring public relations and advertising men might be a necessary
complement to word of mouth – but it would also give influence to people
who are not themselves bereaved parents.

CRUSE began in 1959 as an organisation for widows (Torrie 1987),
but considerable expansion of the vision has occurred since the retirement
of its founder Margaret Torrie in the mid-1970s. Under her successor – a
man, Derek Nuttall – it expanded in the 1980s to include first widowers
and then all bereaved people. With its work widely known and its
counsellors highly respected, CRUSE is now receiving referrals from
other agencies for counselling of more complicated bereavements, which
in turn increases the gap between the highly trained CRUSE counsellor
and the ordinary befriender. In the British welfare state's new contract
culture, there is now the issue of contracts with health and social service
authorities, and the strings contracts will inevitably bring.

In sum, there are two ways in which revival can deal with routinisation.
One is to struggle against it at all costs, with all the attendant risks of
apostolic succession and/or stagnation. The other is to accept routinisation, to manage it carefully in the light of (and even to commission)[2]
sociological research, to resist it in certain specific and carefully chosen
areas (such as ownership of buildings), and to cooperate with new revivalist groups that spring up to meet needs overlooked by the now
established institutions. This second path is certainly being attempted –
yet another example of late-modern reflexivity in which, in this case,

concepts from the sociology of religion have filtered into professional discourse thus enabling the routinisation, with luck without the total depersonalisation, of the hospice. But it means that hospices have to listen not only to patients, but also to sociologists!

FURTHER READING

Goddard, M.K. (1993) 'The Importance of Assessing the Effectiveness of Care: the case of hospices', *Journal of Social Policy*, 22, 1: 1–18.

Higginson, I. (1993) 'Quality, Costs and Contracts of Care', in D. Clark (ed.) *The Future for Palliative Care*, Buckingham, Open University Press.

James, N. and Field, D. (1992) 'The Routinization of Hospice: charisma and bureaucratization', *Social Science and Medicine*, 34, 12: 1363–75.

QUESTIONS

With which revivalist group are you most familiar? Does it show a tendency to routinisation? If so, how? If not, why not?

How might volunteers keep an organisation on its toes?

Is money the root of all organisational evil?

How might qualitative methods be used in audit?

Chapter 12

Disposal

The *Naiad* pulls out of Quay 41, past the sea lions that have colonised this alone of San Francisco's many wharves, out into the bay on a still, foggy August morning, uneventfully until under the Golden Gate Bridge the skipper has difficulty keeping the 50-foot motor yacht on a straight course. Eight thousand miles of ocean seem to want to get through this mile-wide opening, and the turbulence announces the purpose for which we have come – to discharge our cargo of six pounds of ashes into the boundless ocean beyond. A few minutes later the bridge has disappeared in the fog, and we are at the officially designated scattering area. A mere couple of miles from the edge of megalopolis, all we can see is the hint of grey cliffs through the mist. Gerry puts the yacht ever so slowly into reverse, and Alice goes for'd with the half dozen relatives – children, husband, sisters – of the 53-year-old deceased and hands them the container. Memories are shared, tears shed, arms placed around one another, as each scatters a little of the ashes over the bow. Then each flings overboard the roses they have brought, one by one floating away in front of the boat for a second or two before slowly sinking. Alice, drained by the intensity of another unique yet universal farewell that it is her job to facilitate, day in day out, with two more to come this morning, retires aft for a smoke. The party stay on the fore-deck, talking and pondering, as we head back, once more through the turbulence and there suddenly comes the sun and ahead the human world, of city and skyscraper, shining in the morning sunlight, meditation turning to laughter and photography as once again the antics of the sea lions mark our return to Quay 41.[1]

A liminal ritual if ever there was one (Turner 1974): out of the ordinary world and into a ritual world that is immense, mysterious, boundless, unfathomable, with the threshold between the two clearly marked and the return to the ordinary world safe and reassuring. But it is also a distinctly postmodern ritual: a private family group sharing memories that take the place of religious dogma, enriched by an ocean whose symbolism is both ancient and specific to the modern urban culture of West Coast America, Alice the Naiad company employee not directing but facilitating the family, the whole a commercial operation in which an intensely personal experience is bought, at a price.

In many Western societies, life-centred funerals which focus on the unique personality of the deceased are on the increase, and this is consistent with part of the revivalist agenda of bringing the personal into death, dying and bereavement (Walter 1990, especially ch. 20). Unlike the *Naiad* voyage, however, these personal eulogies are rarely integrated into the actual disposal of the body. A moving personal tribute in the crematorium is likely to be followed by the coffin being mechanically removed from view and subsequently pushed by an anonymous workman into the actual cremator with the funeral party long departed from the building. Revivalist funerals are usually strong on talk, and weak on ritual. The discourse is personal, but the disposal remains impersonal.

In Britain where seven funerals out of ten (twice as many as in California) are cremations, few families scatter ashes themselves in a do-it-yourself ceremony. The church wants ashes buried on sanctified ground, while most ashes are actually scattered by crematorium staff without the family present. Revivalist tracts, committed to reforming dying and grieving, usually ignore the disposal of our mortal remains. Amply encouraged to die and to grieve our own way, our remains continue to go the way of the crematorium, the funeral director and the church.

Municipal cemeteries and crematoria in the UK are located within departments such as Public Health or Parks and Recreation, very rarely within Social Services. This reflects the technical nature of their work and their legal remit to dispose of over half a million corpses annually without causing pollution, though individual staff may spend much of their time with bereaved people. When the contract culture was imposed on cemetery maintenance in 1988, there was no guarantee that municipalities would include personal care of bereaved visitors in their specifications; some contracts specify the job simply as a physical matter of gardening. Cemetery managers now have no hands-on responsibility for grounds maintenance; they have become writers of contracts and many of them no longer work on-site. Also, although most contracts have so far been won in-house, there is nevertheless a tendency for labour to become short term and badly paid. Long-standing teams of manual workers that once tended cemeteries and recognised and greeted visitors are inevitably being replaced by short-term contract workers. No hospice contract would allow an absentee manager or flying teams of cleaners who had no time to get to know patients, but this is where cemetery maintenance is going. Revival has yet to touch this part of the death business.

The commercial Victorian cemeteries of urban Britain, unlike many of their American counterparts (Sloane 1991), were not set up on sound financial grounds. Each grave was sold in perpetuity, without any required annual charge for maintenance, so that as the cemetery became full, income dropped to nil and then as relatives of the interred themselves died local interest in the cemetery also waned. Victorian public health legislation made re-use of graves very difficult (something which did not occur in most other European countries in which hygienic re-use is normal). Built originally on the outskirts of the Victorian city, these old cemeteries are now surrounded by houses whose occupants can no longer use them for burial purposes themselves. By the mid-twentieth century, few apart from vandals had any ideas what to do with them.[2]

Attempts to sell or build on these cemeteries, however, leads to outcry, mainly from historical preservation societies and from ecologists who value them as diverse green habitats within otherwise highly built-up areas. Many Victorian cemeteries now have their 'Friends', groups of enthusiasts who spend their weekends clearing the undergrowth and conducting historical tours of the cemetery. They are much less interested, however, in the agenda of revival. They are not noted for supporting the cemetery as a place where local bereaved families can bury their dead or where death can be publicly symbolised, nor for campaigning to reform the burial laws to make continued local use easier. Instead they campaign to preserve the cemetery as a historical and ecological resource; for them the cemetery exists for the sake of flora, fauna and historical tourism. They thereby collude in tying up land that might otherwise be leased by bereaved people, who in London may now have to travel miles out of their own borough to bury their dead (Walter 1990: ch.18). The contrast with the hospice, catering personally for local people as they face death, could not be more striking.

The Victorian cemetery was a *memento mori*, set on high ground to remind every citizen of their final destination; today crematoria are placed out of sight, and nobody wants a funeral parlour next door. Even when the profile of a cemetery or crematorium is raised, it need not be as a *memento mori*. In the *Friends of Nunhead Cemetery Newsletter* (no. 35, September 1991), a teacher describes taking his class of 11 to 12-year-olds to this famous South London cemetery. 'Nunhead has much to offer schools as a cross-curricular resource', he enthuses, 'social history, monument design and symbolism, sketching, photography, creative writing, woodland ecology, tree growth and measurement, fruits and seeds, birds, insects, art from leaves, geology of monuments, architecture, Victoriana, the two World Wars.' But why does he omit the obvious, the intended pedagogic function of the cemetery's Victorian founders, namely the contemplation of mortality? An explanation may lie in his earlier comment that 'Nunhead is atmospheric, and children may react strongly to death, burial and mortal remains. . . . So my briefings to the class emphasised the *living* aspects of the site, rather than the cemetery as such.' The children are frightened of death, or possibly he is, so he diverts them onto natural history instead.

Why has revival failed to touch the corpse the way it has touched the dying and the bereaved? Why, when what is said about the deceased at the funeral is becoming more personal, do the actual procedures for disposing of the body remain locked in the death-denying impersonality of modernity? Various approaches to this question may be found in my book on funerals (Walter 1990), but in this chapter I want briefly to explore the question in the light of Anthony Giddens' observation that ritual has been replaced by discourse.

FROM RITUAL TO DISCOURSE

If modern death is a private affair, and revival encourages the sharing of personal feeling, then neither is conducive to ritual, for ritual is rooted in community and in socially approved not individually expressed emotion, in symbol more than in memory, in action as much as in talk. The neo-modernist, especially the expressivist, seeks not ritual but talk – hence, for example, thc life-centred funeral.

A participant describes his experience of a 'Living with Dying' workshop, run by psychotherapist Christianne Heal. He talks deeply and openly with one who may well be a stranger not only to himself but to the ones he loves, the workshop forming a typically postmodern and temporary group very different from the stable community that underlies traditional ritual.

> Christianne asked us to draw a 'map' and to mark around us all the people who are important to us, living or dead. Then we worked in pairs, one partner listened, while the other had half an hour to say goodbye to all the people he or she had placed on the map. I found this very painful, I think everyone did. It is also beautiful to listen to your partner talking to their friends and family in such a loving and powerful way, expressing the very core of their feelings. Where else would we get the space to say these things to our loved ones, especially those who have died? Funerals serve this function up to a point, and not at all when

it comes to expressing the anger which often accompanies bereavement.

(Albery *et al.* 1993: 59)

Ritual action around the body and within the community is replaced by talk in a group of strangers facilitated by a psychotherapist.

The editors of the book in which this participant is quoted *are* concerned to revive funeral ritual; indeed – through their Natural Death Centre – they are among the very few revivalists to have put the funeral onto their agenda. But the quote does highlight a problem: talking about feelings, expressing anger, is for the expressivist what coming to terms with mortality is *really* all about, and funeral ritual is not as good at that as is group therapy. In which case, why not tip the body into the incinerator *sans* ceremony and go off to psychotherapy instead?

This account of a workshop enabled by a female therapist hints at another reason limiting revival's influence on the funeral: gender. When helping to make a documentary film in a cemetery in Christchurch, Dorset, I was struck that a disproportionate number of those who visited graves were men. As one man said whose son had died in an accident at the age of 19, 'I often pop in here on the way to work and have a smoke with the lad.' This is not a ritual of talk, though he may well talk with his son there; it is essentially a ritual act of solidarity. War veterans do the same: whether or not they talk to their comrades about the old days, they can have a drink in the veterans' association bar with those who have experienced what they have experienced. Like the father sitting on his son's grave on the way to work, the drink is a ritual act of solidarity. Whereas many women deal with stress by talking, many men deal with it by doing, by going off on their own, or by ritual acts of solidarity with other men in the same situation. There are many cultures, South Wales mining villages and the Outer Hebridean Islands to name but two, in which the burial is attended only by the men: they must combine ritual act with practicality and dispose of the body in stoic silence, while the women prepare the tea, talking. Funeral rituals are largely in the hands of men, but we have seen that revival is largely in the hands of women who promote not ritual acts but expressive talk. Though there are now more female funeral directors and women clergy conducting funerals, males predominate. Most female revivalists have simply not seen the public ritual as important as listening one-to-one with the bereaved.

It may be that therapy provides what ritual once did, but more acceptably to neo-modernists. To see why, we can look at an article by Scheff (1977, see also 1979) in which he argues that successful ritual and drama require a certain distancing of emotion among the audience. If the audience are under-distanced from the drama, then they have so identified that they have forgotten that it is a play and are taken over by the emotion; if they are over-distanced they are uninvolved and feel no emotion at all. Between these extremes are dramas with aesthetic distance, in which the audience feel sad or happy but still knows that it is a play – in other words, they become participant observers of their own emotion. In healthy ritual, the accumulation of emotion necessarily repressed in everyday life can be released, accompanied by a sense of control, relaxation and even exhilaration. (Reed's 1978 theory of religious ritual seems rather similar in this respect.)

It seems to me that many forms of therapy do much the same: they enable you both to feel and to label the feelings, to be a participant observer of your own feelings. Like Scheff, many therapists assume the everyday repression of feelings. It now becomes possible to see why therapy and counselling can take over so easily from religious ritual on the deathbed and in the lives of those who grieve. Therapy provides what ritual provides, but needs neither community nor religious belief, and can be purchased at any time. Also, if you want to become a participant observer of your own feelings, therapy is a better bet than ritual because this is the *aim* of therapy but only a *by-product* of ritual, a by-product which cannot be guaranteed.

If funeral rituals do the kind of cathartic effect that Scheff describes (and his work has been challenged by various critics, one of whom points out that many rituals remain popular without having any obvious cathartic effect), any such effects really are by-products. What actually motivates traditional funeral ritual is the need to dispose of the body in an acceptable manner and to dispatch the soul from this world.

In a funeral, there are essentially three actors:

THE SOUL

THE BODY   THE LIVING

Without a corpse to dispose of and a soul to release, funerals would not happen. If all you want is therapy for the living, then you need not a funeral but a therapy session instead. If you are leading a funeral, you must focus on the body and on the soul, and then the living may, possibly, benefit too – but if you focus simply on the living then you will end up with neither therapy nor with a decent funeral (Walter 1990). This, however, is precisely what is happening in more and more funerals, and Farrell (1980) argues that in the USA it has been happening for at least a century: Protestant clergy are not allowed to pray for the soul and the corpse is an embarrassment, so funeral liturgy is rewritten in order to comfort the living. But the result is pseudo-comfort, in which the painful presence of the body is not acknowledged, and feelings of rage and anger cannot be expressed amid the soothing tones of the electronic music and the pink plush carpet.

As I have said in Chapter 10, people go to funerals not in order to comfort themselves but to comfort others, to pay their respects to the deceased, to witness the last exit of the last tangible symbol of the deceased (the coffin or casket), and to pray for the soul. Ultimately they go because they cannot conceive of disposing of a human body as though it were a wild dog's – a funeral is the last statement about a person, an ultimate affirmation of human dignity. Denying a person a proper funeral is reserved for those seen as 'inhuman' – for the Nazis this meant Jews, and for us it means the mass murderers who killed them. To attend a funeral is ultimately about neither therapy nor psychology, it is a statement of the humanity of the one who has died. And that is why people continue to go to funerals, why funerals cannot be defined in terms of whatever therapeutic function they may or may not have for the grieving, and why therapy and the funeral can never be reduced one to the other.

FROM DISCOURSE TO RITUAL

I now consider the following. If people are still going to go to funerals, if funerals are not the same as therapy, yet if we now understand the potential therapeutic effects of funeral ritual and cannot go back on that knowledge, then how can neo-modern funerals be devised that translate discourse into ritual? Not back into traditional ritual, for that was ritual without knowledge of therapy, but into neo-modern ritual? Can the life-centred funeral involve more than talking about the life of the deceased?

Anthropologist Barbara Myerhoff (1982: 129–32) argues that now we know that rituals are not God-given but socially constructed, we are free to construct our own rituals and can do ourselves a favour by so doing. We all have our private rituals, such as burning the picture of the lover who has walked out, but we can also create shared rituals – socially located no longer in community but in ties of friendship and kinship. My own book on funerals is directed to precisely this question, so for now I will simply describe some ways in which funeral ritual is developing. These accounts may seem bitty and piecemeal, but then perhaps that is how postmodern rituals are likely to be. Only on occasion will they attain the spatial, temporal and symbolic coherence of the journey of the *Naiad* through the Golden Gate.

Music is showing significant changes in the British funeral. According to folklorist Vic Gammon (1988), there used to a be a folk tradition of singing at English funerals, a tradition stamped out in the mid-nineteenth century by Anglican clergy wishing to make the funeral an orthodox Christian affair. That is now beginning to change. Naylor's thesis on funerals in the industrial city of Leeds (1989: 215) highlights the growing demand for personalised music in order to give meaning to an otherwise often meaningless ritual, to personalise an often otherwise impersonal ritual, and to provide a vehicle for participation. Typically, mourners ask for the deceased's favourite tune. She also notes the resistance of some clergy to many of the pop songs requested, so clergy and the bereaved are once more struggling over control of funeral music.

Some popular composers are actually writing appropriate songs, not just about love but about love in the context of death. Eric Clapton's 'Tears in Heaven', which won Grammys in 1993 as song of the year, record of the year, and male pop vocal of the year, was written in tribute to his son Conor who at the age of 4 fell to his death from the fifty-third floor of a New York skyscraper. Folksinger Ewan McColl said farewell to his partner Peggy Seeger and his children in the song 'The Joy of Living',[3] which his highly talented musical family played at his funeral and which has now become a favourite at humanist funerals throughout Britain. On Merseyside, a popular funeral song is Liverpool Football Club's informal anthem, 'You'll Never Walk Alone', composed originally for a funeral scene in the musical *Carousel* (Davie 1993). There is also an extraordinarily rich repertoire of classical music written in response to human mortality, from requiems to lieder to grand opera (Walter 1992).

Funeral music substitutes for a genre foreign to the West, namely the lament. Sung at funerals and weddings in the Orthodox tradition in Greece (Danforth 1982: ch. 4) and in the Ingrian folk culture east of the Baltic Sea (Nenola-Kallio 1982), laments provide a language in which fears and negative feelings can be articulated. Ritualised articulation, however, is not the same as what a Western individualist means by 'self expression'. In the Ingrian tradition, for example, substitute names are used: instead of singing 'Mother, I love you', the lamenter sings 'my precious bearer'. When 'The Joy of Living' is sung for anyone other than Ewan McColl, it has this same character, articulating feelings that are akin to, but not exactly those of, the mourners – in other words, providing just that aesthetic distance that is Scheff's prerequisite for ritual.

Negative emotions can also be articulated by *religion*. Pain and despair are recurring themes in the book of Job and in the Psalms, and both guilt and Christ's death place suffering and weakness at the very core of Christianity. A common funeral reading, for example, comes from Psalm 22 (verses 1–2, 14–15):

> My God, my God, why hast thou forsaken me? Why art thou so far from helping me, and from the words of my roaring?
> Oh my God, I cry in the daytime, but thou hearest not; and in the night season, and am not silent . . .
> I am poured out like water, and all my bones are out of joint: my heart is like wax; it is melted in the midst of my bowels.
> My strength is dried up like a potsherd; and my tongue cleaveth to my jaws; and thou has brought me into the dust of death.

This Psalm is like the Eastern lament in naming feelings of despair so that they may be acknowledged publicly, whereas direct personal expression of such feelings would destroy any public ceremony, in our own or any culture.

Why then do so many mourners find the funeral an occasion in which emotion must be stifled? It is in part because mourners have lost touch with the particular religious language in which their emotions are being articulated. It is also in part because of the revivalist belief that feelings have to be expressed directly by the person or at least talked about, but can be articulated no other way. But given the Anglo-Saxon prohibition against expressing strong personal feeling in public, it would seem that the only way such feelings can be articulated in public is ritually; otherwise, they have to be banned in public, and reserved for the privacy of the counselling session. Nevertheless, some clergy are able to use the biblical language of despair and hope, of suffering and joy, to articulate the feelings of even the most secular funeral party; and secular officiants may be hard pressed to find non-biblical poetry that can ritually articulate negative feeling. So traditional religious language can still play an important role in neo-modern funeral ritual.

However there are other non-religious ways of articulating loss in public ritual. The short lines of poetry to be found on gravestones and in *In Memoriam* notices in the local newspaper (examples given in Chapter 1) say what cannot be spoken directly, at least not in public. They too are not self-expression but ritual articulation. Meanwhile, for the upper classes, the famous and the socially mobile, there is the obituary. But working-class culture in Britain, especially in some parts of the north, has in the 1980s developed *the floral tribute* as a way to publicly articulate grief. Florists are asked to make up floral toys, vehicles, books, cushions, footballs, animals, and special colours. Naylor observed this in Leeds:

> Remaining one of the most potent visual cues to death, sole inheritors of the panoply of mutes, feathers, trays, weepers, batons and crepe draperies, flowers tended to mirror the 'type of death' with tragic accidents and sudden deaths attracting the greatest numbers.
>
> (1989: 284)

This cult fuelled the extraordinary covering of much of the Anfield soccer pitch with half a million floral tributes in the week following the Hillsborough disaster (Walter 1991b), and I suspect that the televised coverage of this and similar (if not quite so huge) mass layings of flowers following tragedies have served to promote the cult of the floral tribute at more ordinary funerals.

In more middle-class circles, I have observed that of all the suggestions in my own book on funerals, the one that seems to have been taken up most by readers is for each mourner, or for a representative from each family, to lay a flower on the coffin during the funeral service. The British love flowers and to give someone a flower means 'I love you', so to lay a flower on the coffin is to make a last statement to the deceased, a statement that the reserved British (or at least the English) might not be able to say in public in words. Ritual action says what discourse cannot. Laying not a large wreath but a single flower is an essay in understatement which fits the English temperament.

Though these examples show the evolution of more personalised funeral ritual, the greatest scope for personalisation is not in the primary funeral (the cremation) but the secondary funeral (the disposal of the ashes). It is here that family and friends are most able to do their own thing, especially in the UK where – unlike in many states of the USA – they are legally free to dispose of human ashes how and where they like. Whereas in the USA, ash disposal rituals (like almost everything else) have been substantially commercialised, as in the *Naiad* voyage and more typically in the columbarium, in the UK it is unclear whether they will become commercialised or whether the as yet small number of do-it-yourself family scatterings will increase. Some crematoria sell families a niche in a columbarium in which to store the ashes, a useful source of revenue; but the clear implication of revival is that the family should scatter the ashes themselves, in their own way, at their own time, in a place of their own choosing. Whether commerce or revival will have the most influence on British families pondering what to do with dad's ashes, only time will tell.

FURTHER READING

Walter, T. (1990) *Funerals: and how to improve them*, London, Hodder & Stoughton.

QUESTIONS

Describe, then analyse, the best and the worst funeral you have been to.

In the *Naiad* voyage a physical journey symbolised a personal transition. What kinds of journey or movement have had symbolic power in funerals you have attended?

Why do you think that revivalists have concentrated on caring for the dying and the bereaved rather than for the body or the soul?

Chapter 13

Conclusion
Facing death without tradition . . . but in company

> Yea, though I walk through the valley of the shadow of death, I will fear no evil: for thou art with me.
>
> (Psalm 23)

The question is, though: *what* is the evil not to be feared? and *who* is the thou who art with me? In this last chapter, I review and discuss the somewhat original answers offered by the revival of death. But first let me summarise where the book has taken us.

THE ARGUMENT OF THE BOOK

Part I traced the historical movement from traditional to modern to neo-modern death. Traditional death was based in community and discussed in the language of religion, but in the West this was progressively undermined by increasing individualism. This resulted in a more modern way of death – communal rituals were replaced by privacy for the dying or bereaved person, and the authority of the church was replaced by the authority of the doctor. The much reduced death rate, along with most people going into hospital to die and bereaved people keeping their pain to themselves, has led to the 'dying' of death as an explicit feature of everyday life. The consequent impersonality of dying and the loneliness of bereavement have, however, come under increasing criticism: those who would revive death observe that death is a natural part of life and those whom it touches should not be treated as social lepers. With more people having to live for an extended time with a life-threatening condition (e.g. cancer, heart disease, stroke, HIV), it is less possible to continue with the modern pretence that death does not exist. This revival of death takes individualism to its logical conclusion and asserts the authority of the individual over not only religion but also over medicine: only individuals can determine how they want to die or grieve.

Within the revival lies a tension between two assumptions. The expert ('late-modern') revivalist asserts the right of the individual to know they are dying and to express how they feel; but the expert goes further and insists that individuals *need* to express their feelings, or at least talk about them, and that carers need to create an 'open awareness context' with those who are dying. The more radical ('postmodern') revivalist points to the wide diversity in how human beings encounter death; some individuals for example do not want to know they are dying or choose not to express their feelings of grief – this may work for them and must be respected.

If the individual is to die and grieve in their own way, they can be helped to do so by practitioners only if the latter listen attentively to the individual. In Part II I explored whether institutionalised systems can do this. I concentrated on the hospice movement and to a lesser extent on bereavement counselling, because these are where there is a good chance of attentive listening and they are the heartland of revival. This means that this book is biased towards discussing death by cancer – although it only accounts for around a quarter of deaths in the UK it is the disease that has prompted a more open approach to death. If the individual cannot die their own way when they have weeks, months or even years of warning, it is hardly likely they will be able to do so when they have little or no warning.

Part II concluded that hospice staff and bereavement counsellors have raised the level of attentive listening, but that there are nevertheless major impediments and dilemmas. It is very difficult for practitioners not to be influenced by psycho-social theories that provide reassuring generalisations about how people die and grieve (Chapters 5, 7). Given the urgent physical needs of many dying patients, it is relatively easy for emotional and spiritual distress to be ignored, and many carers even in hospices find it very painful to address such distress (Chapter 6). It is impossible for individuals in a group setting such as a hospice or bereavement group not to be influenced by what they see and hear from others: these are settings not only for listening but also for teaching (Chapter 8). The idea of the autonomous individual, able to do things their own way, implies that he or she has control over events; a deteriorating body, however, often implies dependency, and the tension between control and dependency I explored in Chapter 9. There is also the question, in terminal care (especially when euthanasia is a possibility), in the arranging of funerals and in bereavement, of *which* person is to be listened to (Chapter 10). The very success of hospices as small personal communities threatens to turn them into bureaucratic institutions more akin to the hospitals they were intended to replace (Chapter 11). In Chapter 12 I asked why it is so difficult to arrange funerals that pay attention to the life of the deceased not only in talk but also in ritual.

Part II has implications not only for care of the dying, but also for any attempt at holistic care. The essence of revival is to care for and listen to the whole person, and it is probably true to say that holistic care has entered the mainstream of medicine largely through care of dying people. When medicine that treats the patient as a bundle of physical disease fails to cure, there are only two options: to abandon the patient (which to some degree is what used to happen), or to move towards more holistic care of the mind and soul as well as of the body (which is what increasingly is happening). Part II is therefore a study of the practice of holistic medicine.

A UNIVERSAL FEAR?

Several leading social scientists have assumed that death is inherently terrifying, and that we therefore need the comfort of religion and tradition; without this comfort, we find ourselves disarmed as we face death. Malinowski, for example, wrote: 'Death, which of all human events is the most upsetting and disorganising to man's calculation, is perhaps the main source of religious belief' (1962: 97). Peter Berger (1969) has powerfully restated Max Weber's observation that religion is in large measure the business of keeping at bay the meaninglessness of suffering and the terror of death; in his major work *The Social Construction of Reality*, written with Thomas Luckmann (1967), he considers death as *the* anomic condition and the root cause of the problem of meaning. According to Geoffrey Gorer (1955, 1965), if religion and social norms do not regulate our feelings about death, then these will be expressed in all kinds of unregulated 'pornography'. Ernest Becker (1973) sees mortality as akin to sexuality, a fundamental aspect of bodily nature which if not acknowledged will lurk in the subconscious to terrorise us, a view not far removed from that of Kübler-Ross (1970), for whom to learn that one is dying is so terrifying that one has major psychological work to do in order to accept it. Philippe Ariès is somewhat ambiguous but seems to say that death is so inherently terrifying it has to be tamed through religion and culture. So these leading anthropologists, historians, psychiatrists and sociologists all agree: without tradition, religion and/or hard psychological work, the wild beast of death is untamed and we live in constant if repressed terror.

But there are also dissident voices. Bailey (1979) argues that in the Old Testament death was not to be feared if it was peaceful, at a good age with heirs, and many more deaths today are by this standard good. Bowker (1991) reviews the major world religions, and disputes that they are all preoccupied with relieving the fear of death, early Judaism for one having very little to say on the afterlife. If you are a neo-Freudian like Kübler-Ross or Becker and believe that deep down everyone is petrified of dying, and you meet someone who apparently is not, then you assume they must be denying their fear. But maybe your assumption is wrong and they really are not afraid. Marshall argues that it makes more sense 'to view death itself as a neutral stimulus – something that can be endowed with meanings of different sorts. . . . Any look at comparative religions will tell you this' (1986: 136). Any look at the human life-cycle might also tell you this. Infants have no concept of death, and learn of it as they learn of most things: through experience and observation, within a context of conversations with adults and other children (Anthony 1971). There is therefore scope for wide personal variation in how children come to think about death, which will doubtless continue throughout their life. At the other end of life, Marshall has provided evidence that many older people come to terms with their mortality (Chapter 5). Parsons and Lidz (1967) argue that Americans have a practical, realistic, activist culture which influences their approach to death; hospitals and life insurance salesmen do not 'deny' death, but enable Americans to approach it in the style to which they have become accustomed.

So, *is* it possible to face death without tradition, without ritual, without religion? Is it possible to accept death in a detraditionalised, secular, postmodern society? The revival of death tries to help people do precisely this and presents a fascinating case study. Revivalists claim that modern death, by replacing religion with a narrow medical framework helps our bodies but not our souls – but their postmodern solution merely picks at bits from tradition, ritual and religion; it is not rooted in them. The authority offered in the face of death is the authority not of tradition but of the self, summed up in Frank Sinatra's song 'I Did It My Way'. But does the postmodern self have the authority to look death in the eye, and prove Berger, Ariès, Gorer and the rest wrong? If it does, we have to radically rethink much of our conventional wisdom about death.

If on the other hand the authority of the self proves not to be up to this the hardest of all tasks, those who celebrate postmodernism have to rethink. If the postmodern self can play, make love, consume, tour the world, even go on historical cemetery tours . . . but is unable to face death, then postmodernism cannot last long. Or at least it will continue to be restricted to certain areas of consumer culture, and will be very far from an all-embracing 'postmodern condition'.

What, then, can we conclude about such questions from the foregoing chapters?

COME FLY WITH ME

To change the metaphor from one Sinatra song to another, the evidence of Part II of this book shows that the individual self can die his or her own way, but only in company with others. It is not so much a matter of 'I Did It My Way' as 'Come Fly With Me'. Though most people draw their last breath in an institution, they spend most of their dying – if it is not a sudden death – at home. Within their own family, they create and negotiate their own dying role, drawing on family traditions, past experience, and long-honed personal and family coping styles (Kellehear 1990). Within hospices and other institutional settings committed to patients dying their own way, role models are presented both by staff and by other dying patients; dying is learnt and mutually constructed (Chapter 8). Even when people die their own way, the death has been constructed together with others.

The same is true of the life-centred or do-it-yourself funeral. Such a funeral is not invented from scratch, but is part of an evolving tradition. Often a family member has previously attended a similar funeral or seen one on television, or has nursed the dying person at home and feels it natural to extend the personal care after death to the body, or they have read a book or leaflet about the subject.

Then, after the funeral, what about the injunction to grieve my own way? That too is possible, but likewise not in isolation from the ways of others. When social rules about mourning fell into decay earlier this century, people were left withoout a natural grief process over which they had no control nor total freedom to grieve their own way. Rather, bereaved people find themselves in a network of family members, neighbours, colleagues at work, bereavement counsellors and bookish advice, all of which may offer different notions of what is proper grief, appropriate feeling and acceptable behaviour. Grief is negotiated, perhaps more in postmodern society than ever before (Chapter 8).

Doing it yourself is therefore possible, but only in company. This simple and obvious truth has been somewhat obscured by the successful bid of psychologists who know about not interpersonal but intrapersonal processes to be the experts in death and dying. Coming to terms with my own death or with bereavement is increasingly seen as an inner psychological process in which others are marginal, except to provide 'support' for me as I go through a 'natural' process. I hope the sociological perspective of this book has revealed how partial this picture is, for the process I go through is profoundly affected by the definitions of others in my culture, whether religious, medical or psychological. I can do it myself only with reference to evolving traditions – and in the postmodern world of revival that means with reference to evolving of what is natural and psychologically healthy.

THE COMPANY

The revivalist travels the road down into the valley of the shadow of death, but the journey is not made alone. Who accompanies the dying and the bereaved on this road? Many hospices and bereavement organisations have a logo depicting the dying person held up by caring hands of others – but whose are these hands? If they are those of professionals and of family members, then the journey is a typically modern one, with the traveller having on one side close family members, and on the other the functionaries of the public sphere. Occasionally, as in the disaster in the Welsh mining village of Aberfan in 1966, the journey may be more traditional and the traveller accompanied by an entire community. But in a postmodern world loss is developing a new shape, and may require a new response.

Drawing on his studies of widows, Parkes (1986: ch.1) has described bereavement as 'the cost of commitment': if you love for life, then the death of the other is the price one of you will have to pay. In modernity, with lifelong marriage and the nuclear family seen as the ideal way in which to form and maintain identity, the widow reminds every intact couple of the fate that will one day befall them (Ariès 1981). But with the increasing prevalence of serial monogamy, this is all changing. There are two views as to how it is changing.

Bauman's image is of a postmodern world traversed by nomads. Nothing seems to be 'for life'. Not just changing houses and jobs, but partners and their children:

> they all come and go. . . . Nothing is truly irreplaceable, and thus the tragedy is neither unbearable nor too shattering when things or partners disappear from view. . . . Before we have a chance of becoming widows, too many among us have rehearsed more than once the 'departure' of the putatively 'life-long' partner through divorce or separation. We have played and rehearsed that drama of mortality many times, and we cannot any more clearly see in what way, if any, the rehearsals differ from the 'real' performance.
>
> (1992: 188–9)

We are all so accustomed to loss and change that the ultimate loss is no longer ultimate. Like the nomad, we just up camp and move on once more.

Parkes, however, is pessimistic about the demise of life-long monogamy, for two reasons. First, 'it undermines the quality of parenting and the basic trust which helps children to find the security to tolerate separations and losses later in life' (1986: 18). Second, family and friendship links 'which in the past provided reliable support at times of loss and change' are fragmented by geographical and marital mobility; family are too far away and neighbours barely known. As discussed in Chapter 10, funerals and the role of chief mourner can become bitterly contested, with new spouse and children by previous marriage(s) fighting for recognition for their grief.

This indicates that Bauman's analysis may be over-optimistic. Bauman does not consider whether his 'nomads' have the inner psychological security to brush off repeated losses, nor does he consider the matter of social support. Which view is correct is an empirical question, yet I do not know of any research investigating the effect of serial monogamy on the experience of loss through death. Both Bauman and Parkes agree it is an important question.

They also agree that in postmodernity the fellow travellers in the valley of the shadow of death will not necessarily be the same family and neighbours who accompanied us back in the days of modernity. In traditional and even in modern societies, people who are bereaved find themselves in the company of those family, friends and neighbours who knew the deceased – even if with modernity's increasing uncertainty about how to grieve, these others may have been a source as much of contention as of support. Lopata's (1979) survey of 1,000 Chicago widows identified several who felt they had made bad decisions under pressure from family and friends who were not themselves widows. Without consensus on how to behave as a widow (e.g. whether/when to move house or engage in new relationships), many widows preferred the company of other widows who did not know their husband to friends and family who did. Hence we find the emergence of self-help groups of particular categories of bereaved people, the categories getting more and more specific. The UK newsletter of The Compassionate Friends contains many requests from members seeking contact with others who have experienced more precisely their category of loss. There are now, for example, groups for siblings who have lost a twin, another for parents who have lost a twin, another for parents whose child committed suicide.

What we find, therefore, is a fragmenting of the experience of bereavement. If once there was correct mourning behaviour, finely graded for particular kinds of loss but the gradings publicly known, now we have discrete communities of experience, each believing that no one outside their micro-community can know what they feel. And maybe they are right.

To what extent the members of these self-help groups join because they are or feel more socially isolated than other bereaved people is not yet clear (Stroebe and Stroebe 1987: 228), nor is it clear to what extent they flourish in areas where settled community is a rarity. It is therefore difficult to say whether people join these groups because they lack neighbours and friends, or whether they join because they do have family and friends but do not feel understood by them. It could be both: the collapse of traditional community *and* the breakdown of understanding within the modern nuclear family. Members surely do join because of the collapse of norms as to how to mourn, resulting not in individual freedom to mourn one's own way (as Gorer hoped back in 1965: 64) but in anomie and often misunderstanding within families.

Sometimes family and friends feel that the person needs less personal support because they belong to a self-help group or are attending counselling. Sometimes groups and volunteer counsellors allow the member or client to become over-dependent on them and stay in the group or in counselling long after professional advice would recommend. If a widow is also being bombarded with slogans such as 'only a widow can understand a widow', then she is even less likely to seek support from non-widows in her family or neighbourhood. So *if* there is little support at home, it may not be immediately clear whether this is cause or effect: is she is in counselling because she has little support at home, or has she little support at home because she is in counselling? Either way, help is transferred from the traditional community and/or the modern family to the postmodern temporary group or counsellor.

A new form of association has been developing over the past decades:

> The therapeutic outlook seems to conceive community on the model of associations like Parents Without Partners, a body which is highly useful for its members while they are in a given predicament, but to which there is no call to feel any allegiance once one is no longer in need.
>
> (Taylor 1989: 508)

If the postmodern individual is a nomad, then these surely are postmodern groups *par excellence*, where the nomad spends but a short while before moving on. If such groups complement family, friends and neighbours, this is nothing particularly new. But if temporary groups are a *replacement* for more durable networks, then the metaphor of the nomad seems appropriate.

But it is not entirely clear to what extent membership of these groups *is* temporary. Some members belong to such groups for a long time, ten or twelve years or more. You can live with cancer or be HIV positive for a very long time, and you can feel the loss of your child for ever, which raises the question whether some such groups are providing not a temporary and fragile association but a much longer term association built on something deeper than the special interest groups that characterise modernity or the temporary liaisons that characterise postmodernity. Having cancer or losing a child may provide a deeper sense of communion with others than does a shared interest in golf.

Can death once again, as in traditional society, provide a basis for community, not only between those in similar circumstances, but also between them and at least some of their carers? Young and Cullen (forthcoming) believe it can:

> Death is *the* experience which can make all members of the human race feel their common bonds. The presence of death, for all its terror and bitterness, can also generate the mystical sense of unity with other people which transcends the boundaries of the body and the self. Individualism has no doubt made people feel more separate from each other. . . . But in adversity, and especially in the supreme adversity, something even more fundamental can break through.

If death isolated modern people, maybe some are now beginning to find it reconnects them? My academic interest in the sociology of death has led some folk to view me a trifle oddly, but I have also found it to generate personal as well as intellectual connections with some others, connections of a quality that my previous academic interests never generated. As indeed have the occasions I have talked with or helped care for friends with life-threatening illnesses. To this question of re-connection we will now turn.

A NEW COMMUNITY?

There are examples enough in the twentieth century of the shared experience of loss generating a sense of community or reviving it. The horror of the trenches of the First World War caused some veterans never to want to think about their experiences again, and others to value the solidarity of those years for the rest of their lives. The Holocaust directly led to the establishing of the state of Israel and an entire new society. The Aberfan disaster generated a temporary need to work together which led to a permanent renaissance in Aberfan of community spirit and activity (Miller

1974). The unique sense of identity of the city of Liverpool, born of a sense of shared suffering, has surely been affirmed by the Hillsborough soccer stadium disaster in which so many of its young people died. In San Francisco too, the high proportion of homosexuals who are HIV positive seems to me to have engendered in the city a sense of having a shared problem on which the entire population must work together. More specifically, the Castro district of San Francisco has become an enviable model of community development; cold-shouldered by national chain stores unwilling to be associated with the nation's densest collection of homosexuals, the district has become a veritable treasure trove of interesting, locally owned stores and businesses.

Of course, there are many examples of a shared experience of tragic death as tearing members of a community apart, but there are plenty of examples where loss welds the group. The experience of soldiers under fire is paradigmatic: either group morale collapses and desertion and shell shock ensue, or the group gels and its members later describe these as the best years of their lives – meaning the years when they had the greatest sense of solidarity with others, the greatest mutual trust and loyalty, and the greatest sense of purpose.

The peacetime examples I have just given created or strengthened locally based communities. The AIDS Memorial Quilt is an intriguing project based in one place, 2362 Market Street in the aforementioned Castro district, and rooted in the gay community, but affecting many other places and communities. The Quilt was begun in 1987 by homosexuals, lesbians and their friends to commemorate the lives of individuals who had died of AIDS, and is made up of thousands of three foot by six cloth memorials. By 1992, the Quilt had more than 20,000 memorial panels. Most of the time it is warehoused in Market Street, where new additions are carefully filed and stored in readiness for public displays in symbolic locations such as (in October 1992) The Mall in Washington, DC. Spread out over several acres, it makes a political statement about the rights of homosexuals and the need for a compassionate response to AIDS and is also a focus for the grief of the family and friends of each individual commemorated. To stand holding hands around the panel of a friend or brother (who may well have been black, gay and poor) in a place such as The Mall normally reserved for the commemoration of national heroes gives extraordinary significance to his death. Some of those commemorated are heterosexual, as are many of the friends and family involved in making an individual panel – doing this has been the locus for many more than one family reconciliation. The quilt combines the personal and the political, its symbolism drawing powerfully on two facets of American culture – individuality (in the making of each panel) and the nineteenth-century tradition of quilt making. In uniting male and female, heterosexual and homosexual, parent and child, it shows how death of the most fearful kind can draw people together.

If the person with AIDS is *expected* to be a militant gay, however, the solidarity may be at the cost of freedom to be oneself. One British informant told me, 'The one person I know who has died of AIDS was gay, but this was only a part of his identity, and he wanted to die like anyone else – without becoming a hero or a martyr – but people wouldn't allow him to!' Dying in a leading AIDS hospice where he found some protection from negative images of homosexuality held in society at large, he felt subjected to another prescribed ideology. The ideological AIDS death is, to add another to Ariès' four types, *our death*. Of the two major AIDS units in London, one (the London Lighthouse) is seen by some as gay-dominated, while the other (Mildmay Hospital) is too Christian for some patients – so it may not be so easy for some people with AIDS to die their own way.[1] Is it possible then for death to generate human solidarity without denying human freedom?

Young and Cullen's interviews with cancer patients in East London dying at home suggest that it is. They found that when there are kin living in the house, they do the caring, supplemented by other kin; where kin are non-resident, they do what they can, supplemented by neighbours; and where there are no kin, or no kin able and willing to help, neighbours can be extraordinarily devoted. In most instances carers saw their care, without resentment, as a duty: they were closest to hand and 'could do no other'. The willingness of neighbours to help to such an extent surprised the researchers, perhaps because we imagine neighbourliness in Britain to be a dying art. But it seems not. It is more that neighbours keep a discreet distance when there are kin who can help, and step in when kin are not available. Sickness, especially mortal sickness, can reinforce or even create bonds between neighbours. This has certainly been my own experience in the street where I have lived for the past seventeen years: the bonds between neighbours (almost all middle class, and mobile in that only one was born in the street) have been forged in no small measure by care for residents who have had cancer.

In times past if there was real community in an urban area it was because of the need for people to band together in the face of poverty, suffering and sickness. With the Welfare State and affluence, the basis for community has collapsed: some yearn for urban community but of course no one wants the poverty and suffering that underlay urban community earlier this century. Dying, however, is one form of suffering which will never go away, and it may yet be the surest base for community, even in an affluent society. This may be one of the more important of Michael Young's many contributions to British sociology and to British society; having documented the basis of community in the East End of London and its subsequent destruction by post-war affluence and mobility (Young and Willmott 1957), his current research with people dying of cancer may at last have uncovered an enduring base for community (Young and Cullen, forthcoming).

Not all of us live in the kind of neighbourhoods in which this kind of care is likely, so for the purposes of this argument I would like to expand the definition of my 'neighbour' to mean anyone who is physically near me on a regular basis. We may work in the same office for 40 hours a week, or we may train together three evenings a week for the same sports team, even though we live in different parts of town. Bauman (1989: ch. 7) argues that physical proximity has the potential to generate ethical behaviour. It is much easier to ignore the suffering of someone in another part of the world, or even a distant relative, than to ignore the suffering of someone who shares one's desk, or who lives next door or in the same house. One will be reminded daily of the consequences of refusing to help someone seen daily, but without continued physical proximity the consequences of callousness may be readily forgotten. Bauman suggests that unethical and inhumane decisions can be easily made today because of the long chains of command in modern bureaucracies between those who make decisions and those who have to carry them out and who are in a position to witness the consequences. Neither the concentration camp commander nor the cabinet minister for social security personally witnesses the consequences of his decisions. It is much more difficult to be inhumane towards one whom one is physically near to – so care between friends, colleagues and neighbours is a valuable resource in an increasingly abstract and impersonal society, a resource ignored by such a society at its peril.

However, we may of course grow to hate rather than care for those near us; we can be indifferent towards all kinds of anti-social behaviour so long as it is not indulged in by our next-door neighbour or our office-mate. But the argument still stands that there is an enormous well of goodwill among those who are physically proximate to any one individual, even though it may not be expected from each and every one of them. Proximity may generate hate or it may generate love; much more rarely does it generate indifference.

Tragically, the resource of care by friends, colleagues and neighbours, expressed in the Castro district and in the Quilt, is not encouraged and supported by the British Welfare State. Care of the seriously ill and dying is offered either at great expense in medical institutions or through 'care in the community' – which is a euphemism, because 'community' means either yet more institutions (run by social services or private entrepreneurs rather than the health service) or care in the family. The one thing not supported by the Welfare State is care *by* the community – by neighbours, friends and workmates. This is an opportunity lost, not only for the sake of the sick and dying but also for the sake of community.

> The perpetual fund of good will which death can generate is there, has always been there and will always be there as long as humankind survives. The failing of the collective arrangements we now make is that we draw so parsimoniously on the fund and fail so often to top it up.
>
> (Young and Cullen, forthcoming)

With more marriages ending in divorce and more people living to extreme old age, there will be more people fatally ill and living alone at home, so the question of care by friends and neighbours care will become more and more important.

The Natural Death Centre (Albery *et al.* 1993: 198) has suggested that if neighbours can be encouraged by the police to band together to beat crime by forming Neighbourhood Watch schemes, they can surely be encouraged to band together to care for their own sick, dying and bereaved by forming Neighbourhood Care schemes. One such experiment has been tried in Kent, where neighbours and volunteers were recruited to provide flexible forms of support to both the frail elderly and their carers, with some encouraging results (Qureshi *et al.* 1989; see also Neale 1993). Young and Cullen provide another example, of a Baptist minister who rescued more than one dying inner city church by concentrating on providing good funerals and bereavement follow-up in which bereaved people themselves do much of the work, and from this base the new congregation has found itself at the core of the suffering of the local community. Death thus becomes the motor for congregational life.

The decline of industrial society and of the values that underlay it, the collapse of socialism and the disturbance to the formative years of children through parental separation, all indicate that the coming years may witness a search for new values. A key question is whether this reconstruction will occur, as in modernity, by turning a blind eye to human mortality, or whether the increasing profile of death will form a more realistic context for the formation of values. Illness, especially life-threatening illness, certainly puts things into perspective; it makes the insignificant things *seem* insignificant, surely a necessary condition for any critique of the consumer society, of religion or of patriarchy. The lengthened period of dying so common today, and the forms of association in which some of the dying, their carers and their survivors band together, could yet prove significant for the future shape of society. This is another reason why the funeral should be perceived not as a private affair whose purpose is solely to comfort mourners, but as a public statement that death exists and a reminder to us all to ponder our priorities.[2]

The great danger in the revival of death is that its expressive individualism may take over. Expressing feelings can be a useful corrective to the rationalism, utilitarianism and pragmatism of so much of modernity, but by itself reduces to solipsism in which any knowledge other than of one's own experience is denied (Taylor 1989: 511). Self-help bereavement groups certainly show this tendency, and in Britain volunteer bereavement counselling may now be the most frequent way in which people are introduced to the concepts of popular therapy, with all the attendant dangers of obsessive introspection. The necessary balance to this inward gaze may be commitment to the neighbour.

EXPERTS AND RADICALS

Finally, to return to a question that has run throughout this book. The revival of death takes two forms: the expert (late-modern) strand that would impose a new form of dying and grieving, usually in prescribed psychological stages, and the radical (postmodern) strand that truly believes in leaving it up to the individual to do it their own way.

One should not underestimate the force that has been unleashed as individuals have taken dying into their own hands. The increasing popularity of living wills, the interest throughout the modern world in euthanasia, the publicity given in the UK to the ideas of the Natural Death Centre, the flexing of muscle by American patients, all indicate a vociferous minority of people who want to control their own dying and death. Minority though they be, they cannot but cause doctors to stop and think before paternalistically assuming they know what dying patients want or need.

On the other hand, these vociferous consumers are still dependent on expert medical knowledge; they can challenge professional medicine only through knowing what the doctor knows and more, thus enhancing still further the status of expertise. Articles about death and dying in popular magazines are often by doctors or other professionals, or by journalists who quote them. The revival of death looks less like a consumer revolt than a more sophisticated expert management of the dying and bereaved, with experts propounding knowledgeably on the stages in which people die or the desirability of certain kinds of death. Which then is likely to win out: late-modern expertise, or the self-determining postmodern individual?

The physical diversity of modes of death, from traffic accident to frail old age, indicates that no one idea of the 'peaceful' death can characterise every death. Likewise, the variety of ways of dying, together with the variety of human personality, indicates that not everyone will grieve the same way. However, I know of no historical precedent for a society that leaves people to die and to grieve their own way – all societies seem to have regulated the intense fears and emotions of those who are dying and grieving. Can postmodern society really be different? Can it really celebrate diversity, in death as in life? Or will the expert strand, with its clear ideas about healthy dying and grieving, become the new conventional wisdom?

Geoffrey Gorer (1965: 64) argued that modernity did expect mourners to grieve in their own way, in which case we already have some practice at this, but his research ended up recommending one particular style of grieving – what he termed 'time-limited mourning'. One cannot help but think that Gorer's story will be repeated. In the age of social science, surveys will be conducted into how people die and grieve which will identify those styles that have greater and lesser personal costs, and these results will be fed back into popular consciousness. The systematising tendency of modern social science will counteract the diversity of postmodernism.

There is also the question whether postmodernism can enable carers to live with their inability to control those they care for. Hitherto it has been religions such as Christianity and Buddhism (Chapter 9) that have provided philosophies in which carers could accept their own powerlessness. Postmodernism is a culture born out of the very success of modernism in controlling nature, and I am yet to be convinced that it has the philosophical resources to enable human beings to come to terms with their ultimate powerlessness.

This book identifies some limits to revival. For people to die and grieve their own way, they need carers who can truly listen, and Part II revealed the many reasons why even in the most likely settings such as hospices and bereavement counselling there are limits to listening. As expectations for health care rise and demands on finite resources become greater, the availability of attentive listening is correspondingly reduced even further. But if the revival is to succeed, if communities are to be strengthened and a secure base for values laid, then the struggle to keep on listening cannot be abandoned. And though the postmodern self has chosen a hard path in approaching death its own way, without tradition, I cannot see many of us reverting to paths authoritatively ordained by society or by religion – even if, in order to determine our own way, we may want to know what those once authoritative paths were.

In this book, I have mapped some of the routes currently being explored through the valley and to identify some of the obstacles on the way, in the belief that this kind of sociology may assist at least some travellers and those who accompany them. I hope the belief is well founded.

FURTHER READING

Bauman, Z. (1989) *Modernity and the Holocaust*, Oxford, Polity: ch. 7.
—— (1992) *Mortality, Immortality, and Other Life Strategies*, Oxford, Polity: ch. 5.

QUESTIONS

Summarise the arguments for and against death being a universal human fear. Which position do you find more tenable?

Do you think that the fragmented relationships of the postmodern individual make it easier or harder to accommodate to bereavement? How could this question be tested empirically?

How convinced are you that caring for elderly, sick or dying neighbours can help generate community?

Glossary

Some terms are contentious. I give the definitions as used in the book. Words in *italic* refer to other entries in the glossary.

Advance Directive A statement written by a person in good health, requesting specified forms of *euthanasia* should the person be afflicted by specified incurable medical conditions.

Anomie Normlessness. A situation in which social norms lose their hold over individual behaviour.

Charisma The gift of leadership (more loosely, other personal gifts).

Columbarium A set of niches for containing human ashes.

Community A geographical group (bigger than the family) within which one grew up and within which one still lives.

The Compassionate Friends A self-help organisation of bereaved parents, started in the UK and copied (with greater use of professional advisers) in the USA.

Contract Culture The recent requirement to contract out services previously provided in-house by agencies of the British Welfare State. Contracts are awarded only to contractors who can demonstrate efficiency and value for money.

Cremator Furnace for burning human bodies.

Crematorium The building housing one or more cremators and a chapel for conducting a funeral service. To be found in the UK, ex-British colonies and Europe. In the USA, the building housing the *cremators* is termed a crematory, and is unlikely to contain a chapel.

Cruse – Bereavement Care The UK's biggest bereavement counselling organisation, originally for widows but now for any bereaved person. Has a very substantial programme for training volunteer counsellors.

Denial See *defence mechanism*.

Defence Mechanism Originally coined by Freud to refer to the ego's defences against the unconscious impulses of the id, but used by others to refer to defences against any anxiety. Commonly cited defences against the anxiety of loss (of self or other) are denial and repression. These can be normal and functional in the short run in helping the individual cope with devastating news, but if prolonged can be associated with a refusal to face reality.

De-Traditionalisation The process by which the authority of *tradition* and *community* collapse, to be replaced either by *anomie* or by authority being vested within the self.

Double Coding The combination of modern techniques with elements believed to be traditional in order to create a more consumer-friendly product or service. According to Jencks (1986), a characteristic of *postmodernism*.

Emotional Labour The skilled management of one's own and others' emotions.

Euthanasia Literally, 'good death', but refers to mercy killing. This may be <u>voluntary</u> or <u>involuntary</u>, depending on whether the person's consent has been given; and *active* or *passive*, depending on whether active steps to end life have to be taken, or whether simply withdrawing treatment is sufficient to let a terminal disease take its natural course. The hospice movement practises passive euthanasia in the last hours of some patients, but is strongly against active euthanasia.

Expressivism The belief that it is psychologically healthy to express emotions. Frequently found in *late-modern death*.

GP General Practitioner (UK): the family doctor (through whom referrals must be made to gain access to specialists within the *NHS*).

Hospice An organisation devoted to offering *palliative care* for terminal patients, either as in-patients or at home. The first modern hospice (St Christopher's, London) was founded in 1967.

Ideal Type A construct developed by sociologists that describes a pure form of social organisation. Its aim is to illuminate the more complex forms that actually exist. Example: *traditional, modern, neo-modern death*.

Late-Modern Death The strand of *neo-modern death* that relies on professional expertise to promote the good death and healthy grieving.

Living Will See *advance directive*.

Macmillan Nurse A nurse who visits the home of a cancer patient in the UK in order to advise the patient and family about their concerns, especially pain control. Possibly, but not necessarily, employed by the Cancer Relief Macmillan Fund.

Modern Death The management of the dying within a medical frame;

of the dead within a commercial/municipal frame; and of the emotions of the bereaved within a frame of privacy. The 'meaning' of death is not provided by medicine or religion, but has to be constructed by the private individual

Modernity   A social structure in which production and consumption are clearly separated. It may be said to consist of a public sphere based on technology, rational organisation, efficiency and/or profit; and a private sphere (notably the family) in which are located the generation of meaning and the expression of emotion.

Natural Death Personal, rather than medical or institutional, control over the process of dying. See Albery *et al.* (1993).

Neo-Modern Death   The combination of modern medicine with supposedly *traditional* elements in order to re-create a more personal way of death, disposal and/or grief. See *double coding, natural death*. It has two strands, *late-modern death* and *postmodern death*.

NHS   National Health Service (UK). A health care system for all, funded by taxation and free at the point of access. (Dental care, eye tests, prescriptions and some other services are, however, charged for.) The NHS may now purchase services from independent agencies, such as private *hospices*. See also *Contract culture*.

Palliative Care   Care aiming to relieve pain and symptoms rather than to cure, of particular importance in terminal cases (for whom the term is often reserved). Within palliative care, pain is taken to include emotional and spiritual as well as physical pain.

Participant Observation   A research method used by anthropologists and some sociologists, in which the researcher joins in the group being studied, observing not only their behaviour but also his or her own experience in being a group member.

Postmodern Death The strand of *neo-modern death* that acknowledges wide variability in human responses to death and loss.

Postmodernism   A culture that celebrates individual experience, that no longer believes in overarching 'meta-narratives' (such as religion, science, or progress) but does believe in the authority of the self. Individuals feel free to embrace traditional practices, but these have no authority in themselves and may be as readily discarded as embraced – see *de-traditionalisation, double coding*.

Postmodernity A social structure in which the problem of production (how to tame nature in order to mass-produce goods) has been largely solved, to be replaced by the problem of consumption (how to get people to consume). The power of the consumer increases, and his/her private experience begins to enter the public sphere (compare the increasing power of patients within health care systems), leading to a culture of *postmodernism*.

Practitioner A trained and/or paid carer. In the context of this book, doctors, nurses, clergy, undertakers, bereavement counsellors, etc.

Reflexivity The turning of the action back upon the subject; the continual revising of action, knowledge and beliefs. In *late-modern death*, practices are revised in the light of social scientific (especially psychological) knowledge.

Revival The movement to advance *neo-modern death*, in which modern medicine is combined with a revival of supposedly *traditional* elements in order to re-create a more personal way of death, disposal and/or grief. It is therefore both neo-modern and neo-traditional. See *double coding*, *natural death*.

Revivalist One who believes in *revival*.

Routinisation of Charisma The process of instituting more durable forms of authority within an organisation than the personal *charisma* of its founder.

Spirituality A *de-traditionalised* form of religion in which spiritual understanding is based on personal experience rather on established dogma. See *postmodernism*.

Tradition A form of social organisation in which meaning and rules for behaviour are substantially provided by the *community* and legitimated by religion.

Traditional Death Dying, funerals and mourning governed by rules shared by an entire community and legitimated by established custom.

Notes

1 THE DYING OF DEATH

1 I explore the secularisation of death in much more detail in Walter (1995).
2 A shorter and earlier version of his thesis is found in Ariès (1974).
3 New Age approaches to death reassert the importance of the soul's passage, and arguably constitute a re-sacralisation of death that is finding considerable resonance in some people (Walter 1993a).
4 As a historian of the seventeenth century, Houlbrooke (1989:6–7) argues that Gittings and Ariès overplay the role of individualism in the development of the modern way of death. I am not competent to judge the detailed historical evidence of this particular period, but over the past five centuries the growing influence of individualism seems to me indisputable.
5 I am indebted to Michael Young of the Institute of Community Studies for what follows in this paragraph.
6 These processes are resisted within those minority communities, urban or suburban, in which there are still religious traditions for handling the dying, the dead and the bereaved in particular ways; often this is done not by paid professionals, but by members of the community (Firth 1993a, 1993b). Hindus, Muslims and Orthodox Jews are good examples.
7 There is a considerable sociological literature in the USA on the power struggle between clergy and funeral directors, with the latter triumphing (see e.g. Fulton 1961). We still await a comparable study of the conflicts in the British crematorium, although Naylor (1991) is a useful, and witty, start.
8 Smale (1985) provides a comparative study of British and North American funeral parlour practice.
9 I look at this further in Chapter 10.
10 'A Grief Too Much to Bear', *Evening Standard*, London, 26 March 1993.
11 Se Pleijel (1983) for a Swedish analysis of this trend.

2 THE REVIVAL OF DEATH

1 'Psychological Challenges of the Spiritual Path', talk given at Alternatives, St James Piccadilly, London, 14 December 1992.
2 'Covering the Casket', BBC2, 25 November 1991; see also Awoonor-Renner (1991).

3   THE TWO STRANDS OF REVIVAL

1   See Chapter 7, note 4.
2   *CRUSE Chronicle*, July/August 1993.

4   TRADITIONAL, MODERN AND NEO-MODERN DEATH

1   The term 'dying trajectory' comes from Glaser and Strauss (1968).
2   Paper given by Cas Wouters to BSA Sociology of Emotion seminar, Birmingham, 20 January 1990.
3   'Rites of Passage: (2) Hindus of Leicester', BBC Radio 4, 5 September 1993.
4   Other Compassionate Friends leaflets are more willing to concede that non-expressive and non-talkative ways of dealing with grief can be just as valid as expressive ways.

5   STORIES AND META-STORIES

1   Stage theories of other kinds of loss, such as loss of paid work (Jahoda *et al.* 1972, first published 1933), have also been influential and are subject to many of the same criticisms (see Walter 1985: 99–101).
2   C. M. Parkes, letter to *The Lancet*, 31 May 1986, pp. 1277–8.
3   Produced by The Center for Attitudinal Healing, Tiburon, CA.
4   It was, in fact, the helpfulness of the Zimbabwean model for a group of white English mourners at my own father's funeral in 1985 that first got me critically curious about Western constructions of death, dying and bereavement.
5   Worden's revised definition nevertheless fails to escape the privatisation of grief so typical of modernity. Finding 'an appropriate place for the dead *in their emotional lives*', i.e. privately, is surely not easy. What is noticeable about the Shona and many other African cultures, is that the dead are found a place in *public ritual*, something which can easily be done also in the modern West, as in the memorial service or in the Jewish *Jahrzeit* family ritual (Walter 1990). Hence the African phrase, 'the living dead', refers to the ancestors' presence in the community more than in individual memory.

6   SYSTEMS FOR LISTENING

1   In hospices in the UK, these are usually called *multi-disciplinary*, which is a misnomer since they comprise not academic disciplines but professions. Why this misnomer has taken root, I have yet to fathom.
2   Acknowledgement is made to the *Journal of Advanced Nursing* for permission to quote from Susie Wilkinson 'Factors Which Influence How Nurses Communicate With Cancer Patients'.
3   This second extract concerns a patient coming in for treatment of a recurrence of his cancer, rather than for palliative care.
4   In the UK, all NHS hospitals employ one or more chaplains.

7   EXPECTATIONS AND ASSUMPTIONS

1   Interview with Frank Ostaseski of the San Francisco Zen Hospice Project; see also Ostaseski 1990. Other Buddhist approaches tend to focus more on the non-attachment of the dying rather than the non-attachment of the carer, see Levine (1988) and Rinpoche (1992).
2   It is also, of course, what is involved in the sociological and anthropological method of *verstehen* and in psychoanalysis as conducted by a skilled practitioner.
3   I mean tend. Burnard (1988), for example, commends to nurses both the expressivist approach and a cognitive approach.
4   I hope to develop in a separate article a sociological critique of natural death, pointing out the following: 1) The anthropological data can be read to indicate wide variety as well as consistency in traditional ways of death. 2) The least technologically advanced societies (hunter-gatherer groups) approach death in a remarkably similar way to modern societies. 3) A large number of societies that live close to nature see death as *unnatural* – the result of hexes, witchcraft, supernatural interventions and so on. 4) All societies construct concepts of the good death and it is arbitrary to label some as natural and others as not.

8   THE LISTENING COMMUNITY OR THE DEFINING COMMUNITY?

1   Riesman explored these issues in *The Lonely Crowd* (1950). I suspect that his hope for the future – the autonomous self – has turned out to be more other-directed, looking to others for authority, than autonomous.
2   Carmichael is critical of the obsession with putting a brave face on it, but it seems that sometimes this can make life easier for everyone. Kübler-Ross (1970: ch. 8) gives an extended interview transcript with a patient in which he displays hope work.

9   GAINING CONTROL, LOSING CONTROL

1   Hockey 1990: 183–6 provides a case study of this.
2   There are, however, very substantial criticisms of Becker, notably his assumption that the fear of death is natural rather than culturally and individually constructed.
3   'Primetime', 13 January 1993.

10   WHICH PERSON?

1   Clive Seale, personal communication.
2   For example, 14 November 1992, pp. 224–5

11   ROUTINISATION

1   *Shanti Nilaya UK Newsletter*, October 1992, no. 36, p. 8. In the UK this publication is published by the Elisabeth Kübler-Ross Foundation, Unit 309, Panther House, 38 Mount Pleasant, London WC1H OAP; in the USA by the EKR Center, South Route 616, Head Waters, VA 24442.
2   In the UK, the Trent Palliative Care Centre is a centre for sociological research in this field, especially through the work of its research fellow, David Clark.

12   DISPOSAL

1   Participant observation by author, 1993.
2   See Dunk and Rugg's (1994) valuable survey.
3   Recorded on the album *Items of News*, Blackthorne BR 1067.

13   CONCLUSION

1   *Guardian*, 10 January 1994, p. 10.
2   This paragraph draws on a conversation with Michael Young.

Bibliography

Note: British publication details are usually given in preference to American or European.

Abel, J. (1986) 'The Hospice Movement: institutionalising innovation', *Int. Journal Health Service*, 16: 71–85.

Adams, T. (1990) 'A Model of Multidisciplinary Team Working', *Senior Nurse*, 10, 10.

Ahmedzai, S. (1993) 'A Doctor's View' in D. Clark (ed.) *The Future For Palliative Care*, Buckingham, Open University Press, pp. 140–7.

Ainsworth-Smith, P. and Speck, P. (1982) *Letting God: caring for the dying and bereaved*, London, SPCK.

Albery, N., Elliot, G. and Elliot, J. (eds) (1993) *The Natural Death Handbook*, London, Virgin.

Albrecht, E. (1989) 'The Development of Hospice Care in West Germany', *Journal of Palliative Care*, 5, 3: 42–3.

Andreski, S. (1984) *Max Weber's Insights and Errors*, London, Routledge.

Anon (1970) 'Death in the First Person', *American Journal of Nursing*; reprinted in several places, e.g. *Mud and Stars: report of a working party on the impact of hospice experience on the church's ministry of healing*, Oxford, Michael Sobell House, p.145.

Anthony, S. (1971) *The Discovery of Death in Childhood*, London, Penguin.

Ariès, P. (1974) *Western Attitudes Toward Death: From the middle ages to the present*, Baltimore, Johns Hopkins University Press.

—— (1981) *The Hour of Our Death*, London, Allen Lane.

Armstrong, D. (1984) 'The Patient's View', *Social Science and Medicine*, 18, 9: 737–44

—— (1987) 'Silence and Truth in Death and Dying', *Social Science and Medicine*, 24, 8: 651–7.

Arney, W. R. and Bergen, B. J. (1984) *Medicine and the Management of Living*, University of Chicago Press.

Attig, T. (1990) 'Relearning the World: on the phenomenology of grieving', *Journal of the British Society for Phenomenology*, 21: 53–66.

—— (1991) 'The Importance of Conceiving of Grief as an Active Process', *Death Studies*, 15: 385–93.

Awoonor-Renner, S. (1991) 'I Desperately Needed to See My Son', *British*

Medical Journal, 302 (9 February): 356; also reprinted in D. Dickenson and M. Johnson (eds) (1993) *Death, Dying and Bereavement*, London, Sage.

Bailey, L. R. (1979) *Biblical Perspectives on Death*, Philadelphia, Fortress.

Baudrillard, J. (1990) *La Transparence du Mal*, Paris, Galilee.

Baum, M. (1988) *Breast Cancer: the facts*, Oxford University Press.

Bauman, Z. (1989) *Modernity and the Holocaust*, Oxford, Polity.

—— (1992) *Mortality, Immortality and Other Life Strategies*, Oxford, Polity.

Beck, U. (1992) *Risk Society: towards a new modernity*, London, Sage.

Becker, E. (1973) *The Denial of Death*, New York, Free Press.

Bellah, R. N., Madsen, R., Sullivan, W. M., Swidler, A. and Tipton, S. M. (1985) *Habits of the Heart: individualism and commitment in American life*, Berkeley, University of California Press.

Bendix, R. (1966) *Max Weber*, London, Methuen.

Bennett, G. (1987) *Traditions of Belief: women, folklore and the supernatural today*, London, Penguin.

Berger, P. (1969) *The Social Reality of Religion*, London, Faber.

——, Berger, B. and Kellner, H. (1974) *The Homeless Mind: modernization and consciousness*, London, Penguin.

—— and Luckmann, T. (1967) *The Social Construction of Reality*, London, Allen Lane.

Biswas, B. (1993) 'A Nurse's View' in D. Clark (ed.) *The Future for Palliative Care*, Buckingham, Open University Press.

Blauner, R. (1966) 'Death and Social Structure', *Psychiatry*, 29: 378–94.

Bloch, M. and Parry, J. (eds) (1982) *Death and the Regeneration of Life*, Cambridge University Press.

Bloch, S. (1991) 'A Systems Approach to Loss', *Australian and New Zealand Journal of Psychiatry*, 25: 471–80.

Blythe, R. (1981) *The View in Winter: reflections on old age*, London, Penguin.

Bolton, C. and Camp, D. (1986) 'Funeral Rituals and the Facilitation of Grief Work', *Omega*, 17, 4: 343–52.

Bowker, J. (1991) *The Meanings of Death*, Cambridge University Press.

Bowling, A. and Cartwright, A. (1982) *Life After a Death*, London, Tavistock.

Bradbury, M. (1993) 'Contemporary Representations of "Good" and "Bad" Death', in D. Dickenson and M. Johnson (eds) *Death, Dying and Bereavement*, London, Sage.

British Medical Association (1988) *Euthanasia*, London.

Broadbent, M., Horwood, P., Sparks, J. and de Whalley, G. (1990) 'Bereavement Groups', *Bereavement Care*, 9, 2: 14–16.

Brohn, P. (1987) *The Bristol Programme: an introduction to the holistic therapies practised by the Bristol Cancer Help Centre*, London, Century Hutchinson.

Bruce, S. (1984) *Firm in the Faith*, Aldershot, Gower.

Buckingham, R. W., Lack, S. A., Mount, B. M., Maclean, L. D. and Collins, J. T. (1976) 'Living with the Dying: use of the technique of participant observation', *Canadian Medical Association Journal*, 115 (18 December): 1211–15.

Buckman, R. (1988) *I Don't Know What to Say*, Basingstoke, Macmillan.

Burckhardt, J. (1960) *The Civilisation of the Renaissance*, New York, Mentor.

Burnard, P. (1988) 'No Need To Hide', *Nursing Times*, 84, 24 (15 June): 36–8.

Campbell, C. (1987) *The Romantic Ethic and the Spirit of Modern Consumerism*, Oxford, Blackwell.

Canguilhem, G. (1978) *On the Normal and the Pathological*, Boston, D. Reidel.

Cannadine, D. (1981) 'War and Death, Grief and Mourning in Modern Britain', in J. Whaley (ed.) *Mirrors of Mortality*, London, Europa.

Carlisle, J. (1992) 'Terminal Care Limited for AIDS', *Nursing Times*, 88, 15: 7.

Carmichael, K. (1991) *Ceremony of Innocence: tears, power and protest*, London, Macmillan.

Carson, V. B. (ed.) (1989) *Spiritual Dimensions of Nursing Practice*, Philadelphia, W. B. Saunders.

Cartwright, A. (1990) *The Role of the General Practitioner in Caring for People in the Last Year of Their Lives*, London, King's Fund.

Charmaz, K. (1980) *The Social Reality of Death*, Reading MS, Addison-Wesley.

Charnes, L. and Moore, P. (1992) 'Meeting Patients' Spiritual Needs: the Jewish perspective', *Holistic Nursing Practice*, 6, 3: 64–72.

Churchill, L. (1979) 'The Human Experience of Dying: the moral primacy of stories over stages', *Soundings*, 42, 1.

Clark, D. (1982) *Between Pulpit and Pew: folk religion in a North Yorkshire fishing village*, Cambridge University Press.

—— (ed.) (1993a) *The Future for Palliative Care*, Buckingham, Open University Press.

—— (ed.) (1993b) *The Sociology of Death*, Oxford, Blackwell.

Clarke, M. (1978) 'Getting Through the Work', in R. Dingwall and J. McIntosh (eds) *Readings in the Sociology of Nursing*, Edinburgh, Churchill Livingstone.

Clegg, F. (1987) *Decisions at a Time of Grief*, London, Memorial Advisory Bureau, unpublished manuscript.

Cleiren, M. (1991) *Adaptation After Bereavement: a comparative study of the aftermath of death from suicide, traffic accident and illness for next of kin*, Leiden University, DSWO Press.

Collick, E. (1986) *Through Grief: the bereavement journey*, London, Darton, Longman, Todd/CRUSE.

Consumers' Association (1986) *What to Do When Someone Dies*, London, Hodder & Stoughton.

Coombs, R. H. and Powers, P. S. (1976) 'Socialization for Death: the physician's role' in L. Lofland (ed.) *Toward a Sociology of Death and Dying*, Beverly Hills, Sage.

Corr, C. (1991) 'A Task-Based Approach to Coping with Dying', *Omega*, 24, 2: 81–94.

Crowther, T. (1993) 'Euthanasia', in D. Clark (ed.) *The Future for Palliative Care*, Buckingham, Open University Press.

Danforth, L. (1982) *The Death Rituals of Rural Greece*, Princeton University Press.

Davie, G. (1993) 'The Pilgrimage to Anfield' in I. Reader and T. Walter (eds) *Pilgrimage in Popular Culture*, Basingstoke, Macmillan.

Davies, J. D. (1990) *Cremation Today and Tomorrow*, Nottingham, Alcuin/GROW Liturgical Study 16.

Detmer, C. and Lamberti, J. (1991) 'Family Grief', *Death Studies*, 15: 363–74.

Dickenson, D. and Johnson, M. (eds) (1993) *Death, Dying and Bereavement*, London, Sage.

Dinnage, R. (1990), *The Ruffian on the Stair: reflections on death*, London, Viking.

Docherty, D. (1990) 'A Death in the Family', *Sight and Sound*, Spring.

Douglas, C. (1983) *A Cure for Living*, London, Hutchinson.

Draper, J. W. (1967) *The Funeral Elegy and the Rise of English Romanticism*, London, Frank Cass.

du Boulay, S. (1984) *Cicely Saunders*, London, Hodder.

Duda, D. (1987) *Coming Home: a guide to dying at home with dignity*, Santa Fe, Aurora.

Dumont, R. G. and Foss, D. C. (1972) *The American View of Death: acceptance or denial?*, Cambridge MS, Schenkman.

Dunk, J. and Rugg, J. (1994) *The Management of Old Cemetery Land*, London, Shaw & Son.

Durkheim, E. (1915) *The Elementary Forms of the Religious Life*, London, Unwin.

Elias, N. (1982) *The Civilising Process*, vol. 2, Oxford, Blackwell.

—— (1985) *The Loneliness of the Dying*, Oxford, Blackwell.

Engel, G. I. (1961) 'Is Grief a Disease?', *Psychosomatic Medicine*, 23, 1: 18–22.

Farrell, J. J. (1980) *Inventing the American Way of Death, 1830–1920*, Philadelphia, Temple University Press.

Feifel, H. (1988) 'Grief and Bereavement: overview and perspective', *Bereavement Care*, 7, 1: 2–4.

Feinstein, D. and Mayo, P. E. (1990) *Rituals for Living and Dying*, San Francisco, Harper & Row.

Field, D. (1984) 'Formal Instruction in United Kingdom Medical Schools about Death and Dying', *Medical Education*, 18: 429–34.

—— (1986) 'Formal Teaching about Death and Dying in UK Nursing Schools', *Nurse Education Today*, 6: 270–6.

—— (1989) *Nursing the Dying*, London, Routledge.

—— and Travisano, R. (1984) 'Social History and American Preoccupation with Identity', *Free Inquiry in Creative Sociology*, 12, 1: 51–6.

Firth, S. (1993a) 'Approaches to Death in Hindu and Sikh Communities in Britain', in D. Dickenson and M. Johnson (eds) *Death, Dying and Bereavement*, London, Sage.

—— (1993b) 'Cross-cultural Perspectives on Bereavement', in D. Dickenson and M. Johnson (eds) *Death, Dying and Bereavement*, London, Sage.

Fitchett, G. (1980) 'It's Time to Bury the Stage Theory of Death and Dying', *Oncology Nurse Exchange*, 2, 3.

Foucault, M. (1973) *The Birth of the Clinic*, London, Tavistock.

—— (1977) *Discipline and Punish: the birth of the prison*, London, Allen Lane.

—— (1979) *The History of Sexuality*, vol. 1, London, Allen Lane.

Fowler, J. (1981) *Stages of Faith*, San Francisco, Harper.

Fox, R. (ed.) (1980) *The Social Meaning of Death*, special issue, *Annals of the American Academy of Political and Social Science*, vol. 447, special issue.

Frankl, V. (1987) *Man's Search for Meaning*, London, Hodder & Stoughton.

Freud, S. (1984) 'Mourning and Melancholia' in S. Freud, *On Metapsychology*, London, Pelican Freud Library, vol. 11: 251–67.

Fulton, R. L. (1961) 'The Clergyman and the Funeral Director: a study in role conflict', *Social Forces*, 39: 317–23.

—— (ed.) (1976) *Death and Identity*, Bowie MD, Charles Press.

Gammon, V. (1988) 'Singing and Popular Funeral Practices in the Eighteenth and Nineteenth Centuries', *Folk Music Journal*, 5, 4: 412–47.

Germain, C. P. (1980) 'Nursing the Dying: implications of Kübler-Ross' staging theory' in Fox, R. (ed.) *The Social Meaning of Death*, special issue, *Annals of the American Academy of Political and Social Science*, vol. 447.

Giddens, A. (1990) *The Consequences of Modernity*, Oxford, Polity.

—— (1991) *Modernity and Self-Identity*, Oxford, Polity.

—— (1992) *The Transformation of Intimacy*, Oxford, Polity.

Gilligan, C. (1982) *In a Different Voice: psychological theory and women's development*, Cambridge MS, Harvard University Press.

Gilmore, A. and Gilmore, S. (eds) (1984) *A Safer Death*, London, Plenum.

Gittings, C. (1984) *Death, Burial and the Individual in Early Modern England*, London, Croom Helm.

Glaser, B. and Strauss, A. (1965) *Awareness of Dying*, Chicago, Aldine.

—— (1968) *Time for Dying*, Chicago, Aldine.

Glover, J. (1988) *Causing Death and Saving Lives*, London, Penguin.

Goddard, M. K. (1993) 'The Importance of Assessing the Effectiveness of Care: the case of hospices', *Journal of Social Policy*, 22, 1: 1–18.

Goffman, E. (1968) *Asylums*, London, Penguin.

—— (1974) *Frame Analysis*, Cambridge MS, Harvard University Press.

Goody, J. (1959) 'Death and Social Control Among the LoDagaa', *Man*, 203: 134–8.

Gorer, G. (1955) 'The Pornography of Death', *Encounter*, October.

—— (1965) *Death, Grief, and Mourning in Contemporary Britain*, London, Cresset.

Greenall, B. (1988) 'Books for Bereaved Children', *Health Libraries Review*, 5: 1–6.

Grey, M. (1985) *Return from Death*, London, Arkana.

Hacking, I. (1975) *The Emergence of Probability*, Cambridge University Press.

Hafferty, F. (1991) *Into the Valley*, New Haven, Yale University Press.

Hamilton, M. P. and Reid, H. F. (1980) *A Hospice Handbook*, Grand Rapids, Eerdmans.

Harre, R. (ed.) (1986) *The Social Construction of Emotions*, Oxford, Blackwell.

Harrison, J. (1992) *Aspects of Spirituality*, University of Wales College of Medicine, Cardiff, Master of Nursing unpublished thesis.

Hartley, J. (1992) 'Accession', *Sunday Times Review*, 26 January.

Hawkins, A. H. (1990) 'Constructing Death: three pathographies about dying', *Omega*, 22, 4: 301–17.

Hertz, R. (1960) *Death and the Right Hand*, London, Cohen & West (1907).

Higginson, I. (1993) 'Quality, Costs and Contracts of Care', in D. Clark (ed.) *The Future for Palliative Care*, Buckingham, Open University Press.

Highfield, M. F. and Cason, C. (1983) 'Spiritual Needs of Patients: are they recognised?', *Cancer Nurse*, 6: 187–92

Hill, S. (1977) *In the Springtime of the Year*, London, Penguin.

Hinton, J. (1980) 'Whom Do Dying Patients Tell?', *British Medical Journal*, 281: 1328–30.

Hoad, P. (1991) 'Volunteers in the Independent Hospice Movement', *Sociology of Health and Illness*, 13, 2: 231–48.

Hochschild, A. R. (1973) *The Unexpected Community*, Englewood Cliffs, Prentice Hall.

Hockey, J. (1986) *The Human Encounter with Death*, Durham University, unpublished PhD thesis.
—— (1990) *Experiences of Death*, Edinburgh University Press.
—— (1993) 'The View From the West: reading the anthropology of non-western death ritual', paper prepared for the conference 'The Social Context of Death, Dying and Disposal', Oxford.
Holloway, J. (1990) 'Bereavement Literature: a valuable resource for the bereaved and those who counsel them', *Contact: Interdisciplinary Journal of Pastoral Studies*, 3: 17–26.
Honeybun, J., Johnston, M. and Tookman, A. (1992) 'The Impact of a Death on Fellow Hospice Patients', *British Journal of Medical Psychology*, 65: 67–72.
Hospice Information Service (1993a) *1993 Directory of Hospice Services, London*, St Christopher's Hospice.
—— (1993b) 'Where People Die and Hospice Provision', Fact Sheet 7.
Houlbrooke, R. (ed.) (1989) *Death, Ritual and Bereavement*, London, Routledge.
—— (1993) 'The Puritan Death-bed', paper given at conference, 'The Social Context of Death, Dying and Disposal', Oxford.
Howarth, G. (forthcoming) *Deathwork*, Amityville, NY, Baywood.
Hull, R., Ellis, M. and Sargent, V. (1989) *Teamwork in Palliative Care*, Oxford, Radcliffe Medical Press.
Hunt, M. W. (1989) *Dying at Home: its basic 'ordinariness' displayed in patients', relatives' and nurses' talk*, Goldsmiths College, University of London, unpublished PhD thesis.
—— (1991a) 'Being Friendly and Informal: reflected in nurses', terminally ill patients' and relatives' conversations at home', *Journal of Advanced Nursing*, 16: 929–38.
—— (1991b) 'The Identification and Provision of Care for the Terminally Ill at Home by "Family" Members', *Sociology of Health and Illness*, 13, 3: 375–95.
—— (1992) 'Scripts for Dying at Home – displayed in nurses', patients' and relatives' talk', *Journal of Advanced Nursing*, 17: 1297–1302.
Huntingdon, R. and Metcalf, P. (1979) *Celebrations of Death: the anthropology of mortuary ritual*, Cambridge University Press.
Ignatieff, M. (1990) *The Needs of Strangers*, London, Hogarth Press.
Illich, I. (1976) *Limits to Medicine*, London, Marion Boyars.
——, Zola, I. K., McKnight, J., Caplan, J. and Shaiken, H. (1977) *Disabling Professions*, London, Marion Boyars.
Jacik, M. (1989) 'Spiritual Care of the Dying Adult', ch. 10 in V.B. Carson (ed.) *Spiritual Dimensions of Nursing Practice*, Philadelphia, W.B. Saunders.
Jacobs, J. (1899) 'The Dying of Death', *Fortnightly Review*, New Series 72: 264–9.
Jahoda, M., Lazarsfeld, P. F. and Zeisel, H. (1972) *Marienthal*, London, Tavistock.
James, N. (1989) 'Emotional Labour: skill and work in the social regulation of feelings', *Sociological Review*, 37: 15–42.
—— (1992) 'Care = Organisation + Physical Labour + Emotional Labour', *Sociology of Health and Illness*, 14, 4: 488–509.
—— and Field, D. (1992) 'The Routinization of Hospice: charisma and bureaucratization', *Social Science and Medicine*, 34, 12: 1363–75.

James, V. (1986) *Care and Work in Nursing the Dying: a participant study in a continuing care unit*, Aberdeen University, unpublished PhD thesis.

Jameson, F. (1991) *Postmodernism: or, the cultural logic of late capitalism*, London, Verso.

Jencks, C. (1986) *What is Postmodernism?*, Art & Design.

Jupp, P. (1990) *From Dust to Ashes: the replacement of burial by cremation in England 1840–1967*, London, Congregational Memorial Hall Trust.

—— (1993) *The Development of Cremation in England 1820–1990: a sociological analysis*, London School of Economics, unpublished PhD thesis.

Kalish, R. A. (1980) *Death, Grief and Caring Relationships*, Monterey CA, Brooks Cole.

—— and Reynolds, D. K. (1981) *Death and Ethnicity: a psychocultural study*, Farmingdale NY, Baywood.

Kamerman, J. B. (1988) *Death in the Midst of Life: social and cultural influences on death, grief and mourning*, Englewood Cliffs, Prentice Hall.

Kastenbaum, R. (1975) 'Is Death a Life Crisis?' in M. Datan and L. Ginsberg (eds) *Life-Span Developmental Psychology*, New York, Academic Press.

—— (1979) '"Healthy Dying": a paradoxical quest', *Journal of Social Issues*, 35, 1: 185–206.

—— (1988) '"Safe Death" in the Postmodern World', in A. Gilmore and S. Gilmore (eds) *A Safer Death*, London, Plenum.

Kavanagh, D. G. (1990) 'Towards a Cognitive–Behavioural Intervention for Adult Grief Reactions', *British Journal of Psychiatry*, 157: 373–83.

Kearl, M. C. (1989) *Endings: a sociology of death and dying*, Oxford University Press.

Kearney, M. (1992) 'Palliative Medicine: just another specialty?' *Palliative Medicine*, 6: 39–46.

Kellehear, A. (1990) *Dying of Cancer: the final years of life*, Chur, Harwood Academic.

—— and Fook, J. (1989) 'Sociological Factors in Death Denial by the Terminally Ill', *Advances in Behavioural Medicine*, 6, 527–37.

Kfir, N. and Slevin, M. (1991) *Challenging Cancer: from chaos to control*, London, Routledge.

Klass, D. (1981) 'Elisabeth Kübler-Ross and the Tradition of the Private Sphere', *Omega*, 12, 3: 241–65.

—— and Hutch, R. (1985) 'Elisabeth Kübler-Ross as a Religious Leader', *Omega*, 16: 89–109.

Kübler-Ross, E. (1970) *On Death and Dying*, London, Tavistock.

—— (ed.) (1975) *Death: the final stage of growth*, Englewood Cliffs, Prentice Hall.

—— (1991) *On Life After Death*, Berkeley, Celestial Arts.

Kuhn, T (1962), *The Structure of Scientific Revolutions*, Chicago University Press.

Lanceley, A. (forthcoming) 'Emotional Disclosure' in A. Richardson and J. Wilson-Barnett, (eds), *Research in Cancer Nursing*, London, Scutari.

Lasch, C. (1977) *Haven in a Heartless World: the family beseiged*, New York, Basic Books.

—— (1978) *The Culture of Narcissism*, New York, W. W. Norton.

—— (1985) *The Minimal Self: psychic survival in troubled times*, London, Pan.

Leaman, O. (1993) 'Religious Affiliation and the Concept of Death', paper given at conference on 'The Social Context of Death, Dying and Disposal', Oxford.

Lendrum, S. and Syme, G. (1992) *The Gift of Tears*, London, Tavistock.

Levine, S. (1988) *Who Dies? an investigation of conscious living and conscious dying*, Bath, Gateway.

Lichter, I. (1991) 'Some Psychological Causes of Distress in the Terminally Ill', *Palliative Medicine*, 5: 138–46.

Lindeman, E. (1944), 'Symptomatology and Management of Acute Grief', *American Journal of Psychiatry*, 101: 141–8.

Lister, L. (1991) 'Men and Grief: a review of research', *Smith College Studies in Social Work*, 61, 3: 220–35.

Littlewood, J. (1983) *Loss and Change*, Leicester University, unpublished PhD thesis.

—— (1992) *Aspects of Grief*, London, Tavistock/Routledge.

—— Pickering, M. and Walter, T. (forthcoming) 'Public Death'.

Lofland, L. (ed.) (1976) *Toward a Sociology of Death and Dying*, Beverly Hills, Sage.

—— (1978) *The Craft of Dying: the modern face of death*, Beverly Hills, Sage.

Logue, B. L. (1991) 'Taking Charge: death control as an emergent women's issue', *Women and Health*, 17, 4: 97–121.

Lopata, H. Z. (1979) *Women as Widows – Support Systems*, New York, Elsevier.

Loudon, J. C. (1981) *On the Laying Out, Planting, and Managing of Cemeteries and on the Improvement of Churchyards*, Redhill, Ivelet Books (1843).

Lund, D. A. (ed) (1989) *Older Bereaved Spouses*, New York, Hemisphere.

Lunn, L. (1990) 'Having No Answer', in C. Saunders (ed.) *Hospice and Palliative Care: an Interdisciplinary Approach*, London, Edward Arnold.

Lynn, J. (1985) 'Ethics in Hospice Care', in *Hospice Handbook*, Rockville MD, Aspen Systems Corp.

McIntosh, J. (1977) *Communication and Awarenes in a Cancer Ward*, London, Croom Helm.

McManners, J. (1981) *Death and the Enlightenment*, Oxford University Press.

Malinowski, B. (1962) 'The Role of Magic and Religion' in W. H. Lessa and E. Z. Vogt (eds) *Reader in Comparative Religion*, Evanston, Row Peterson (1931).

Marris, P. (1958) *Widows and Their Families*, London, Routledge.

—— (1974) *Loss and Change*, London, Routledge.

Marshall, M. (1991) 'Advocacy Within the Multidisciplinary Team', *Nursing Standard*, 6, 10 (27 November): 28–31.

Marshall, V. W. (1980) *Last Chapters: a sociology of ageing and dying*, Monterey CA, Brooks/Cole.

—— (1986) 'A Sociological Perspective on Ageing and Dying' in V. W. Marshall (ed.) *Later Life: the social psychology of ageing*, Beverly Hills, Sage.

Martin, B. (1981) *A Sociology of Contemporary Cultural Change*, Oxford, Blackwell.

May, C. (1990) 'Research on Nurse–Patient Relationships', *Journal of Advanced Nursing*, 15: 307–15.

—— (1992) 'Individual Care? Power and subjectivity in therapeutic relationships', *Sociology*, 26, 4: 589–602.

Mayne, M. (1989) 'Exploring Spiritual Needs', paper given at Regents College London, 6 July.

Mellor, P. (1993) 'Death in High Modernity' in D. Clark (ed.) *The Sociology of Death*, Oxford, Blackwell.

—— and Shilling, C. (1993) 'Modernity, Self-Identity and the Sequestration of Death', *Sociology*, 27, 3: 411–32.

Miles, S. H. and August, A. (1990), 'Courts, Gender, and the "Right to Die"', *Law, Medicine, and Health Care*, 18, 1–2: 85–95.

Miller, J. (1974) *Aberfan: a disaster and its aftermath*, London, Constable.

Mitford, J. (1963) *The American Way of Death*, London, Hutchinson.

Moody, R. (1975) *Life After Death*, Covington GA, Mockingbird Books.

Mor, V., Greer, D. S. and Kastenbaum, R. (1988) *The Hospice Experiment*, Baltimore, Johns Hopkins University Press.

Morley, J. (1971) *Death, Heaven and the Victorians*, London, Studio Vista.

Mount, B. and Scott, J. (1983) 'Whither Hospice Evaluation?' *Journal of Chronic Disabilities*, 36, 11: 731–6.

Mount, F. (1982) *The Subversive Family*, London, Cape.

Mulkay, M. and Ernst, J. (1991) 'The Changing Profile of Social Death', *Archives Europ. Sociol.*, 23: 172–96.

Myerhoff, B. (1979) *Number Our Days*, New York, E. P. Dutton.

—— (1982) 'Rites of Passage: process and paradox', pp. 109–35 in V. Turner (ed.) *Celebration: studies in festivity and ritual*, Washington DC, Smithsonian Institution Press.

—— (1992) *Surviving Stories: reflections on Number Our Days* in M. Kaminsky (ed.) *Remembered Lives: the work of ritual, storytelling and growing older*, Michigan.

National Association of Health Authorities and Trusts (1991) *Care of People with Terminal Illness: report by a joint advisory group*, Birmingham Research Park.

National Health Service Management Executive (1992) *Health Service Guidelines*, HSG 92 (2), London.

Naylor, M. (1989) *The Funeral: the management of death and its rituals in a northern, industrial city*, Leeds University, unpublished PhD thesis.

—— (1991) 'The Role of a Minister at a Funeral', paper given to The Churches' Group on Funeral Services at Cemeteries and Crematoria, Birmingham, 20 October.

Neale, B. (1993) 'Informal Care and Community Care', in D. Clark (ed.) *The Future for Palliative Care*, Buckingham, Open University Press.

—— and Clark, D. (1992) 'Informal Palliative Care: the needs of informal carers of terminally ill people', paper given at the Third Palliative Care Research Forum, Glasgow, 7–8 October.

Nenola-Kallio, A. (1982) *Studies in Ingrian Laments*, Helsinki.

Novack, D. H., Plumer, R., Smith, R., Ochitill, H., Morrow, G. and Bennett, J. (1979) 'Changes in Physicians' Attitudes Toward Telling the Cancer Patient', *Journal of the American Medical Association*, 241, 897–900.

Noyes, R. J. and Clancy, J. (1983) 'The Dying Role' in C. Corr and D. Corr, (eds) *Hospice Care: Principles and Practice*, London, Faber.

Office of Fair Trading (1989) *Funerals*, London.

Oken, D. (1961) 'What to Tell Cancer Patients: a study of medical attitudes', *Journal of the American Medical Associaion*, 175: 1120–8.

Ostaseski, F. (1990) 'Living with the Dying', *Inquiring Mind*, 6, 2: 8–11.

O'Toole, M. (n.d.) *What to do When a Child Dies*, Amersham, Bucks, Society for Mucopolysaccharide Diseases.

Palouzie, A.-M. (1985) 'Aspects of the European Dying Process', *Social Science and Medicine*, 20, 8: 851–3.

Paradis, L. and Cummings, S. (1986) 'The Evolution of Hospice in America Toward Organisational Homogeneity', *Journal of Health and Social Behaviour*, 27: 370–86.

Parkes, C. M. (1972/1986) *Bereavement: studies of grief in adult life*, London, Tavistock.

—— (1980) 'Bereavement Counselling: does it work?', *British Medical Journal*, 281 (5 July): 3–6.

—— (1990) 'Risk Factors in Bereavement: implications for the prevention and treatment of pathologic grief', *Psychiatric Annals*, 20, 6: 308–13.

—— and Weiss, R. (1983) *Recovery From Bereavement*, New York, Basic Books.

Parsons, T. and Lidz, V. (1967) 'Death in American Society' in E. Shneidman (ed.) *Essays in Self-Destruction*, New York, Science House.

Pennells, M. and Kitchener, S. (1990) 'Holding Back the Nightmares', *Social Work Today*, (2 March): 14–15.

Perakyla, A. (1988) 'Four Frames of Death in a Modern Hospital' in A. Gilmore and S. Gilmore (eds) *A Safer Death*, London, Plenum.

—— (1989) 'Appealing to the "Experience" of the Patient in the Care of the Dying', *Sociology of Health and Illness*, 11, 2: 117–34.

—— (1991) 'Hope Work in the Care of Seriously Ill Patients', *Qualitative Health Research*, 1, 4: 407–33.

Peterson, E. A. (1985) 'The Physical, the Spiritual: can you meet all of your patients' needs?', *Journal of Gerontological Nursing*, 11: 23–7.

Pleijel, H. (1983) *Jordfastning i stillhet* (Funeral Strictly Private), Lund, Saml. o. stud. till Svenska Kyrkans Historia.

Ponzett, J. and Johnson, M. A. (1991) 'The Forgotten Grievers: grandparents' reactions to the death of grandchildren', *Death Studies*, 15: 157–67.

Porter, R. (1989) 'Death and the Doctors in Georgian England' in R. Houlbrooke (ed.) *Death, Ritual and Bereavement*, London, Routledge.

—— (1990) untitled in R. Dinnage *The Ruffian on the Stair: reflections on death*, London, Viking.

Prior, L. (1989) *The Social Organisation of Death*, Basingstoke, Macmillan.

Prior, L. and Bloor, M. (1992) 'Why People Die', *Science As Culture*, 3: 346–74.

Qureshi, H., Challis, D. and Davies, B. (1989), *Helpers in Case-Managed Care*, Aldershot, Gower.

Rando, T. (1984) *Grief, Dying, and Death: clinical interventions for caregivers*, Champaign IL, Research Press.

Rawlings, M. (1979) *Beyond Death's Door*, Nashville TN, Thomas Nelson.

Reader, I. and Walter, T. (eds) (1993) *Pilgrimage in Popular Culture*, Basingstoke, Macmillan.

Reed, B. (1978) *The Dynamics of Religion*, London, Darton, Longman & Todd.

Rees, W. D. (1971) 'The Hallucinations of Widowhood', *British Medical Journal*, 2 October: 37–41.

—— and Lutkins, S. G. (1967) 'Mortality of Bereavement', *British Medical Journal*, 4: 13.

Retsinas, J. (1988) 'A Theoretical Reassessment of the Applicability of Kübler-Ross's Stages of Dying', *Death Studies*, 12: 207–16.

Richardson, R. (1984) 'Old People's Attitudes to Death in the Twentieth Century', *Society for the Social History of Medicine Bulletin*, 34: 48–51.

—— (1989) *Death, Dissection and the Destitute*, London, Penguin.

Rieff, P. (1966) *The Triumph of the Therapeutic: uses of faith after Freud*, London, Chatto & Windus.

Riesman, D. (1950) *The Lonely Crowd*, New Haven, Yale University Press.

Ring, K. (1980) *Life at Death*, New York, Coward, McCann & Geoghegan.

Rinpoche, S. (1992) *The Tibetan Book of Living and Dying*, London: Rider.

Roberts, E. (1989) 'The Lancashire Way of Death' in R. Houlbrooke (ed.) *Death, Ritual and Bereavement*, London, Routledge.

Rodgers, B. and Cowles, K. (1991) 'The Concept of Grief: an analysis of classical and contemporary thought', *Death Studies*, 15: 443–58.

Rose, N. (1989) *Governing the Soul: the shaping of the private self*, London, Routledge.

Rosenblatt, P. (1983) *Tears, Bitter Tears: Nineteenth century diarists and twentieth century grief theorists*, Minneapolis, University of Minnesota Press.

Rowell, G. (1974) *Hell and the Victorians*, Oxford, Clarendon.

Roy, D. (1992) 'Measurement in the Service of Compassion', *Journal of Palliative Care*, 8, 3: 3–4.

Saunders, C. (1965) 'The Last Stages of Life', *American Journal of Nursing*, 65 (March): 1–3.

—— (1970) 'The Moment of Truth: care of the dying person' in L. Person (ed.) *Death and Dying*, Cleveland, The Press of Case Western Reserve University.

—— (1988) 'Spiritual Pain', *Hospital Chaplain*, March.

—— (1990a) *Beyond the Horizon: a search for meaning in suffering*, London, Darton, Longman & Todd.

—— (ed.) (1990b) *Hospice and Palliative Care: an interdisciplinary approach*, London, Edward Arnold.

—— (1992) 'Voluntary Euthanasia', *Palliative Medicine*, 6: 1–5.

Scheff, T. (1977) 'The Distancing of Emotion in Ritual', *Current Anthropology*, 18, 3: 483–505.

—— (1979) *Catharsis in Healing, Ritual and Drama*, Berkeley, University of California Press.

Schulz, R. and Aderman, D. (1972) 'Clinical Research and the Stages of Dying', *Omega*, 5, 5: 137–43.

Seale, C. (1989) 'What Happens in Hospices?', *Social Science and Medicine*, 28, 5: 551–9.

—— (1990) 'Caring for People who Die: the experience of family and friends', *Ageing and Society*, 10, 4: 413–28.

—— (1991a) 'Communication and Awareness About Death', *Social Science and Medicine*, 32, 8: 943–52.

—— (1991b) 'Death from Cancer and Death from Other Causes: the relevance of the hospice approach', *Palliative Medicine*, 5: 12–19.

—— and Addington-Hall, J. (1994) 'Euthanasia: why people want to die earlier', *Social Science and Medicine*, 39(5): 647–54.

—— (forthcoming, a) 'Dying at the Best Time', *Social Science and Medicine*.

—— (forthcoming, b) 'Euthanasia: the role of good care', *Social Science and Medicine.*

Sennett, R. (1993) *The Fall of Public Man,* London, Faber.

Shelly, J. (1982) 'Spiritual Care – planting seeds of hope', *Critical Care Update,* 9, 12: 7–17.

Shields, R. (1991) *Places on the Margin,* London, Routledge.

Silverman, D. (1987) *Communication and Medical Practice: social relations in the clinic,* London, Sage.

—— (1989) 'Making Sense of a Precipice: constituting identity in an HIV clinic' in P. Aggleton, G. Hart and P. Davies (eds) *AIDS: Social Representations, Social Practices,* Lewes, Falmer.

Simpson, M. (1979) *Dying, Death and Grief: a critical bibliography,* New York, Plenum.

—— (1987) *Dying, Death and Grief: a critical bibliography,* University of Philadelphia Press.

Sklar, F. and Hartley, S. F. (1990) 'Close Friends as Survivors', *Omega,* 21, 2: 103–12.

Sloane, D. C. (1991) *The Last Great Necessity: cemeteries in American history,* Baltimore, Johns Hopkins University Press.

Smale, B. (1985) *Deathwork,* University of Surrey, unpublished PhD thesis.

Smith, A. M., Eve, A. and Sykes, N. P. (1992) 'Palliative Care in Britain and Ireland 1990 – an overview', *Palliative Medicine,* 6: 277–91.

Spottiswoode, J. (1991) *Undertaken with Love,* London, Robert Hale.

Stannard, D. (1977) *The Puritan Way of Death,* New York, Oxford University Press.

Stoddard, S. (1989) 'Hospice in the United States: an overview', *Journal of Palliative Care,* 5, 3: 10–19.

Stoll, R. (1989) 'The Essence of Spirituality' in V.B. Carson (ed.) *Spiritual Dimensions of Nursing Practice,* Philadelphia, W.B. Saunders.

Stroebe, M. (1992) 'Coping with Bereavement: a review of the grief work hypothesis', *Omega,* 26, 1: 19–42.

Stroebe, W. and Stroebe, M. (1987) *Bereavement and Health,* Cambridge University Press.

Sudnow, D. (1967) *Passing On: the social organisation of dying,* Englewood Cliffs, Prentice Hall.

Sweeting, H. and Gilhooly, M. (1991) 'Doctor, Am I Dead? A review of social death in modern societies', *Omega,* 24, 4: 251–69.

Sykes, G. (1965) *The Society of Captives,* New York, Atheneum.

Taylor, C. (1989) *Sources of the Self: the making of modern identity,* Cambridge MS, Harvard University Press.

Taylor, H. (1987) 'Hospice Care and Non-belief', *THS Health Summary,* 4, 6: 4–5.

Taylor, Liz McNeill (1983) *Living with Loss,* London, Fontana.

Taylor, Lou (1983) *Mourning Dress: a costume and social history,* London, Allen & Unwin.

Thomas, J. (1978) 'Last Word', *Social Work Today,* 9 May.

Tocqueville, A. de (1969) *Democracy in America,* New York, Doubleday Anchor.

Torrens, P. (1986) 'U.S. Hospice Between Two Worlds', *Journal of Palliative Care,* 2, 1: 6–8.

Torrie, M. (1987) *My Years With CRUSE*, Richmond, Surrey, CRUSE.

Townsend, P. (1964) *The Last Refuge*, London, Routlege.

Troeltsch, E. (1931) *The Social Teaching of the Christian Churches*, vol. 2, London, Allen & Unwin.

Troubridge, Lady (1926) *The Book of Etiquette*, Kingswood, Surrey, The World's Work.

Turner, R. H. (1976) 'The Real Self: from institution to impulse', *American Journal of Sociology*, 81, 5: 989–1016.

Turner, V. (1974) *The Ritual Process*, London: Penguin.

Van Gennep, A. (1960) *The Rites of Passage*, University of Chicago Press (1909).

Vanstone, W. H. (1982) *The Stature of Waiting*, London, Darton, Longman & Todd.

Veatch, R. and Tai, E. (1980) 'Talking About Death: patterns of lay and professional change', in R. Fox (ed.) *The Social Meaning of Death, Annals of the American Academy of Political and Social Science*, vol. 447, special issue.

Vernon, G. (1970) *Sociology of Death*, New York, Ronald Press.

Wadsworth, J. S. and Harper, D. C. (1991), 'Grief and Bereavement in Mental Retardation', *Death Studies*, 15: 281–92.

Walton, I. (1987) 'Terminal Care of the Elderly and Bereavement Counselling', *The Practitioner*, 231 (June): 869–73.

Walter, T. (1977) 'Emotional Disturbance – what does it mean?' *Social Work Today* (26 April): 8–10.

—— (1979) *A Long Way From Home*, Exeter, Paternoster.

—— (1985a) *All You Love Is Need*, London, SPCK.

—— (1985b) *Hope on the Dole*, London, SPCK.

—— (1990) *Funerals: and how to improve them*, London, Hodder & Stoughton.

—— (1991a) 'Modern Death – taboo or not taboo?', *Sociology*, 25, 2: 293–310.

—— (1991b) 'The Mourning After Hillsborough', *Sociological Review*, 39, 3: 599–625.

—— (1991c) 'Settling the Spirit', *Bereavement Care*, 10, 1: 4–5.

—— (1992) 'Angelic Choirs: on the non-secularisation of choral music', *The Musical Times* (June): 278–81.

—— (1993a) 'Death in the New Age', *Religion*, 23, 127–45.

—— (1993b) 'Sociologists Never Die: British sociology and death', in D. Clark (ed.) *The Sociology of Death*, Oxford, Blackwell.

—— (1995) *The Eclipse of Eternity – religion and death in the modern era*, Basingstoke, Macmillan.

Wambach, J. A. (1985) 'The Grief Process as a Social Construct', *Omega*, 16, 3: 201–11.

Wattis, J. (1990) 'Practice Makes Perfect', *Nursing the Elderly*, July/August.

Waugh, L. (1992) 'Spiritual Aspects of Nursing: a descriptive study of nurses' perceptions' in *Cancer Nursing, Changing Frontiers: spiritual and ethical issues*, Proceedings of the 7th International Conference on Cancer Nursing, Vienna, 15–16 August.

Wilkes, E. (1991) 'How Do We Measure the Quality of the Environment and the Autonomy of the Patient in the Hospice?' in Royal College of Physicians of London, *Palliative Care: Guidelines for good practice and audit measures*.

Wilkinson, S. (1991) 'Factors Which Influence How Nurses Communicate with Cancer Patients', *Journal of Advanced Nursing*, 16: 677–88.

Williams, R. (1989) 'Awareness and Control of Dying: some paradoxical trends in public opinion', *Sociology of Health and Illness*, 11, 3: 201–12.

—— (1990) *A Protestant Legacy: attitudes to death and illness among older Aberdonians*, Oxford University Press.

Willoughby, R. (1936) *Funeral Formalities and Obligations: what to do when a death occurs*, Universal Publications.

Wilson, I. (1987) *The After Death Experience*, London, Corgi.

Wood, J. (1976) 'The Structure of Concern: the ministry in death-related situations' in L. Lofland (ed.) *Toward a Sociology of Death and Dying*, Beverly Hills, Sage.

—— (1977) *Expressive Death – the current deathwork paradigm*, University of California at Davis, unpublished PhD thesis.

Worden, J. W. (1991) *Grief Counselling and Grief Therapy*, 2nd edn, London, Routledge.

Wortman, C. B. and Silver, R. C. (1989) 'The Myths of Coping with Loss', *Journal of Consulting and Clinical Psychology*, 57, 3: 349–57.

Wouters, C. (1990) 'Changing Regimes of Power and Emotions at the End of Life: The Netherlands 1930–1990', *Netherlands Journal of Sociology*, 26, 2: 151–67.

Wright, M. (1981) 'Coming to Terms with Death: patient care in a hospice for the terminally ill' in P. Atkinson and C. Heath (eds) *Medical Work: realities and routines*, Aldershot, Gower.

Yamamoto, J., Iyiwsaki, T. and Yoshimura, S. (1969) 'Mourning in Japan', *American Journal of Psychiatry*, 125, 1660–5.

—— (1970) 'Cultural Factors in Loneliness, Death, and Separation', *Medical Times*, 98: 177–83.

Young, M. and Cullen, L. (forthcoming) *The Presumption of Immortality: a study in East London*.

Young, M. and Willmott, P. (1957) *Family and Kinship in East London*, London, Routledge & Kegan Paul.

Index